Governance Unbound

Public Services, Players and Rules of the Game

Governance Unbound

Public Services, Players and Rules of the Game

R.N. GUPTA

AAKAR

GOVERNANCE UNBOUND: Public Services, Players and Rules of the Game
R.N. Gupta

First Published 2014

ISBN 978-93-5002-316-7

Published by
AAKAR BOOKS
28 E Pocket IV, Mayur Vihar Phase I, Delhi 110 091
Phone : 011 2279 5505 Telefax : 011 2279 5641
aakarbooks@gmail.com; www.aakarbooks.com

In association with
INSTITUTE FOR DEVELOPMENT AND COMMUNICATION
Sector 38 A, Chandigarh 160 014
Phone : 0172 262 5941, 466 0038
idcindia@idcindia.org, www.idcindia.org

Printed at
Saurabh Printers Pvt Ltd, New Delhi

To
Friends and colleagues
Dr. Pramod Kumar and Mr. Janak Raj Kundal
and my ever supportive wife
Vijaya

Contents

PART III: Beta Services: Social and Economic Regulations

PART IV: Delta and Gamma Regulations: Positive and Negative Public Goods

PART V: Alpha and Omega of Public Services

Preface

The journey that culminated (it could even be the beginning) with the present work could be said to have been serendipitous. An association with a Commission on Governance Reforms set up by a State government prompted a number of recommendations which, it was zealously hoped, would prove to be critical 'game-changers'. However, the typically serene and status quoist flow of the governmental functioning did not allow any ripples to be formed. One is reminded of Laurence J. Peter of *The Peter Principle* fame: "Bureaucracy defends the *status quo* long past the time when the quo has lost its status".

The Central and the State governments in India are committing an increasing share of government revenues for providing administrative, civic and social services to citizens - civic services, school education, health and many others, even though the outlays may not be adequate in absolute terms. Despite additional resources, participatory processes and extensive consultations with the NGOs, economists, sociologists and others in policy making, the outcomes of public policy or specific services generally continue to be below par. Infusion of business tools and practices, skills and capacity building, restructuring of agencies, re-engineering and performance measurement do not appear to be making much difference either, in terms of outcomes or improving the experience or the opinion of citizens. Various 'best practices' and models have also failed to provide adequate momentum for governance to 'take off'. Something seems to be amiss.

Here, then, is the process of discovery of that 'missing link', the micro 'operational' 'rules of the game' which appear to be much more relevant for delivery of public services than macro policy, macro rules and institutions, resources, delivery structures and sophisticated performance measurement tools such as the RFD (Results Framework Document - the latest initiative by the Government of India). I hope that the policy advisers, policy makers and the middle level officials who are responsible for designing these micro rules and institutions for specific sectors, programmes and policies, would, even though they may not accept the hypothesis, at least appreciate the logic of the specific institutional interventions proposed in the case of different services and regulatory areas of public governance. In any case, one major advantage of the proposed approach – redesigning the rules and institutions of interaction and exchange in the public services to align them with the incentives and behaviour of the agents and actors involved – is that the feedback on results and outcomes is almost instantaneous. Unfortunately, despite having a large number of autonomous and 'sovereign' states, India has been unable to provide scope for diversity and experimentation in public governance. This seems to be primarily due to the increasing centralisation of resource allocations by the Government of India which appears to have resulted in uniformity and rigidity in the design and implementation of most of the programs. This has also encouraged (as explained in Chapter 3) the somewhat 'lazy' and 'automatic' System I responses from the state bureaucracy - to comply with the form of the laid down rules and procedures, rather than innovate and experiment.

Needless to say, while the operational rules and institutions in the governance markets are important, that does not mean that macro policy and institutions do not matter; they are and will continue be relevant. Given, however, the wide consultations and inclusive processes which today go into policy making, the policy design and macro institutions are rarely a problem in governance. There is a need rather to look into micro interactions and exchanges and the relevant rules and institutions which shape and affect the behaviour and incentives of the actors engaged in the processes of governance in the case of different public services and regulations.

Apart from micro 'rules of the game', by which I mean rules

governing 'play of the game', the second point of focus is the 'human' players – officials as well as the citizens – engaged in various governance exchanges and interactions. There is a general belief in the innate rationality of *Homo sapiens* expressed in the 'rational agent' model or the 'rational choice theory'. Psychologists have, however, pointed out a number of cognitive and emotional biases and limitations which may lead to irrational responses. Further, the context of a service or regulation generally determines the nature of the exchange and its outcome and is in a way, the playing field for the complex interplay of the rules and the players—rational agents, no doubt, but with all their cognitive and affective limitations and biases.

It is all very well to understand and appreciate these issues or to think that one does so, but I don't think I would have been able to complete this work without the simultaneous availability of an 'ivory tower' of academia—the Institute for Development and Communication, Chandigarh—which has an interesting culture, and refrains from pushing or even 'nudging' the faculty. I got tremendous support and help from the faculty and staff at the IDC especially some friends to whom this book is dedicated—so much so that only my humility restrains me from attributing the faults and deficiencies (and there will be many) to them.

Introduction
Public Governance: Actors, Incentives and 'Rules of the Game'

The hypothesis of the book is easily stated, though may be not so easily demonstrated. Public governance, in general discourse and practice, has been mostly about the macro aspects of economic and social policies and practices. This focus on the big picture, the wood rather than the trees, is not uncommon. Economists and even the intelligentsia have been similarly pre-occupied with macro economics and it is only recently, thanks to behavioural economists, that micro economic approaches to human behaviour have been rehabilitated to some extent. It is proposed that the discourse and practice in the case of public governance, as distinguished from corporate governance, need to shift from macro governance—macro aspects of public policy, such as the formulation processes, resources, structures and organisations—to micro governance—the 'small' transactions, interactions and exchanges among the actors, public officials and the citizens. The playing fields where these exchanges take place are, in a way, the governance markets for different public services and regulations. A detailed exposition of the premise and the approach is provided in Chapter 3 and the issues have been explored in subsequent chapters in the course of an empirical analysis of different public services and regulations. It may, however, be appropriate to focus on some key dimensions of the basic premise.

Governance Interactions: 'Play of the Game'

One, the interactions of the government and private actors, in the course of delivery of public services, do get a mention, but mainly as 'case studies' of implementation or delivery mechanisms of policy. Some authorities tend to focus on the attributes of good government—transparency, 'steering' capacity, equity, the orientation and objectivity of the government agents etc. The route to understanding and improving public governance, however, appears to lie through 'micro governance', the public agent-citizen interactions, exchanges and transactions, the 'play of the game' on the 'playgrounds' of different public services. Acemoglu[1] points out the need to attend to the micro market failures as these may lead to macro institutional failures. Micro failure in the governance markets may similarly result in the failure of public policy. Micro governance, however, is not just the implementation 'tail' of the policy frame; it is rather the core of public governance. Charles Cadwell, in the Preface to *Power and Prosperity*,[2] refers to Mancur Olson's contribution in identifying the main springs, the 'jugular' of the social and economic structures, and his somewhat disparaging remarks about some 'researchers having an instinct for "capillaries" rather than the "jugular"'. In public governance, however, the micro interactions taking place in the 'capillaries', the micro governance markets, are many a time, all that matter for the success or failure of governance.

Micro governance neither demands nor hopes for omnibus policy designs and solutions, even in the broad sectors of health or education. The problems of absenteeism, of quality of education etc., are subject to different incentives and a single strategy may not be applicable for ensuring attendance of the students as well as that of the teachers. A vegetable market is very different from a share market. While free bed nets may be a solution for malaria, free medicines may not be enough for AIDS and even tuberculosis—the patient in the former case may not even volunteer, and in the latter, may not consume the antibiotics as per the required protocol. Governance exchanges are embedded in the specific context of public regulations and services.

'Rules of the Game'

Two, the use of the term 'rules of the game' as an alternate to 'institutions' has come into popular use, thanks to the emerging discipline of New Institutional Economics which emphasises the importance of political, social and legal institutions for economic development. We are concerned with the micro institutions and 'rules of the game', which govern interaction among the players, provide for pay offs and sanctions and affect incentives. Some examples are the rules for the issue of yellow and red cards for the fouls committed in the game of football and in golf, the circumstances in which a player may incur a specific penalty. Unlike macro rules about design and structure which are stable and fundamental (e.g. eleven players for each team in the game of football but five in basketball), these rules about 'play of the game' can change over time, depending on how effective or otherwise they turn out to be in responding to the evolving game strategies of the teams and their coaches. The asymmetry between the macro institutions of a public policy and its 'field' outcomes, may therefore need to be addressed primarily through the micro rules and institutions, which influence and affect behaviour of the parties to governance exchanges—government agencies/actors and the citizens/private parties—directly and immediately. The formal 'rules of the game' can have a trajectory independent of their history, unlike macro institutions which are much more 'path dependent'; in the language of the chaos theory, the rules, rather than actors, can change the 'initial conditions' and boundaries of behaviour.

Actors, Incentives and 'Biases'

Three, micro rules and institutions, which in the case of public governance, are mostly formal and codified, need to address the incentives not only of the citizens but also of the 'street level' government agents and actors. Most of the civil servants spend their official careers, drafting tens or hundreds of micro rules (technically known as 'delegated legislation') which may sometimes generate perverse incentives among the private actors involved, as we shall see. Incentives of the government agents are left, however, to be managed by the generic rules of conduct which are divorced from the context of specific situations and services and the incentives these call into play. Socially wasteful outcomes of perverse incentives are sometimes generated by well-intentioned motivational measures. A Power Utility in Punjab provided incentives to the staff in the thermal power generation stations in the 1980s, to raise the PLF (plant load factor). The result? There was widespread reluctance to back down generation, say during the rainy days of winter, even when required by the regional grids. Coal companies have been provided incentives in their contracts with the power utilities companies to supply about 90 per cent of the committed coal deliveries. These incentives, however, resulted in the coal companies merrily loading wagons even when the thermal plants had surplus coal and did not want further consignments. The social waste caused by such incentives in the case of the sub-prime mortgage crisis in 2008–09, as also the stock options given to the CEOs, has been well-documented.[3] Ariely explains the rationale, or rather the irrationality, of bonuses for the CEOs: *'Why Big Bonuses don't Always Work'*.[4] The mid-day meals programme in India is an example of a functional incentive for encouraging attendance of children, though the same incentive has no impact on the attendance of teachers. In the absence of market clearing prices, there is a need to consider the aspect of incentive compatibility while designing micro institutions and rules for the governance markets.

Four, the design of micro rules needs to take note not only of the material incentives of the agents, but also their affective, intuitive, and cognitive biases and dispositions. Self-interest, it is generally agreed, is material in economic interactions, even though one may not go as far as the economist Gary Becker, who argued that economic incentives govern social and even family interactions. Material and economic motivations of the actors are no doubt relevant in public governance. We need to consider, however, not only the rational self-interest and material incentives of the *homo economicus* but also the actual behaviour and incentives of the *Homo sapiens*. Experimental psychology and behavioural economics have thrown light on these dark zones of human interactions and exchanges but we have yet to extend this knowledge and understanding to the area of public governance.

Affective and emotional biases do matter in social interactions but may not be relevant in most of the situations of public governance. On the other hand, cognitive 'heuristics' and 'biases' may be much more relevant for governance exchanges than for the economic markets, as the frame of utility for the parties (private and government agents) is neither clearly defined nor always purely economic. My first exposure to this dimension was in a power utility company in Punjab in the 1990s. Power supply to the agriculture sector was not free, but the State of Punjab had a flat rate (Rs. X per HP—Horse Power—of the tubewell motor). The records showed an overwhelming number of motors to be of 3 HP, whereas the pressure of the water-guzzling paddy crop had led to most of the motors having been actually upgraded to 5 HP by the farmers; the official procedure for upgrading of the motors was not only expensive but also tortuous. The question for the utility was: 'how to identify such cases and levy higher charges'? Random checks, penalties, and exhortations were not helpful. The utility company finally adopted, after trial and error, a new strategy: instructions were issued that all motors would be billed at 5 HP, unless any farmer declared to the utility company that he/she had a 3 HP motor, which claim could be verified and power supply disconnected in the case of false claims. The farmers in Punjab are a strong lobby and, as such, managed through political pressure to have the period provided for exercising the option extended twice. But, ultimately they acquiesced in the default option; their System I (some expressions and terms used in the Introduction—'System I', 'Nudge' etc.—are explained in Chapter 3 in order to avoid repetition) was too strong!

Prohibitions, Bans and 'Nudges'

Five, there is a need to adopt an approach based on 'nudges' and mild incentives to address the irrationality and biases of the human actors rather than depending, as the rule makers mostly tend to do, on mandatory and absolute 'bans' and restrictions.

In the unique context of governance exchanges in the public services, as distinguished from the economic and social interactions, the nature of such 'nudges'—'patrimonial' or 'asymmetrically patrimonial' or 'dictatorial' —need not worry the designers of rules as much as it seems to bother the founders of the 'Nudge' school, Thaler and Sunstein.[5] The nature of 'nudges' and, if at all, to what extent do they constrain the choices, need not be driven by ideology. Instead, the objectives of the policy, and the outcomes desired, need to shape their direction and structure. A 'kick', for example, may be in order in the case of the 'criminals' (at least some of them). While 'patrimonial nudges' advocated by Thaler may be appropriate to social exchanges, 'nudges'— benevolent or otherwise—in the case of the governance markets, have to be compatible with the incentives of the actors involved. These interventions need to factor the complexity, not only of cognitive biases, but also the usual 'econ' incentives and 'nudges' need to be structured by the outcomes desired. Sometimes, the very design of the governance mechanisms can be the instrumental 'nudge', especially in the case of the public goods—promoting the public sector for universal school education but the private sector for higher and quality education, as indicated later.

Some of the governments, such as, the US Federal Government and the UK Government have recognised the need to incorporate these perspectives in the policy and design of rules. An excellent summary of the salient findings and applications, in various public policy areas, such as, credit cards, healthcare, loans for students, savings plans has been provided by Sunstein.[6] The purpose here is to see whether we can do something similar in the context of India, and more importantly, in the context of specific situations of governance interactions and exchanges in the public services. The character of exchanges in public governance is distinct as compared to social and economic markets. The 'agency' problem in governance interactions is especially relevant. In the absence of a tangible or proximate Principal, the problem is likely to be much worse, a product of (lack of) information and the hierarchical complexity of the agency involved. This, however, warrants focus, not so much on supervision and monitoring of outputs, as is usually sought to be done, but on addressing incentives, especially those of the bureaucrats. Their jobs are rarely on the line, transactions are multiple and mostly complex and outputs are not easily measurable. The elements of organizational, institutional, and personal risk and profit and loss that are common in the private sector are missing in the case of government officials and employees. That adds to the tendency to resort to naïve interventionism leading to iatrogenic and unintended harm, inflicted by the 'medicine' devised for the citizen 'patients'. *The Economist*[7] provides some instances of 'nudges', especially, by the UK Behavioural Insight Team. However, as pointed out in the example cited there (the tendency by the Anglo-Saxons to comply more readily with the social norms than the French), a uniform 'choice architecture' or 'frame' may not be appropriate for different situations. Specific public services, given their unique context, may require different rule design for structuring the choice of the citizens. This focus on micro services may incidentally also lead to micro transparency and accountability, lower transaction costs, and decreased subjectivity.[8] Despite patronage and support by governments and academics, the potential of nudges in public governance is yet to be fully explored. In any case, this dimension appears to be conspicuous by its absence in India. Probably, the application needs more 'domain' knowledge than the 'experts' can possibly have. The book is an attempt to address this deficit.

Structure of the Book

The approach is unfolded in the context of various public services, which cover most of the areas of governance interactions in the micro markets of public governance, ranging from basic and contingent services (Alpha), social and economic regulations (Beta), social public goods, such as, health/ education (Delta), crime, pollution, and other public 'bads' (Gamma), and the services directed at the economically and socially vulnerable sections of the society (Omega). The main omissions are the judicial and justice systems and taxation.

Chapter 1 provides a broad perspective on the dimensions of governance, how the different agencies and the academics view its relevance and the long journey from 'command and control' to inclusive governance. Chapter 2 provides perspectives on public governance shared by the Central and State governments in India (which provide a lead in many areas of human interactions mainly through the Plan documents), the NGOs, and the academics. The focus in India has mostly been on the areas of macro policy. The 'interactive' aspect of public governance has generally remained neglected. Chapter 3 explains the approach adopted in the present work and how the present models and theories of governance, statistical models and best practices, are of little help, not only in the design of the rules and institutions for public services but even in understanding them. Also explained therein is the relevance of looking into the interactions and situations 'nested' in their micro context—micro rules, local jurisdictions, actors' incentives, behaviour and outcomes. The main contributions of the economics of 'market failure' and behavioural economics are briefly indicated to provide a broad frame of reference for an analysis of the governance exchanges which take place in the course of delivery of public services.

Chapter 4 provides a broad classification of the public services and areas of governance interactions—alpha, beta, delta, gamma and omega services—each of which needs a different frame of understanding and analysis in view of the different dimensions of behaviour and incentives involved, as well as invoked, by the 'rules of the game'.

Chapters 5 to 23 relate to different services and regulations, across the spectrum of public services that have been identified for detailed analysis. Chapter 10 and 15 outline the broad approach which may be adopted in the case of Alpha and Beta services respectively. Chapter 24 includes a miscellany of examples and instances which may warrant the approach suggested; some of these are only tentative suggestions, as in the case of the pharmacological narcotics, as it has not been possible to evaluate the options exhaustively. Instances given, however, make it quite clear that the illogical rules and instructions, which never had, nor do they now, any rationale, continue to be extant despite the radically changed context. Some concluding observations are provided in Chapter 25.

'Long and Fat Tails' in Public Governance

One is tempted to describe micro governance in the metaphor of the genome; the number of public services and interactions is diverse and large, and the genes (rules) are subject to mutations and changes, not due to the struggle for survival and the need for adaptation, but the competence and disposition of the hidden 'rule makers' (cf. *The Blind Watchmaker* by Richard Dawkins), and the enforcers, the RNA messengers, who sometimes deliver toxic proteins to the organism. The rule-making processes and the governance codes are much more susceptible to intervention before the organism or an organ emerges fully formed. The design of micro institutions and 'rules of the game' may, therefore, need attention as they are critical to the outcomes, whether of policy or public satisfaction. Chris Anderson[9] has been instrumental in drawing public attention to the 'niches' on the 'long tails', rather than the mainstream 'hit' products, and to the shift, due mainly to the Internet, from the 80/20 rule to the 98 per cent rule: the large number of 'niche' products on the 'long tail' account for much more than 20 per cent of the turnover/profits. Public services are the historical 'long tails', each a niche and mainstream product in its own right, but swamped by the more fashionable and convenient macro policy and institutional 'hits'. This is probably a function of the 'availability' heuristic; macro policy and macro institutions get most of the public attention, as well as media coverage. Micro governance interactions in the 'capillaries' of different public services are, in fact, the 'fat and long' tails and the 'mainstream hits' in public governance. This area, however, appears to have been relegated to the pedestrian and low value 'implementation' and left to be attended to by the 'street level' officials. Hypotheses and theories about the front desk or 'cutting edge' governance interactions—whether in terms of agent incentives, or their skills and capacity, or the problems of bureaucratic mode of management,[10] or character of the organisation[11]—tend to converge on popular macro issues of structure and organisation, while the diversity and complexity of specific services, transactions, exchanges, and interactions tends to be ignored.

Designing 'Rules of the Game' for 'Humans'

Suggestions about the design of rules, the 'frame' and 'choice architecture', are based on a sort of triangulation of my personal experience and observations: a) as part of the government regulatory apparatus; b) as a client in a regulated public utility as well as the private sector; and c) as an observer outside the heat and dust of the interactional playgrounds and battlefields (during my association with the Governance Reforms Commission of a State Government). Contrary to what may be generally believed, the commercial public sector is as much, if not more, bothered and affected by the government regulations as the private sector. For instance, the ill-equipped regulatory staff has the authority to approve the commissioning of power sub-stations which might have been constructed and supervised by very well qualified professional staff of a Power Utility.

These procedural and operational rules appear to be somewhat casually drafted. It is probably the 'availability' heuristic which accounts for this. As Kahneman remarks,[12] 'people tend to assess the relative importance of issues by the ease with which they are retrieved from memory and this is largely determined by the extent of coverage in the media.' This bias can extend from selectivity in 'major issues' to the sub-issues of a particular policy or event. The officials tend to keep, within their sights, the major enunciations and goals of the policy, for example that four times the market price is payable for compensation, or that 70 per cent of 80 per cent of the people affected have to be consulted, under the recently passed *Land Acquisition and Rehabilitation & Resettlement Act* in India. They are likely to forget the nitty-gritty of defining the process for getting the approvals required, and to ensure that the approval process does not become a mere formality and is not captured by the interest groups. Even the NGOs, who would have participated enthusiastically in drafting and piloting the bill, may not demonstrate any keenness to be associated with the rather lowly and pedestrian process of rulemaking. As Milton Friedman has remarked,[13] they would have moved to their next macro policy area of interest.

Mahatma Gandhi tried to recall the face of the poorest person while deciding on a new policy or initiative. The Food Security Act, 2013, attempts the impossible task of recalling all the 70 crore faces who are hopelessly merged in a crowd of over 125 crore. The problem with the macro policies which are designed to improve the welfare of the individuals (humans rather than atoms) who constitute the masses is precisely this; the only way to translate the impact is to refer to numbers, not faces. Most of the civil servants are, of course, exposed to 'street level' governance during the initial years of service. The district level officers are, in a way, 'street level' bureaucrats despite their status—there is little hierarchy below; people can and do interact with them directly and they happen to be always in the firing line—whether the DC or the SSP or the district head of a department. However, as William Wordsworth would put it ('Ode to Immortality'), the 'shades of the prison house (committee rooms and office suites) begin to close' on the 'growing boy', as he gains in seniority; the 'street' links are lost as he enters the elite area of directive, constitutional and macro governance and policy, develops amnesia about the street level interactions, and shifts from 'faces' to 'numbers'. The humble attempt here is to reactivate the memory of 'faces' of the human actors—agents as well as citizens, engaged in governance interactions.

I confess the book may be somewhat lacking in the rigour of academic analysis, but hopefully, the suggestions, the incentive compatible 'nudges' and similar interventions which form the core of the book, will make up for the lapse. Governance has a rather short history as indicated in Chapter 1. It is quite likely to suffer the fate of the Neanderthals, and be swamped by the 'proactive' and determined governments, the 'tough States'. It is through 'nudges' and similar positive strategies for incentive compatible institutions and rules that it may retain or be able to establish its relevance. While making this assertion, one might possibly be expressing the bias of 'overconfidence'. In any case, one is in good company. That's the reason the readership of Kahneman is the office crowd at the 'office water cooler'. As he remarks, it is 'much easier as well as more enjoyable to identify and label the mistakes of others, than to recognise our own.'[14]

Incentives and biases of the state agents, who design the micro rules and institutions, appear to be especially relevant. As such, it is to them, the 'Mudbloods', rather than the policy 'Wizards' of Harry Potter's world that the suggestions are addressed with the hope that their dormant system II may be activated. Many of the interventions and 'nudges' can be accommodated without requiring new laws and can be a part of what is known as 'delegated legislation'. It would be appropriate to clarify that the proposed suggestions and 'toolkits' are primarily with reference to the context of public services in India, even though some of these may be helpful elsewhere too as 'best practices'.

PART I

From Government To Governance

Chapter 1 provides a brief account of the journey from the 'command and control' States and governments—absolute, oligarchic, or democratic—to collaborative and 'interactive' governance and points out some areas of concern for its 'survival'. In Chapter 2, the theory and practice of public governance is discussed within the administrative and political context of India and its states. The rationale of the framework, the salience of micro institutions and rules of public policy, which govern interactions in the 'market' for public services, are outlined in Chapter 3. An attempt has been made in Chapter 4 to classify different public services and regulations (alpha, beta and so on). This classification provides the basis for analysis of different services in the subsequent chapters.

1

Public Governance: The Four Dimensions

Governing mechanisms and structures of state-citizen relationships have been generally influenced by the political and economic ideologies of the time. The political philosophy of Hobbes—'an authoritarian sovereign to command and control the inherently selfish nature of human beings and destructive competition in the quest for power leading to "war"'[1]—has dominated the design and organization of the organs of State for over 300 years. This has continued despite Locke and J.S. Mill, for whom liberty of individuals took primacy over the government and the State. The Parliament and other semi-democratic (only propertied classes had a vote) systems replaced the authoritarian sovereign in due course but continued with the same approach to the state-citizen relationships, a bond of the 'stick', penalties, and punishment. Governance norms and institutions provided little space for cooperation and collaboration, and the citizen-government interactions continued to be mediated through control—whether of children in school or of soldiers on the battlefield—exercised to satisfy whims of the rulers or interests of the powerful. That seems, for example, to be the reason for the rules documented by Adam Smith[2] for restricting the migration of the poor from one parish to another; migration of the poor was prohibited not in their interest but that of the landlords and for control of the wages. Incidentally, that is, probably, the first recorded instance of 'gaming' of these regulations by the public authorities—the parishes—as well as the poor.

The economic ideology originated with Adam Smith's

'invisible hand' of the market, bringing about socially desirable outcomes through individual actions dictated by self-interest of the parties. The State was required to confine itself to 'tolerable administration of justice, peace, and supply of public goods'.[3] Taxation, which has been a distinctive feature of most of the modes of organization of the State—monarchic, democratic or oligarchic—was minimal and derived its justification primarily for funding State actions for fighting wars and maintaining peace and order. Economic markets were left to their own devices and were manipulated sometimes by the clever 'bakers' who managed to sell bread without making any, as in the case of the 'Mississippi Bubble' in France.[4] A detailed account of these manipulations and the mob frenzy which added to the Bubbles has been provided by Charles Mackay;[5] over five hundred tents had to be set up by Jack Law, the architect of the Mississippi bubble, at specially leased promises to handle the hordes of aspirants wanting to buy shares. The State rarely stepped in or intervened except when powerful political or elite interests were threatened, as in the case of the Corn Laws or the ban on cotton imports.[6] For the limited areas of government-citizen interaction, however, the iron hand of the State was very much in evidence. *Laissez fair*e in economic areas and an iron fist in the administration of justice and public order, were the two 'horses' pulling the governance 'cart', to use the metaphor of Benkler, who has provided[7] a brief but excellent account of these developments.

The Welfare State

There was a change in this worldview after the First World War and the Great Depression of the 1930s. The problems of hyperinflation in the Weimar Republic, the collapse of the financial and labour markets, and the Deep Depression in the USA, were attributed to the inability of the State to control and regulate the free markets (though this has been subsequently shown to be erroneous by Friedman and Anna Schwartz in *A Monetary History of the United States;* they argued that the culprit was a sharp decline in the country's money stocks controlled by the Federal Reserve.)[8] The surge in government expenditure was also aided by the Keynesian ideas of stimulating demand through public expenditure and by the bloated bureaucracy, a by-product of government regulations and programmes to enforce or implement them. Extensive regulations were made by the State, covering not only the economic, but even the social activities of its citizens. The post-World War II period witnessed a massive increase in public expenditure and in the staff of the executive agencies administering them. Ferguson remarks:[9] 'If the welfare State was conceived in politics, it grew to maturity in war.' Not all of this expansion could possibly be justified by ideology. Quite a bit appeared to be 'free riding' (although expensive for the tax payers) on the Keynesian wagon. In the UK, the 'night watchman State was soon swamped by the pressures built up for a proactive government for introducing compulsory education, laws for safety at work, tax-funded libraries and welfare; a more active State became the answer in the later half of the 20th century.'[10] Even Harold MacMillan, the conservative Prime Minister, talked about 'advancing rapidly on the road to conscious regulation.'[11] The State came to be viewed as necessary, not only for its core functions, but also for ensuring economic and social well being of its citizens; it became the 'welfare state'. No doubt, some elements of social security (such as pensions in Germany) existed earlier, but these were driven more by political or production motives rather than a commitment to help the working class; the system of compulsory 'State health insurance and old age pensions' was introduced by Bismarck in Germany in 1882 'for motives which were far from altruistic.'[12]

'De-inventing' Government

In the 1970s, the State lost its colours; it was unable to address stagflation, a disastrous combination of inflation and unemployment. A new messiah, Milton Friedman, had emerged. He advocated abolition of the role of government not only in economic markets, but even for the core Adam Smithian functions of providing public goods, generally agreed to be under provided by the free markets. Milton Friedman was of the view that most of the government departments—FDA, energy, et cetera—had no rationale;[13] he questioned not only the government being in business and production, but even in regulation—a paradigm of 'minimum government' described as Capitalism 3.0 by Kaletsky.[14] Daniel Stedman Jones[15] refers to this period as the second phase of neoliberalism that broadly consisted of 'monetarism, de-regulation and market-based reforms'. The Washington Consensus of John Williamson included tax reform, trade liberalization, privatization, de-regulation, and strong property rights. It epitomized the shift as a strategy for economic growth and development but also became a catalyst for minimum government and market fundamentalism—de-inventing government and withdrawal of the government from the baggage it had piled onto itself in the earlier era, by running businesses and manufacturing activities and appropriating the 'commanding heights of the economy'. Whatever remained of government was required to be re-invented[16] through privatization, disinvestment, the PPP (public private partnership) mode for public utilities and infrastructure, including even outsourcing of the basic government functions, such as social security, as in Argentina. The governance-business cycle entered a period of depression.

The extreme views of Milton Friedman for minimum government, however, had few followers—academics or practitioners—in the sphere of public governance. Barring Chile, this ideology, coupled with the magic pull of the markets, mostly translated into denationalization of public enterprises, and positioning of the bureaucrats as managers who organized residuary government activities as business—the New Public Management in the UK under Margaret Thatcher.[17] Political, economic and public management structured around the freedom of individuals, free markets and minimum government, pinned down the 'Leviathan' of Hobbes, even though now viewed as a benevolent entity.

Experiments with Governance: the National Health Scheme (NHS)

The history of reform in the unique health institution in the UK —the NHS—since its inception in 1946 epitomizes the changing perspectives over time.[18] It was set up on the basis of a report by Sir William Beveridge ('medical treatment to be provided to all citizens by a national health service'). From its inception till the 1970s, the focus was on internal reforms, efficiency, personnel, scope, and other organizational and administrative issues; mental health was covered in the 1950s; in 1962, the District General Hospitals were set up as the area specific focal points. The New Public Management (NPM) under Margaret Thatcher included NHS reorganization through abolition of the area health authorities in 1982. The Griffiths Report of 1983 focused on 'staff efficiencies and other resources of the NHS'. The *1988 White Paper-Working for Patients (NHS reforms)* proposed to introduce a distinction between the providers of care, GP fund-holders, a State-financed 'internal market' and the incentives for the GP's in order to drive service efficiency and a focus on patients as customers. The Labour Government added the issues of equity and quality to the 'business' innovations like the Hospital Star Rating system. There was decentralization of control from regional authorities to Strategic Health Authorities (SHA's) and Primary Care Trusts. The new conservative government has restored the state quo ante and abolished the SHAs through the NPM has not been fully abandoned. The 'third way' of running the NHS was 'neither command and control system of the 70s, putting the needs of the institutions ahead of patients' nor 'the divisive internal market system of the early 90s.[19] History of the NHS illustrates 'path dependence' in what the governments do, and how one can rarely divorce the present from the past in practice, despite the prevalence of differing ideologies and perspectives over time.

The New Paradigm

That was the context in which the concept of governance made a silent and unobtrusive entry in the early 1990s—a paradigm characterised by individualization rather than atomization and the need for the government to engage and collaborate, rather than administer and rule. This paradigm shift appears to have been aided by various developments. 'Both handed' economists had provided evidence of the limitations and failure of economic markets. The unitary State model—'command and control' view of the government functioning—which wished away the incentives and motives of the individuals, groups, and public agents, was itself shown to be subject to severe limitations by the 'public choice' theory and 'agency' and 'information' problems. Arrow's 'Impossibility Theorem[20]' and 'paradox of voting'[21] indicated major problems of preferences in political and social choices even in the fully democratic systems.

The limitations of a system of command in full control and the failure of governments in whatever limited activities they engage in, appear to have led to the gradual evolution from *laissez faire*, 'welfare', and 'minimum government', to good governance. 'Governance' has been described by Ayyar[22] as one of the three major paradigms of the 1990s, but its definition and meaning remain ambivalent. The ball appears to have been set rolling with the following definition: 'Governance is concerned with creating the conditions for ordered rules and collective action, often including agents in the public and non-profit sectors, as well as within the public sector. The essence of governance is its focus on governing mechanisms—grants, contracts, agreements—that do not rest solely on the authority and sanctions of government.'[23] Kooiman[24] identifies the key features of governance as the 'totality of the interactions in which public and private sectors participate in diverse, complex and dynamic situations'. For Newman, governance is 'a shift from hierarchies and markets to networks; from formal authority of the State power to steering and coordinating, from actions of the State to interplay of plural actors.'[25] Michael Hill and Peter Hupe,[26] quoting Selznick,[27] trace the change from a focus on organization and management to a 'responsive adaptive mechanism' of institutions, described by them as a natural product of social needs and pressures, as against an organization which suggests a bare, no-nonsense system of coordinated activities: 'a selective [neo] interventionism, replacing private finance initiatives and competitive tendering of the Margaret Thatcher era by public private partnership and best value.' The authors refer to a 'multiple governance framework—constitutive, directional and operational governance'—relating it to systems, organizations and individuals respectively, with rule design and context design relevant to the first two, and management to operational, 'street level'[28] governance.

Some of the academics consider governance as a natural extension of the NPM; governance in the Municipal areas of Mexico, for example, is projected practically as an application and extension of the NPM philosophy.[29] Newman has captured the bewildering variety and overlap in the concept of governance.[30] There were, of course, differences between the NPM and the 'third way' of the Labour Government; as she remarks, the Public sector under Thatcher was 'a target for reform rather than an agent for change. The transition from hierarchies to markets under the NPM to the networks under the Labour Government was, however, partial; the "third way" of the Labour Government did not abandon the NPM but, instead, sought to effect efficiency through the processes of involvement of public as well as private actors'.

Academic 'competition' has also led to some maverick interpretations and an obsession with quantification. One of these defines governance in terms of orderly rules of transaction among the private actors and a "rational choice neo-institutional model of political transactions"[31]; rule compliance is determined not by culture (social capital norms), nor by context (evolutionary institutionalism of Huntingdon) but by the decisions of the actors regarding rule compliance determined by the 'perception of potential rewards, risk and comparison of likely outcomes'—in other words, an extension of the rational agent model to governance interactions. Governance in the area of Crime is measured by a somewhat constipated indicator of the Rule of Law—a simplistic but quantitative 'number of murders and riots'. The academic world, thus, seems to present 'governance' as a 'witches' brew', rather than a 'recipe based cake'.

There is, apart from the academics, an influential group of what one may describe as practicing academics, especially economists, who have to engage in the discourse on governance, while designing or suggesting economic policies for growth, development, and equity at the global and national levels. Joseph Stiglitz[32] refers to governance as 'the quality of the public and private institutions, which, in turn, is related to how decisions get made and in whose interest'. He remarks on the psyche of the global policymakers who blame faulty implementation for the failure of strategies and policies and stresses the fact that the policies have to be implemented by ordinary mortals, which the policy fails to take note of. Implementation failure is, in other words, a failure of policy. Prescriptions, however, seem to follow a well-defined macro, global or national bias, with little concern for the interacting parties and the playgrounds of governance interactions. One can ignore for the moment the somewhat unfair label given by Taleb;[33] 'Stiglitz syndrome' is described as 'lack of penalty from bad recommendations (made by the practicing academics) causing harm to others, while they themselves have no skin in the game'. Local institutions and preferences of citizens tend to be neglected. Dani Rodrix,[34] however, stresses the relevance of national and local cultures, social and economic institutions, preferences and practices, and the need to respect this micro diversity, rather than the utopian macro and global governance. As we shall see, the national and the State governments need to respect the local context and institutions, not only in the economic, but also in the governance markets, rather than looking for, as they tend to do, a single macro model of governance for the diverse areas of citizen-government interaction.

Governance Attributes and Indicators

Outside the *'Groves of Academe'*, the concept was adopted with religious zeal by a number of multilateral organizations in the 1990s. The approach, however, was somewhat tangential to that of the academics. It was more of a convenient paradigm for promoting free markets, democratic governments or, at least the minimal democratic practices even in the totalitarian regimes, as a pre requisite for development aid and other assistance and was generally used interchangeably with good responsive government. The Sustainable Governance Indicators[35] for the OECD countries have a 'status index' (democracy, economy, employment, social affairs, security, and resources) and a 'management Index' (steering capability, policy implementation, institutional learning, and accountability). Only a couple of these would refer to governance *per se*. The Sustainable Governance Indicators 2008 developed by Bertelsmann Stiftung,[36] the BTI, rates countries across a number of factors that cover the structure of the State apparatus, mainly in areas of political and administrative management. The BTI is concerned with macro aspects of political and economic institutions of different countries and does not appear to be amenable to application at the sub-national level. If the BTI were to be calculated for the different Indian States for example, it would not indicate major differences, especially in terms of 'stateness', 'social safety nets', 'respect for human rights' (some of the BTI indicators), as the states in India follow similar formal rules and institutions. Many of the factors may also be beyond the competence, jurisdiction, or the resources of the state governments. Social safety nets may be constrained by resources, electoral systems by the Constitution. The BTI is a comprehensive index and may be a good guide to the state of governance and to the 'capacity of countries for reform' and readiness for integration with the European Union, but is unlikely to provide an instrument for analysis and improvement in the areas of concern to the common citizens in countries like India.

The Ibrahim Index of African Governance[37] covers safety and the rule of law, participation and human rights, sustainable economic opportunity, human development—in other words 'good government'. Major countries like the US or the UK, which profess to carry the 'White Man's Burden', also focus on the macro political and economic institutions. The Millennium Challenge indicators of the US Government[38] include social and economic policy as well as some of the governance attributes, such as control of corruption, government effectiveness, et cetera. The Transparency International's *Perception of Corruption Index (CPI)* is primarily concerned with corruption in governance transactions. A country can only hope for improvement in its standing and score; the data provided, however, is of little help. The World Bank has also developed governance indicators,[39] and country assessments are updated regularly. The UNDP has even published a technical guide on governance indicators[40] to facilitate the process. The country rankings, however, mostly indicate marginal changes over time in the case of different countries—a step dance of Tweedledum and Tweedledee.

There are various other indicators and rankings provided by the 'Competitiveness Index': 'Ease of Doing Business' and so on, mostly focused on economic regulations, apart from some attributes of 'governance'. The approach of most of the organizations is in a way judgmental and from an outsider's perspective. This is not a criticism as the purpose of these indicators is precisely this—to assess for the global community or a particular government, the standing of different countries, and thus help the outsiders in making choices and decisions with regard to economic, strategic and social engagement with a specific country—involvement, investment, aid, relocation, ideological support, and so on.

Relevance of the Indicators

These measures and assessments may be very relevant for the agencies concerned, but may not be meaningful for public governance at the 'street' level of interaction of the government agents with the citizens which may, indeed, matter more than the macro policies and institutions. The indicators are statistical approximations, rather than quantitative measures, based as they are on a large number of independent surveys, carried out by different organizations, as in the case of the World Bank index. It is difficult to make use of the data except in a comparative (inter-country) context. The indicators also cleverly sidestep the issue of the nature of political institutions due to the inherent contradictions of the approach; political stability may be less of a problem in China than in India where one would expect transparency and public engagement to be more visible. Different countries have their unique context, structures and constitutional, legal, and transactional frameworks; the attribute-based approach of the international and global agencies is generally confined to the national level sectors, and organisations—environment, health and economic, political and bureaucratic systems. Or they may focus on specific components and attributes of national governance—the rule of law, freedom, transparency, equity et cetera. Most of the indicators and surveys on which these are based rely on formal processes, rules, protocols, and institutions rather than actual practices, are mostly based on perceptions of the 'jet set', national and international, and may not reflect the common citizens' views, interests, and experience. For countries like India, therefore, where the State governments/provinces are sovereign in major areas of citizen interaction, and hence, the locus for governance, these indices appear to be of little use as similar surveys across different States are not carried out and/or are too expensive. One can imagine the difficulty when even a comparative picture of performance of the States in India in respect of the MDGs (Millennium Development Goals) is not compiled annually; the data was published after a gap of about 15 years and is based mostly on secondary data such as the NSS surveys.[41]

Governance indicators, based as they are on a compilation of assessments by other agencies, represent to some extent the 'hearsay' fallacy. They are based on 'inadmissible evidence' and do not provide a roadmap for changes/redirection. Individual countries can only hope that a future survey will show them in better light, without being aware of the specific and concrete steps needed to bring about those results. Further, as in the case of surveys on corruption, topicality and accidental events can distort trends. In case of India, for example, the debate and progress on the draft of the Lok Pal Bill may be considered a positive development by some of the opinion leaders, while others may discount these surges in the debate. They may be more influenced by scams, such as the 2G, which surfaced at the same time. And these factors may not necessarily cancel each other. Productive comparisons of the government institutions and practices across various countries may also be difficult, as the total context of the cultural, political, economic, and social institutions within which specific interactions and transactions take place is different. International organizations concerned with governing structures and processes at the national and global levels are oriented more towards macro policies, and hence, may use governance sometimes as a non-economic instrument for promotion of the values of political democracy, minimum government and free markets. There is a tendency to conflate good governance with good government, a mix of ideology—economic and political freedom, equity, and justice—with some infusion of transparency and participation. These are some of the problems that have led to the approach adopted in the present work, as explained in a subsequent section.

Business Management in Public Governance

Approach to public management has been primarily influenced by contemporary political and economic ideologies and paradigms. In the twentieth century, however, business management and the practices and precepts of the corporate management have also played a role and influenced perceptions about how governments should manage their day to day business of governing—right from the Taylorite 'time and motion' studies to Maslow's 'hierarchy of needs' with its focus on employee motivation, McGregor's Theory X and Theory Y, 'management by objectives', 'down sizing' in the 1970s, 'reinventing' in the 80s and re-engineering in the 90s. These inputs from the business world in the later half of the 20th Century were mainly in the direction of efficiency of resource use and cost effectiveness. Business practices, honed and driven by competition, were expected to improve public governance. Governing was to be conducted as business, using minimum resources for producing the required outputs while spurring privatization of governing activities. 'Preachers'[42] as well as practitioners have, however, confined themselves to macro policies, statutes and rules—whether *laissez faire* of Friedman or interventionism of Jeffrey Sachs. The area of micro management and implementation of such public policies continued to be a 'black box' comprising obedient public officials, who were expected to extend the implementation or delivery of policy in the directions required by the policymakers. The complexities of the behaviour of the government agents and the public were rarely appreciated. If some rules created a problem or the objectives were not achieved, the solution was sought in changing the rules, re-orienting 'disposition' of the bureaucrats, or building the 'capacity' of officials.

The models of administrative behaviour in public organizations—span of control, time and motion studies etc.—were themselves based on assumptions of obedient and rational agents. The 'government as business' model, designed on the NPM, appears to have been effectively demolished not only by an appreciation of the agency and information problems, but also by the actions of the rationally self interested agents causing collapse of economic markets; it has been difficult to justify the self regulating market model in the face of crises in the Savings and Loans market in the US in the 80s and the dot.com bubble in the 90s. Bureaucrats, instead of eliminating transaction costs, the rationale for the existence of a firm,[43] may multiply them and still not deliver. The *coup de grace* appears to have been delivered by the failure of the free financial markets as demonstrated by the sub-prime mortgage crisis of 2008–09.

Interactive Governance: a Convergence?

The fable of the 'six men of Indostan, who went to see the elephant,'[44] touched different limbs of an elephant and came to very different conclusions about what the elephant is (knee for a tree, ear for a fan, tail for a rope, and so on), well illustrates the limitations of biased perception:

'Though each was partially in the right,
And all were in the wrong!'

Governance can also mean different things to different people, agencies, and organizations—corruption (or lack of it) to Transparency International, efficiency to civil servants, transparency to the RTI activists, freedom and democracy to the international donor organizations. Some writers,[45] however, notice a shift towards interactive governance after the financial crisis of 2008-2009, with the governments starting to operate in an interactive mode with the private actors and entities. Interactive governance is defined[46] as 'the complex process through which a plurality of social and political actors, with diverging interests, interact in order to formulate, promote and achieve common objectives'. Unlike the four dimensions of governance discussed above—time and the three dimensions of space, occupied by the academics, the 'policy fragilistas' (Taleb[47]), and the governments and international organizations —governance at micro interactive levels needs to be viewed as more of a *'gestalt'* experience, which neither wishes away government—'governance without government'-nor governance—'government as business'. Public governance has to include actors outside the government apparatus as part of the governing process, and governing activities need to be viewed in a cooperative (like the Linux or the Wikipedia[48]) rather than a competitive or a coercive frame. Interactive governance is a 'legitimate alternative to hierarchy and markets that are based on a context dependent and issue-specific choice of a particular combination of governance mechanisms.'[49]

Governance, thus, needs to emerge from the ashes of the traditional bureaucratic theories, in its new avatar of 'interactive' governance. There appears to have been little change however, in the public discourse and the preoccupation of the governments with the macro policy seems to continue. The old paradigm of public management and public administration seems to dominate in practice, if not in discourse. It continues to wrestle with the need to reconcile various models of rational agents, 'bounded rationality', 'predictably irrational'[50] agents, Principal-agent problems, inconsistency of 'public choice', and the cognitive biases of the System I humans—the public, the second rung of rulers ('Auxilliaries' of Plato) and the 'street level' bureaucrats. Governance markets, unlike economic and social interactions, have yet to internalize the insights provided by the 'market failure' and 'information' economists, and of course, the behavioural and experimental psychologists. Available models, whether outcome-oriented or process-oriented, have little to offer to the practitioners. A somewhat similar situation prevails in India as we hope to show in the next chapter.

2

India: 'Planning' for Governance

There does not seem to be much by way of evolution of 'governance' in India after Chanakya, who is extensively quoted in Indian literature on governance, and that too mainly on the issue of corruption. One reason could be the absolutist rulers, who did not have to seek any public mandate and could get away with whatever they thought fit, with some of them taking good care of the people and some others, akin to characters from the book by Dewan Jermany Dass,[1] who has written about the seamy side of Indian monarchs in pre-Independence India. The British, after some halting attempts at social reforms, became primarily concerned with law and order, consolidating their hold on the country, extracting revenues, feeding the English industry, guarding against being 'absorbed' by Indian culture, and bequeathing to the bureaucracy of independent India the dubious legacy of keeping distance from their 'masters', the public. The only aspect of interactive governance that the British had and that the successive governments in India and its states have carried on is the complaint and grievance redress system, however ritualistic and inefficient. Open *darbar*s are held by the Chief Ministers where pedestrian issues, which need not have arisen in the first place, are raised, but rarely resolved. An example is given later. It is a pity that the Chief Ministers have to camp in the villages to see the situation and do mine sweeping of citizen complaints and problems. Governance continues to be a *mai baap*, 'patrimonial' exchange.

The 'Official' Version

There has been little focus till recently on the need and obligation of the government agencies and actors to involve private actors and citizens in the business of government—policymaking, implementation, and oversight. There is no reference to governance in the 9th Plan and it appears to have become an instrument of public policy only in the 10th Plan, only after the term had come into circulation in the international fora; as usual in India, this also had to be planned and initiated by the government. This public policy document drew attention to good governance in the following terms:

> Governance relates to the management of all such processes that, in any society, define the environment which permits and enables individuals to raise their capability levels on the one hand, and provide opportunities to realize their potential and enlarge the set of available choices, on the other. These processes, covering the political, social and economic aspects of life, impact every level of human enterprise, be it the individual, the household, the village, the region or the nation. It covers the state, civil society and the market, each of which is critical for sustaining human development. The state is responsible for creating conducive political, legal and economic environment for building individual capabilities and encouraging private initiative.

That is even more confusing than the scenario projected by the academics referred to in the previous chapter. The only thing left for God and the people themselves is religion! Governance is broadly identified with 'good government' and its macro, political, social, and economic policies; and good government goes much beyond Adam Smith's modest expectations from the government. Minimum government is not for the Indian Government; it is rather an aggressive, a 'no child left behind' policy in governance!

A more practical approach is, however, visible in the 11th Plan:[2] 'As a democratic country, a central feature of good governance is the constitutionally protected right to elect government at various levels in a fair manner, with effective participation by all sections of the population. This is a basic requirement for the legitimacy of the government and its responsibility to the electorate'. It refers to attributes of: a) *Transparency and accountability* ('The government at all levels must be accountable and transparent. Closely related to accountability, is the need to eliminate corruption, which is widely seen as a major deficiency in governance. Transparency is also critical, both to ensure accountability, and also to enable genuine participation'); b) *Efficiency and effectiveness* ('The government must be effective and efficient in delivering social and economic public services, which are its primary responsibilities'); c) *Decentralization* ('Governments at lower levels can only function efficiently if they are empowered to do so. This is particularly relevant for the PRIs, which currently suffer from inadequate devolution of funds as well as functionaries to carry out the functions constitutionally assigned to them'); d) *Rule of Law* ('An overarching requirement is that the rule of law must be firmly established. This is relevant not only for relations between the government and the individuals, enabling individuals to demand their rights but also for relations between individuals or businesses. A modern economic society depends increasingly upon complex interactions among private entities and these interactions can be efficiently performed only if legal rights are clear and legal remedies for enforcing these rights are swift'); and e) *Fairness* ('The entire system must function in a manner which is seen to be fair and inclusive. This is a perceptional issue but it is real nonetheless. Disadvantaged groups, especially the SCs, STs, minorities and others, must feel that they have an equal stake and should perceive an adequate flow of benefits to ensure the legitimacy of the State').

There is a shift in the focus from inputs to outcomes in the areas of government-citizen interaction and the need for e-governance in basic services—'online record of the land rights, computerized land registration, computerized transfers, computerization of the social security schemes, birth and death certificates, proof of residence, issue of ration and ID cards', and so on. The National e-Governance Plan (NeGP) was approved in May 2006 with the following vision:[3] 'Make all government services accessible to the common man in his locality, through common service delivery outlets and ensure efficiency, transparency and reliability of such services at affordable costs to realize the basic needs of the common man'.

The major difference from the 'computerization' initiatives of the past is the focus on delivery of services to the citizens, rather than internal systems and processes. The Second Administrative Reforms Commission (ARC) Reports reflect this focus, especially on ethics, transparency, citizen participation through the self-governing PRI's, the legal and directional policy interventions, and on the macro level programmes and resources. The unstated assumption seems to be that all the areas of citizen-government interaction are subject to the same set of interventions, a sort of uniform, across the board 'assembly line' system for different services, whether in terms of transparency or participation or fairness or (removal of) corruption. The refreshing focus, at the level of discourse, at least, is on the basic services and e-governance. A draft bill on the Citizen Charters and grievance redress, Citizens Right to Grievance Redress Bill, 2011[4] is under process, though contemplated under certain naive assumptions about 'one size fits all' rules and laws, sidestepping the context of different areas of interaction and service delivery. In practice, simplifying and 're-engineering' of processes has meant obsession with the reform of procedures. Subsequent to the recommendations of the National Knowledge Commission on identifying and simplifying important processes and services, the state governments were asked to set up 'process re-engineering' committees (we have referred earlier to the influence of business management on governance!). The recommendations of a Punjab committee set up for this purpose reflect this obsession with simplifying/eliminating internal procedures—reducing steps of internal processes in one case, say from 17 to 5 and so on, to provide quick service delivery. A citizen, however, is not bothered whether 15 officials deal with a service or only one, but is concerned only about how quickly he or she gets the final product from the agency. Issues of transaction costs for the citizens, who don't have to be bound by the structure of internal processes, tend to be neglected. Incentives and motivations—economic, material, or social—of the government agents as well as the public, which generally structure interactions and their outcomes, are ignored. Simplification of internal processes would, it is hoped, itself lead to a change in the structure of interaction and improved quality of experience, without the systems having to take note of the dispositions, cognitive and other biases and behaviour of the parties—government agents and citizens, not to speak of the transaction costs.

Instead of open-mindedness and experimentation in seeing 'what works', the focus is increasingly on more and more uniform command and control systems. Thus, the latest Plan, while noting some problems in the functioning of the regulatory institutions for various sectors—water, power, health, et cetera —seeks to impose 'super regulators' to streamline and harmonize the regulatory systems, ignoring the distinct character and context of different domains. Regulatory authorities for technical education and medical education have been, on occasion, responsible for governance failure—especially in regard to corruption in granting affiliation/ recognition— ending with the prosecution of the top officials of both the organizations. A macro super regulator, it is assumed, will be more objective, conveniently forgetting the higher probability of the 'multiplier' in information problems and 'information cascades' due to vertical distance. It appears from newspaper reports, however, that the proposal may be mercifully dropped. When the 'centre does not hold', a 'central core' is sought to be created. The governments in India and its states seem to consistently ignore the problem of 'regulatory capture' that was brought to the policymakers' attention by George Stigler[5] 40 years ago. The government agencies appear to have problems with incorporating these inputs in their operational and policy systems, unlike the private sector, which due to competition, has to internalize the relevant academic and experiential inputs provided by the researchers, academicians, and consultants. As indicated in the previous section, the state agents have 'no skin in the game'.

One other aspect of regimentation of the governing processes and mechanisms is the accountant's perspective adopted by the Ministries in Government of India specifying minor processes and procedures of various programmes, tending to divert attention of the state bureaucrats from outcomes to (mainly accounting rather than financial) processes. In the course of a study of Haryana Watershed Development Programmes,[6] the officials confessed off the record that, in view of the limited working season and the cash system of budgeting, they had to 'manufacture' the records to complete the elaborate pre-requisites, in order to ensure the release of funds and sanctions in time, sometimes even completing the paperwork ahead of the activity, apart from having to resort to the common factor for approval of projects-'speed money'.

The proposed Bill on Citizen Charters and Redress of Grievances[7] is another instance of macro level policy and rules which tend to ignore specific transactions and their nature. The Bill requires display of time and service standards, the names of officers responsible for grievance redress and a state-level commission. However, the legislation ignores the distinctive character of various public services and the crucial role that the transaction costs play, as is shown later. Coase's[8] remark about the diversity of economic transactions in the modern world is appropriate for governance transactions. Uniform and simplistic solutions, however, are offered, whether for a residence certificate or FIR registration. Some of these need physical delivery, while other cases require only documentation. A driving licence, for example, may notionally take 15 days to deliver, but is subject to a driving test being passed; that can take whatever time (up to 12 hours) on the day fixed, as indicated subsequently, but is not factored into the process of e-governance or the citizen charters which may provide a total timeline, say of 15 days; the problem of one whole day wasted for the test—a process that could easily be similarly simplified if looked into as a separate transaction—is ignored. This is apart from the problem mentioned later of a higher correlation between bribes, rather than skills, and getting the licence. A draft bill (Electronic Delivery of Services Bill 2011[9]) proposing to make online delivery of all the services mandatory, was circulated among the states, thus effectively eliminating choice not only of the states but even of the customers—all in the name of good governance!

Best Practices

Apart from the planned and dictated routes to good government, much is made of 'best practices'. A GoI document[10] lists 46 best practices (some of these have been listed below) in different states of India. The Administrative Reforms department has also come out with some good publications on the theme.[11] What may not be immediately obvious is that the e-registration project for example in Punjab (listed below), with which I am familiar, is trying to reinvent the wheel in its own way, not adopting the best practice, say of Karnataka. Though Punjab was one of the first states to start with computerization of land records in early 1990s, it has only recently managed to digitize the land records. The same is the case with the e-governance initiative in transport in Punjab; a system different from what is in operation in Delhi is being adopted. There is little evidence of transfer of any of the best practices from one state to another.

Best Practices – Indian States

Name of the Best Practice	*State/Organisation*
Bhoomi	Karnataka
e-Registration (SARITA)	Maharashtra
e-Registration (PRISM)	Punjab
e-Registration (STAR)	Tamil Nadu
Treasury Information System	Karnataka
Treasury Information System	Tamil Nadu
e-Treasury Mission Mode Project	
Urban Governance Innovations in Municipal Administration – Surat Municipal Corporation	Gujarat
Innovations in Transport Sector – Computerization in Transport Department in Punjab	Punjab
Sickle Cell Anemia Control Programme	Gujarat

Source: DPARP GoI; Addressing the Challenges of Public Service Delivery – background note for a conference.

The fact is that the states are 'reinventing' the best practice models in their own way, for reasons not of different context, but just trying to be different. This is an area where some uniformity might be more helpful, but the same is generally avoided.

A Planning Commission document[12] lists 'best practices' in a number of sectors such as education, in different states. Most of these, far from being replicated, have disappeared without any trace of their legacy, as I happen to know in one or two cases. There has been some focus on transparency and participation in the 1st decade of this century; the RTI Act is in position but, as will be seen later, the law in its present form may not succeed in empowering the citizens in their day-to-day interactions. Costs, especially in terms of transaction costs incurred, can be disproportionate to the gains; attributes such as transparency are rooted in the context of micro citizen government interactions and public services, and may not be always amenable to macro management and interventions.

Quantification of Governance: Models and Indicators

Multilateral and other international organizations, as indicated earlier, generally confine their perspectives to specific issues—democracy, freedom, business friendliness—and most of these are undertaken in a comparative framework vis-à-vis other countries. In-country surveys are mostly about specific issues such as corruption, transparency, or investor-friendly policies. As in the case of business innovations, the 'first mover' advantage is temporary. The RTI has now become universal; so has the institution of the Human Rights Commissions. The International Convention on Bribery has been (almost) universally adopted. Inter-country assessments tend to be based primarily on the existence of such formal institutions prompted by common concerns—of human rights, freedom of enterprise, equity, protection of vulnerable and differently challenged sections, and so on. One reason for the rather sterile quality of surveys is the overriding objective to build a macro model, irrespective of its relevance to the 'playing fields'. A Report on Governance[13] looks into the functioning of the legislators, courts, and the government performance in education, health, agriculture, and decentralization. An annexure thereof lists the time taken to discuss the bills during the year 2008–09, varying from 15 hours to as low as three seconds, which indicates, according to the Report, the lack of focus and attention devoted by the legislators of the two houses of Parliament. This, however, could also be due to efficient functioning of the Parliament and the cooperative consultations that go on behind the scenes, or the sheer play of interests on different issues or even a lack of substance. Similarly, huge arrears of the court cases (over 4 million—3.2 million civil and 0.8 million criminal) do not indicate anything by themselves; the civil and criminal laws and the rules may be ambiguous or the problem may be what we call poor 'law and order', or the judicial entities could be non-functional or understaffed. We don't compare institution and disposal of cases among the different states/courts which may show substantial variations from the best to the worst—variations, therefore, not explained by the standard explanations and factors of staff, defective laws and systems which are generally common within a particular state and almost similar even across the states in India. Most of the quantitative analyses seek to project 'averages' and 'totals', rather than variations.

An interesting study[14] claims to have abandoned the complex statistical approach of the World Bank in developing governance indicators based on '310 variables derived from 33 different agencies totalling some 1000 plus data points'. The authors dispose similarly, the GoI's DARPG[15] document comprising 123 indicators across five dimensions, as being too complicated, based on processes rather than outcomes, and requiring expensive survey work. The study lists its own indicators, mostly consisting of socioeconomic outcomes (power consumption, water supply coverage, development expenditure —a sort of extended HDI), but the same study is surprisingly economical in the case of complex areas of judicial service delivery (only one factor, the disposal of cases), Law & Order (three factors, namely police strength, complaints, violent crimes) and Legislature (only two factors, proportion of women and legislators with criminal charges). The problem with the study's own 20 indicators covering outcomes of various services—education, health, law and order, et cetera—is that one has to struggle to identify the 'governance' components. The report is a compilation of the indicators of 'good government' with a focus on what the governments do and on the outputs, which are easily quantifiable, such as, completion of trials, et cetera. There is no logical relationship between the indicators and governance. The number of charge-sheeted legislators in different states (an indicator adopted in the study) may be just an accidental factor.

Bimal Jalan[16] illustrates the polymorphic nature of governance in India; it consists of a grid of political, economic, and social policies and management in government, the relations of bureaucrats and ministers, their accountability, and responsibility. This is apart from the preferred course-privatization—for service delivery, advocated by the author. The quality of governance is, however, expressed in the interactions between the citizens and the government agents, a never-ceasing conflict, which may be resolved sometimes, but as in the economic markets, will never end.

Iterations on Miserable Governance

Citizen Report Cards by the PAC (Public Affairs Centre), Bangalore, is a refreshingly different initiative and the only example we know of a time series on governance, concerned with governance interactions. A report[17] that provides an assessment of the impact of citizen report cards (CRCs) on the performance of public agencies in the city of Bangalore, indicates positive impact of the CRCs, especially in transparency, and to some extent, improved quality of delivery in a couple of specific areas (such as tax assessment). The CRC rated agencies rather than services, but as will be seen, it is possible to have different services at different levels of satisfaction and an aggregate measure may not be an effective tool for capturing the diversity of specific services; each service has its unique context of rules, actors, incentives, social mores, and so on. The Report indicates some problems (an average of three visits to the officials to solve a problem, poor grievance redress, and corruption) that persisted in the CRC-2 which was taken after 5 years, but averages mask the variations in the case of different services and agencies. These limitations are also demostrated by a similar exercise adopted in Ethiopia.[18] It was conducted to assess satisfaction in the case of services for health facilities, water supply, et cetera. Different population groups or the regions may, however, face different dimensions of a problem regarding the same public service. In the case of drinking water, for example, the issue may be of quality somewhere and that of quantity elsewhere. Efforts to assess aggregate satisfaction across different problems, a 'satisfaction index' (though, no doubt, this is important in a general way), thus, leads to a general recommendation in the Study like 'Access to protected water supply service must be improved'. There seems to be a need to move beyond physical resources and their outputs to the processes and outcomes of governance interactions and exchanges.

Governance in the North Western States: A Conventional Evaluation

The Institute for Development and Communication (IDC) conducted two studies with which I was associated, in the north-western states of India: one on urban governance in Punjab[19] and the other on governance in the rural peripheries of the States of Punjab, Haryana, and HP.[20] The Study on Urban Governance adopted the attribute approach and looked into the areas of public and civic services within the domain of the urban local bodies, and the issues of efficiency, effectiveness, responsiveness, equity, participation, fairness, et cetera. The six selected Urban Local Bodies (ULBs) were paired in three sets; the focus was on comparative assessment of governance in the two ULBs in each set having similar demographics. The Study on Governance in the Rural Peripheries[21] selected three adjoining villages (one in each of the States of HP, Haryana, and Punjab) located at the peripheries of their respective districts and states. The studies show some interesting results regarding the state of governance as perceived by the citizens and assessed during the study.

Masses and Leaders: Conflicting Choices

Though the priorities in respect of the physical and social infrastructure are context and location-specific, broadly, these are water supply, maintenance of roads and streets, solid waste disposal, and street lighting in that order. So far as the civic infrastructure is concerned, the priorities are dictated by the location-specific problems and can change from place to place. City transport, parks, storm water drainage, which are the favourites with the urban planners, do not figure among the top priorities. It would appear that programme-specific national and state priorities may result in an inappropriate use of resources, through adoption of uniform programmes, for example for storm drainage, across different towns and cities, instead of concentrating the available resources in a specific ULB for addressing the major deficiencies and priorities of civic infrastructure, which bother citizens the most. In the rural areas, the citizen priorities are water supply, health, and physical connectivity/transport. The responses are location-specific but education takes a back seat in urban as well as rural areas. An interesting finding was the disjunct between the perceptions of the elected councillors and the public in regard to what should be the local priorities.

Infrastructure: O&M and Investment

An interesting finding was that the sheer absence of civic infrastructure/desired service is more acceptable than the day-to-day irritants experienced by the citizens while making use of the civic facilities and infrastructure claimed to be provided. People tend to adjust more easily to a product's/service's absence than to its unpredictable and varying quality, once it is provided. Absence of storm drainage is noticed only on a day of heavy rain but the piled up solid waste on the streets can be a daily nuisance. Civic infrastructure exists but people are unsatisfied—potholed roads, dysfunctional street lighting systems, and water supply systems adequate only for the ground floor residents. This is probably the reason why the (lack of) civic infrastructure is perceived as less of a problem in the rural areas—'no claims made'—than in the urban areas.

Management and O&M (Operation and Management) of infrastructure services appear to be more important than investment thereon. There is a case for putting on ground, a base level of services rather than scrappy bits of infrastructure through extensive, rather than intensive, use of resources—streets paved in one locality, drains in another. That was the fate of the *Sunder Gram* (beautiful village) project renamed *Nirmal Gram* project later, under which over Rs. 800 crores were spent in the 1990s in Punjab; the expenditure was mostly ill planned, without much lasting impact as an IDC evaluation[22] has shown.

Responsiveness to Citizens

Grievance redress systems appear to be absent even in the urban areas. Only one of the six cities (mainly due to a local initiative, the district Suvidha Centre, which incorporated this function) had a proper complaint *recording* system. About 85 per cent of the complainants had to make personal visits for getting their complaints recorded/addressed, with 50 per cent of respondents making two to three visits; official responses do appear to need an exogenous stimulus. One basic component of responsive governance, responsiveness in the case of complaints, is generally missing; even the systems of recording, let alone response, are non-existent. People prefer to approach the authorities one or more levels removed—vertically or horizontally—from the appropriate official in the hierarchy. There is, thus, a disorganized 'forum shopping', with the authorities right from the President of India/the CM down to the District Magistrate being flooded with (many a time) routine complaints which are required to be looked into, say, by an Executive Engineer or even a JE, and sometimes posed for resolution in the personal contact programmes—*Sarkar apke dwar* (government at your doorstep) in Haryana or *Sangat Darshan* (face to face with the people) in Punjab.

A number of states (Bihar, MP, Delhi, Punjab) have sought to address the problems of service delivery through the Right to Public Service Laws, but this may only result in diluting the responsibility of the massive hierarchies that exist. The laws seek to create apex Commissions for addressing problems of timely delivery of basic services that are really required to be addressed at the 'front desk'. We do need an 'ombudsman' for public governance but not in a lateral relationship to the lowly official of an agency but rather in a vertical relationship to the agency and its head (for example, an 'ombudsman' for local bodies, when the Chief Executive and not a draftsman is answerable to the 'ombudsman'). These institutions ignore the heavy transaction costs incurred by the individuals for seeking redress of their problems in the case of services where 'speed money' will be only a fraction of these costs, as indicated later. That is the reason for a five member Commission in one of the states having an average of two to three revisions per member over a full one year period, and most of these were being taken up *suo motu*! Even the number of first and second appeals is rather limited.

Participation: Local Councillors Excluded

In the urban areas, 65 per cent of the respondents reported that there was little encouragement in precept or practice from the leadership or the officials in the ULBs for participation of the citizens. What is still more surprising is the fact that even the municipal councillors felt the same way and reported a general practice of exclusion, even of the elected councillors, from major decision-making and implementation areas. A similar picture was observed in the rural areas where the sarpanch, generally in collusion with the panchayat secretary, rules the roost. In the three periphery villages of the three states, only 33 per cent of the respondents indicated some element of participation in the public affairs with 53 per cent reporting little improvement in this regard over time. However, there is substantial variation among the three villages—little participation in one state to 62 per cent in another. The latter is mainly due to more carefully planned and properly structured Gram Sabha meetings in that state as compared to the other two, as well as a minimal (administrative) resource support provided to the Gram Panchayat that was absent in others.

Bureaucratic Efficiency

The O&M expenditure on water supply and sewerage per unit of population/connection among the selected six ULBs could vary by a factor of 10. Officials were completely unaware of such major variations. There is no platform for information on comparative performance, no benchmarking, and such vital data is not even compiled by the ULBs, let alone compared and monitored. These variations in cost efficiency had to be calculated in the Urban Governance study. What is not measured tends to be neglected. And, this is very true for governance in India.

Good Governance: An 'Accidental' Phenomenon

Governance in India, as viewed by the governments, the NGOs and the academics, seems to consist of a mix of macro economic and social objectives—poverty elimination, growth, development, and organizational efficiency (judiciary, legislature, executive, PRIs) rather than the 'how' of the business of governing. The attribute-based approach does not appear to be very helpful in improving governance for specific services and sectors. Good practices appear to emerge from instances of personal commitment, and instead of spreading, start fading away sooner than later. This appears to be happening in one of the ULBs studied where the quality of outputs in the Suvidha Kendra has deteriorated after the departure of its 'champion', the Deputy Commissioner. There is little evidence of the adoption of best practices across local jurisdictions even within the same state even though the context—institutional, social, administrative, and political—remains the same.

Accident and chance appear to play a role in shaping governance practices and performance. In one of the cities in the Urban Governance Study, for example, there was not only prompt service delivery but also effective grievance handling and this appeared to be due to the effective positioning of a Suvidha Centre as a single window even for civic problems, usually left to the ULBs, and personal follow up thereon. In another ULB, a lowly official who helped systemize and computerize various records was instrumental in projecting a positive image of the ULBs performance among the citizens. It would appear that the 'champions' need not necessarily be in the leadership positions, and anybody can make a difference. There was no evidence of any national or state-level political or administrative initiative being taken except in one of the states in the Rural Governance Study, where attention to proper structuring of the panchayat functions and provision of much-needed staff for administrative housekeeping, appeared to have made a difference in respect of the village concerned in improving the area of panchayat functioning. The overall picture, as viewed by the citizens, reflected by and large poor governance despite some islands of excellence.

From Attributes and Indicators to Interactions

A number of civil servants including the economists have devoted a lot of space to governance in their books and memoirs, focusing on macro policies and reforms. Bimal Jalan, for example, in a chapter on Crisis of Governance,[23] refers to problems in the implementation of government policies—the vitiated environment within which policies are made, the rural-urban divide, poverty, misuse of subsidies, and the contrast between the stagnant public sector (poor public services, staff costs, appropriation of resources by the departments rather than the public, indiscipline among officials) and the vibrant private sector. The solutions offered are in some ways contradictory: restoration of the State/Central authority, coupled with delegation and decentralization of powers, internal reforms of the bureaucracy, and individual responsibility and autonomy of the ministers (notwithstanding the coal scam/telecom auctions). Unfortunately, the private sector is no longer vibrant and is now appealing to government for the 'stimuli' to be continued. Some others advocate a 'champions' approach based on a model of their own image as bureaucrats. Performance in different areas and jurisdictions, in respect of the attributes of governance, varies widely across services, locations, and outcomes, and appears to be a function of the context-specific factors.

One major problem with the attributes approach is the somewhat confusing picture it provides of 'governance'—akin not even to the partial reality of the elephant, as mentioned in the last chapter, but to an abstract mathematical aggregation. The Studies mentioned were aimed at generating an easy and comprehensive governance index relevant for the local governing jurisdictions in India, but while it was possible to manufacture one, it would have been somewhat artificial, a statistical construct divorced from reality. The performance in different areas does not reflect a 'normal distribution'—of a 'Gaussian' bell curve—and instead, consists of 'fat tails', or 'statistical boulders', except for the one constant, corruption. This was the case whether one considered the six ULBs of Punjab or the three contiguous villages in three states, or responses for most of the areas of interaction and public service functions—birth and death certificates, construction approvals, grievance redress, O&M expenditure, et cetera. The tools of statistical analysis, based on averages and standard deviations, did not appear to be very useful, either for analysis or for initiating reforms.

We had initiated the two studies with high hopes of developing a time-series for governance in the north-western states, based broadly on the World Bank indicators and a 'cutting edge' focus on the citizens. We, however, came to the conclusion that carrying out such surveys would not only be expensive but also futile. We may be publishing the same miserable data year after year and snatch at the 'straws in the wind'—best practices, best districts, the best management models—for some lessons. As Abhijit Banerjee and Esther Duflo[24] remark, 'Talking about the problems of the World without talking about some accessible solutions is the way to paralysis rather than progress.' Generally, there is a tendency to pack in one group under 'governance' practically everything that the governments do; macro policies in the areas of redistribution and reduction of poverty, justice, the rule of law, infrastructure, electoral processes, civil and police organizations, entities, public service delivery, and interaction with the citizens. A concerted attack on all these fronts of poor governance, as well as the national issues of internal and external security, as one author[25] seems to do, appears to be a pathetic appeal to the elites, the 'white men' of India, to come out and do something for 'them'. Such a wide canvas leads to a 'planner's rather than a 'searcher's approach. We appear to be seeking comprehensive solutions covering all the possible fronts of government policies and action, even though in Easterly's words,[26] 'we can't get twelve cent medicines to children dying of malaria'.

Only a modest objective is proposed here—how to reach to the people what *they* want, rather than what *we* want for them. It is now *de rigueur* to propose solutions to the tricky problems of public service delivery in the frame of experiments and randomized trials, Easterly[27] refers to the Progresa program in *Mexico* which provides cash grants to the mothers, provided they keep their children in the school and also have regular health checks; how it was adopted after a randomized trial over two groups of villages, with the 'control' villages getting no benefits. The problem seems, however, not so much of the lack of evidence of the effectiveness of these small steps, but the planners' (utopian) social engineering frame, which diverts attention from the more 'modest, doable steps'. For the citizens, each interaction and transaction is a microcosm for governance, a sort of 'homunculus' compressing the governance totality in that interaction. Governance would need to be explored through a detailed mapping and analysis of its unique sites and structures—something similar to the mapping of 23,000 genes, across the twenty three chromosomes of the human genome and not simply counting their numbers and deriving meaningless averages and deviations across the 'exons' intermingled with a much larger number of the non functional 'introns'. Meaningful public governance in India needs to focus on and explore the 'play of the game', the areas of public private interactions within their micro context, rules and institutions.

3

Incentives, Behaviour and 'Rules of the Game': A Framework

It would be apparent from the brief account of governance provided in the previous chapters—theory and practice across different countries, academics, governments, multilateral organizations, and friendly or critical practitioners—that there is generally a tendency to refer, or even defer, to global or national macro perspectives and judgments when looking for explanations of failure or mantras for success. Governments and the practicing academicians focus mostly on the macroeconomic, political, judicial, administrative and structural reforms, which Williamson calls the 'first order governance institutions'.[1] The interactions and exchanges between the government agencies and the citizens, played out at the cutting edge on the playgrounds, the 'governance markets', have been the 'blind spots'; their salience is rarely appreciated. One problem is that good governance tends to be viewed against the shifting landscape of economic and political ideologies and beliefs—the Hobbesian stick, the pragmatism of Alexander Pope ('for forms of government let fools contest/what ever is administered best, is the best'), the interventionist New Deal, 'managerialism' and the NPM of 1980s, 'reinventing of government'[2] through outsourcing of activities to the private sector/PPP's, *laissez faire* or minimal government of the Milton Friedman/Chicago School. It is rarely possible, however, for governments, especially in the pluralistic democracies, to adopt a single-minded approach or a uniform model across all areas of governance activities and the result is a 'path dependent' and incremental 'brew'. The global discourse is concerned mainly about the pan-national institutions and systems—political, economic, and social. National priorities are about the macroeconomic, social, and political policies and institutions. Even the 'middle kingdoms'—the states in India—are obsessed with macro policies and governance systems, and devote little attention to the governance playgrounds where the micro processes and interactions actually take place. Micro governance appears to have been elbowed out by macro public policy.

Cassidy[3] quotes Galbraith (*The Affluent Society*): 'To a far greater degree than is commonly supposed, functions accrue to the state because as a purely technical matter, there is no alternative to public management.' And as indicated, it appears to be now in a 'bubble' phase, especially in India with regulations demanded, or contemplated, for lighter school bags and preschool education (as per a recent report, a law for the latter has been proposed by the Central Government!) Some of these ventures evidently go beyond the modest necessity highlighted by Galbraith. Various surveys and studies however indicate little change in the 'governance capital'—trust and cooperation in governance exchanges—or the outcomes of intense rule making. On the other hand, in some areas such as corruption, public engagement, effectiveness, and efficiency, the quality of governance may have deteriorated over time. Searching for good governance is like *Waiting for Godot*. It appears to be constrained by the very space occupied, like air in a balloon. One brings in the RTI Act for transparency but finds the non-RTI space of information compressed. You go after the 2G spectrum allocation in India, but discover the natural gas and coal blocks allocations going awry. Botswana in Africa and Bihar in India may improve, but governance in Nigeria and the Indian state X (it may not be politically correct to name such states) deteriorates.

Bell Curves and Statistics

The problems with an attribute-based approach may be compounded by the inherent limitation of statistical methodologies, the common route for building models. Statistical approaches based on scoring and normalization techniques have sometimes found correlations, say, between the GDP growth and corruption.[4] The Governance Index developed by the World Bank, a much respected and quoted index, assesses governance across different countries for a number of attributes. It is, however, difficult to derive meaningful average, median, and other statistical parameters—the standard measures of assessment and cataloguing—across a large number of interactions, activities, outputs, and outcomes that involve human beings and their diverse incentives and motives on the two sides of exchange (the government and the citizens). Even the Gross National Happiness Index, which appears closer to the day-to-day experience and aspirations of the citizens, has ended up being averaged. One can as well try devising an index for the 'average' *Homo sapiens* on the basis of averages spread across the dimensions of physique (the Body Mass Index), personality (five attributes), intelligence (IQ), and other features! It may be more prudent to study the specific markets and exchanges rather than bank upon, to take an analogy, the discredited quantitative models to predict the movement of the share markets. Indicators of socioeconomic outcomes do not trace a normal 'bell' curve across different services, contexts, and jurisdictions, administrative and geographic; the 'fat tails' tend to predominate on both sides of the 'bell'. Sometimes claims are made about the ability of experts to integrate such 'fat tails' or 'black swans'[5] into the domain of quantitative analysis. Ian Bremmer and Preston Keat seek to do so in the area of political risk, which exhibits mostly 'fat tails'.[6] Barring such optimistic exceptions, we generally wish away these oddities out of the structure of analysis and prognosis.

While describing the bell curve as a 'great intellectual fraud', Taleb[7] quotes Poincare: 'physicists tended to use the Gaussian curve because they thought mathematicians believed it a mathematical necessity; mathematicians used it because they believed that physicists found it to be an empirical fact.' Stephan J. Gould[8] remarks in an aptly titled essay ('The Medium is not the Message') that the 'Platonic heritage .... leads us to view statistical measures of central tendency wrongly, indeed opposite to the appropriate interpretation in our actual world of variation, shadings and continua; variation is the hard reality, not a set of imperfect measures of a central tendency.' This is probably very true of the statistical and indicator based models of governance.

In the case of governance interactions and exchanges, given their complexity and variation, this approach may not be fruitful. Matt Ridley[9] points out the futility of the exercise to identify the 'average' human genome, based on a proposed study of the genes of 200 individuals; each person's genome is not only unique but also constantly evolving through interaction with the environment, including parasites and viruses. That seems to be the case with governance exchanges. One problem with the correlation between X and Y, say between corruption and delivery of services or between citizen satisfaction and transparency, is that a study depends on specific data/area/period chosen for the purpose, but the same can be and generally is demolished by the same weapon. A sample may not be representative of the universe in respect of the attributes to be measured and sometimes the data for the universe itself cannot be measured objectively. *The Times of India* published a news item,[10] which refers to a five-year study whose findings negate an earlier and widely accepted correlation between the distribution of vitamin A and antihistamines in schools and improvement in the mortality rates and cognitive development of children. We shall mention another example later regarding correlation between specific factors favoured by different researchers and reduction in the crime rate in the USA in the 1990s. Dehejia *et al*[11] provide valuable insights into the pitfalls of statistical data based on surveys—whether about elections, the incidence of Aids in India, or malnutrition among children. They provide the instance of the 'missing women' study by Amartya Sen, which was re-examined in a subsequent study, on the distribution of 'missing women' across the Indian states, by Debraj Ray and Siwan Anderson; the latter describe Sen's study as a 'one dimensional' explanation of equating 'missing women' with women never born. Such averaged macro data tend to ignore the diversity of causes of the missing women across local jurisdictions and can rarely be fruitful inputs for locally appropriate interventions, which need to be related to (maybe) just one out of the many significant causes of failure. Taleb has demonstrated the problem of spurious correlations in respect of events and phenomena that have multiple variables, leading to exponential increase in correlations—'the more variables, the more correlations that can show significance in the hands of a "skilled researcher"'[12]—described by him as 'The Tragedy of Big Data'.

Theories of social interaction in the area of public governance tend to be based on 'representative' samples picked up from diverse and unique contexts. One needs only to imagine Charles Darwin trying to understand the process of evolution, based on the averages and standard deviations of the beak sizes of finches on the islands of the Galapagos! In public governance, more than in evolutionary biology, a focus on specific exchanges and transactions may be more helpful in understanding good 'governance'. A pragmatic approach can then be developed for designing appropriate institutions, rather than seeking arbitrary statistical patterns and coherence across 'complex, diverse and dynamic'[13] governance interactions. These interactions and exchanges do not appear to have *a priori* norms or standards; there is need therefore, as advocated by Harford,[14] to study the variations and make a selection based on what works and in which context.

Myth of Best Practices

The magic of 'best practices' and their adoption by other governing jurisdictions is also unlikely to be useful as seen in the last chapter. Chile's governance model covers a wide field of economic and social policies and is a model for free market ideology, not governance. The Botswana model is primarily about natural resource management, apart from the adept, but to some extent, also fortuitous handling of the ethnic and colonization issues, as explained by Acemoglu.[15] Dani Rodrix mentions the shifting preferences for policy models—Scandinavia in the 1970s, Japan in the 1980s, the US in the 1990s: 'the very idea of a winner is suspect in a world when nations have somewhat different preferences'.[16] Good governance outcomes appear to need a unique amalgam of men, resources, context, and chance, difficult to emulate, or even deconstruct, in a way an 'emergent' property, a characteristic of the complex systems. Adoption of sector or attribute-specific best practices outside their specific contexts may not even be helpful; there is little evidence of the adoption of best practices, and if adopted, of their survival outside the cocoons of their birth. It is easy to appreciate the difficulty of adopting international best practices to fit the local context. Toolkits for transparency or participation based on idealistic assumptions and models of best practices tend to either wither away in alien contexts or inflict unintended damage like foxes and rabbits, imported into Australia.[17] This apart, the recipients of the gift of 'best practices' show little enthusiasm. The passivity in adopting the 'foreign' practices can be contrasted with the business innovations that have to be zealously protected through patents and other means. In the case of governance practices, the national and state agencies are exhorted and beseeched even by the patent holders, the originator governments and the 'champions'; no royalty is payable, but there are still no takers! The Ahmednagar experiment in the open district administration and the Surat one in waste management are rarely talked about now. The micro credit model of the Grameen Bank in Bangladesh—an obvious success in a neighbouring country—is struggling to find its feet in India, despite government support, even in terms of funding. In fact, there could be no better illustration than provided by Yunus;[18] he is himself sceptical of the spread of the model in alien contexts, and hence, his reluctance to partner with the multilateral agencies for extending it to other countries.

One reason the 'best practices' are at a discount could be a lack of competition. In the economic markets, innovations which provide the first mover advantage are soon competed away; in the governance markets on the other hand, there is little incentive for government agents to adopt them; they rarely face the pressure of competitive survival. Best practices seem to be like genetic mutations that originate in specific contexts and environments and help in 'survival', but may not work elsewhere. We may as well engineer a 'sickle cell' mutation to control malarial in India; the sickle cell syndrome while offering some protection against the malarial parasites, possibly the cause of the genetic mutation in Africa, causes grave problems of its own[19]. The difficulty of adopting best practices is well illustrated by Shankkar Aiyaar[20] in the example of the introduction of hybrid seeds for the Green Revolution in India in the 1960s; it took a unique combination of men (the Agriculture Minister, the Prime Minister, and even the Private Secretary to the Agriculture Minister), moment and resources to successfully introduce the same in India.

It would appear that the statistical models of the characteristics, attributes and traits of governance, 'best practices', or even the socioeconomic indicators, may not be of much help in devising tools to improve the quality of governance for the citizens and the parties impacted by the governance processes-macro or micro. We may need a different framework based on 'governance' as 'operational' and 'interactive' governance, which addresses the 'event horizon' at the point of interaction of the government and the citizens.

State and Governance Failure

Success stories—'best practices' and/or an optimum mix of attributes—may not be helpful as seen, and it may be more appropriate to study failure, following the trajectory of economics from the equilibrium models and 'economics of bliss' to the economics of 'market failure'.[21] Tolstoy has been quoted by many writers in this context: 'Happy families are all alike; every unhappy family is unhappy in its own way' (*Anna Karenina*). Jared Diamond,[22] while explaining the phenomenon of seemingly suitable species like zebra not being domesticated, indicates six reasons why some animals were not domesticated. None of the reasons concern the skills of the people inhabiting various regions: (a) diet; (b) growth rate; (c) problems of captive breeding; (d) nasty disposition; (e) disposition to panic; (f) social structures. *Any one of these is sufficient for failure whereas all of them may be required for successful domestication.* As Diamond remarks, "we tend to seek single factor explanations of success.

For most important things though, to quote him, *success requires avoiding many separate possible causes of failure*". Take another example from health. A lot of things need to be in order for the health of organisms—food, environment, genes. Take out one small component and a health problem appears, say scurvy due to vitamin C deficiency or an infection which needs specific medication; what is relevant is the unique cause of failure, not the case histories, diet, or genes of healthy people. Tim Harford's subtitle for his book, *Adapt—Why Success Always Starts with Failure,*[23] appears very appropriate in the context of public governance. We need to study failure in order to achieve success.

Wikipedia defines 'governance failure' as government intervention causing a more inefficient allocation of goods and resources than would occur without intervention. Some writers[24] describe governance failure as a policy failure, a failure of exchange through imposition of transaction costs, which should be zero; it is claimed that generally government intervention may result in 'double market failure', that is, 'market failure resulting in bureaucratic mal function—government failure through inefficient interventions'. It is also suggested by them that generally the issues of externality et cetera justifying government intervention, have a spurious rationale and the transaction cost is a more appropriate concept for deciding the scale and nature of interventions to optimize trade and output. The example of successful operation of the privately managed light houses is given to illustrate that even in the case of public goods government intervention may not be appropriate or even required. Instances given in the chapters that follow indicate such 'double market failure' in a number of public service areas. Market failure may be necessary but is not a sufficient justification for government intervention.

It is necessary to differentiate 'state failure' from 'governance failure'. State failure is concerned with macro level political and economic institutions; it occurs due to the collapse of the national authority due to factors such as external or internal conflict and physical violence and is characterized by violence, human rights violations, absence of the rule of law and autocracy. As Stephen D. Krasner says, 'failed, weak, incompetent, abusive, national authority structures, lead to failure and inadequate governance.'[25] The paper refers to the report of a Task Force which studied the cases of 'state failure' —136 cases for the years 1955-1998—and attributes state failure to one of the following types of internal political crises: revolutionary war, ethnic war, adverse regime change and genocide. The primary causes of state failure are stated to be 'partial democracy, trade closure, low levels of economic well being, high infant mortality rates'. State failure is captured in the macro indicators covering socio-economic areas and security —corruption, deterioration of infrastructure, unregulated borders, declining GDP, rampant crime, currency volatility, failure of basic political, economic and social institutions and the dominant extractive character of the remnants of the state which survive.

State failure obviously includes governance failure, as there is little space for public governance in such chaos. Governance 'failure' on the other hand can occur even in regimes with sound political and economic institutions. Unlike state failure, governance failure does not leave easy clues, as will be seen later; it needs a Sherlock Holmes to unravel them. It is somewhat akin to 'market failure'; the latter refers not to the collapse of all the economic markets (generally a case of state failure) but specific segments thereof—financial, share markets, real estate or (the academic model of) the 'used car'[26] market. In fact, the 'used car' analogy may be useful in explaining the relevance of micro governance within a specific context. This market, contrary to the model's prediction, is flourishing in India, thanks to competition and the various *jugaadu* (innovative solutions to problems) practices, which address information problems of the purchasers. One such institution is of the middlemen, who now dominate the market and have a reputation to sustain; it is these middlemen who mostly buy and sell in the second hand car market, pocketing the 'arbitrage'.

Market Failure and Governance Failure

The economics of market failure has enriched our

understanding of the functioning or collapse of economic markets and the play of incentives. Insights provided by the studies of information asymmetry ('used car' market failure), 'bounded rationality' (Herbert Simon), 'externalities' (Pigou) and, of course, the problem of monopolies have enriched the barebones classical approach to economic transactions and have exposed the utopian assumptions of the equilibrium and welfare theorems. In the governance exchanges and interactions involving material incentives, uneven information would appear to play a major role, as will be seen; other factors causing market failure, such as the monopoly character of the exchange, are in fact a defining feature of most of the governance exchanges. One can add the problems of disinterest/'rational ignorance' of the public, vested interests, disaster myopia, short sightedness and a host of others which have been brought to the grudging attention of the policymakers by behavioural economists and experimental psychologists. Governance failure is similar to the imperfect but functional markets; exchanges do take place but are not positive sum games under conditions of perfect competition and complete information. Governance failure imposes avoidable costs on society, individuals and the state mostly in terms of transaction costs, is reflected at the junction of interaction and exchange in the market for services provided by the state, and is service and context specific. Failure in the 'used car' market points to the need for addressing information asymmetry and it is the market which provided the solution as indicated in the case of the used car market in India. The failure of credit markets similarly requires the relevant incentives of the parties to be addressed[27]. In the case of public governance, however, we tend to favour omnibus 'snake oil' solutions across the board for the public services markets, whether in terms of information or participation or efficiency or all of them put together. Such solutions and magic remedies are likely to be iatrogenic and cause more harm than good.

Macro Policy and Institutions

Economic, social and political policies are no doubt important for the social and economic development of countries and their populations. Primacy, however, needs to be given, not to an abstract concept of a country's population, but its living and breathing constituents—citizens and juridical entities, corporates and businesses. There is a reason for looking into the bread and butter issues of relevance to them. Economists and sociologists alike stress the role, which the political, economic, and social institutions play in the growth and development of countries and communities. North[28] focuses on the economic institutions, Avner Greif[29] on the religious and cultural institutions whereas Acemoglu[30] is concerned mostly with the political institutions, 'inclusive' or 'extractive', and the way they determine the prospects of growth and development. There is also a debate on whether these institutions can be moulded (Jeffrey Sachs) or are deterministic (Easterly).

Apart from the lack of unanimity on the role of institutions, the tendency for governments is to bite more than one can chew in the case of macro policies and programmes. The corporate sector, at least, has one overarching objective—profits. Public interest on the other hand may be getting children to school or reducing infant mortality or helping the poor survive. In many of these, tried and tested methods of intervention are rarely available and even experts differ, as can be seen from the violent tenor of debate in India on the Food Security Bill or on government investment in higher education and so on. The most governments can do is throw money at these problems and hope for the best. Funding from the tax pool covers a large number of good, bad, and indifferent programmes and schemes. One wonders what the results would be of a regression analysis (that is, after controlling for other factors) for such schemes—a regression analysis to assess correlation, say between the funds under the National Rural Health Mission and the outcomes. The macro level fiscal imbalances however are a more popular theme, while at the sector level, the same academics might favour the governments turning out the not so deep pockets, say for education or health or other personal pet ideas, known as the 'endowment effect' among psychologists. The Lok Pal bill passed by the Indian government recently is one of the few examples of attention to macro as well as micro rules—how the Lok Pal is to be constituted, the process of enquiry, investigation and prosecution, rights of the persons under enquiry, et cetera. Most of these issues were left unsettled in the earlier drafts, which were driven either by single-minded idealism or political opportunism. This appears to be an excellent example of the 'wisdom of the (political) crowds', comprising different parties and interests, expressed in the final report of the Select Committee, which was the basis for the final bill.

Micro Institutions: 'Play of the Game'

We need, therefore, a framework built around interactions taking place in the course of public services between the citizens and the government and its agencies—framework centred around 'play of the game' and the interactions of the players in the specific context of objectives, situations, rules of exchange, motivations, incentives, and other boundary conditions relevant for 'operational governance'. Governance interactions may need to be analysed within their micro contexts of institutions, rules and incentives of the parties. There is not much by way of 'aggregate' demand, across different public services, to warrant Keynesian style macro interventions. The quantum universe of micro individual interactions, exchanges and transactions, can also help in understanding macro governance in the policy and directional areas. The latter is important but we need to be concerned more with the 'business' and play of governing, rather than the agenda setting/decision-making of the Board of Management, the top government agents responsible for policy making and direction.

In the 'playing fields' of micro governance markets, exchanges, and interactions, the inputs and outcomes are easy to ascertain and correctives possible due to real time feedback. One problem with the governance transactions, however, is that, unlike economic markets, there is no competition, and therefore, no automatic feedback on the outcomes of the transactions. One needs therefore to make efforts and develop clever information systems to get the feedback. In advertising for example, one traditionally gets feedback, sometimes from increased sales, but mostly through queries and responses. And there is only one reliable way for getting a reliable feedback—the experience of the citizen, the other party to the exchanges taking place on the streets and at the front desks. These micro exchanges and interactions in public governance, however, tend to get a short shrift. This is not surprising when one considers that even microeconomic markets tend to be treated similarly; such issues are considered trivial. We now know Akerlof for his path-breaking work on information asymmetry, but the article was rejected by three prestigious journals—as they deemed it to be concerned with a trivial subject matter, the used car market—before it was finally published in 1970.[31] Economic markets are generally about tangible goods and services, labour, money/credit, and other factors. Micro exchanges and markets, in public governance, mostly concern what we call public services—whether delivering some value or product to the citizens, or extracting value from them as in taxation. The nature of various public services is elaborated in the next chapter.

Governance Regimes and Jurisdictions

A macro/national perspective in a vast country like India may not even be feasible. India has a distinctive federative structure with sovereign states; the latter are important players and account for most of the public governance exchanges. Concerns of the common man are mostly within the domain of state government and the self-governing local institutions. The Central Government does play a major role in areas of social and economic policy but it is mainly through control over the purse and the broad contours of policy objectives. All major governance interactions, at the middle and cutting edge levels, remain within the domain of the state government and the local bodies. The national government is dependent on the states for the 'last mile' delivery even in respect of areas under its jurisdiction. The 'play of the game' in the case of public service interactions is carried out within the governance jurisdictions at the middle and micro levels—the states and the sub-state jurisdictions/PRI's (urban and rural). The sub-national jurisdictions in India are relevant as there is a uniform and common infrastructure of the political, social, economic and administrative structures and rules, which make comparisons much easier, one state to another, and among the districts or other similar jurisdictions in a state. This may not be possible in the case of the nation states, as the underpinnings of the institutions in different countries may provide too diverse a canvas and context to factor in, and one may only hope to have a bird's eye view rather than a 'worm's eye view', favoured by the founder of the Grameen Bank.

In the case of the schemes funded by the Government of India, the agents responsible for carrying out the activities are spread out across the states and the complex hierarchies, thus multiplying the agency and information problems. The people who help make policy in government, have much on their plate and as Friedman remarks,[32] move on to their next favourite, once a particular policy/legislation is done. Results take a long time coming and even then, one is not sure to what extent the results of 'moderate success' are due to policy, or accident, or a regression to the mean. Most of these involve complex factors and it is difficult to judge the efficacy of governance inputs on the basis of outcomes, such as in the areas of malnutrition or infant mortality. Policy in such areas is a sort of 'Ponzi Scheme', though rarely exposed; the persons to be benefitted do not pay for it and the taxpayer does not know and/or is not bothered.

Due to factors such as the mobility of labour and its migration across different governing jurisdictions—states within a particular nation state—the local governing entities are getting more and more diverse, as various ethnic, social and cultural groups move into the local communities. This requires incorporation of these minorities' needs and priorities in the policies of the governing units. It is no longer sufficient to plan for their limited but vital contribution to the society as outsiders and in isolation (as in the case of Jews in Venice[33]). The issues of diversity and multi-ethnicity matter more for governance at the middle and micro levels, but may tend to be neglected. This is another reason for a focus on the local governing jurisdictions.

Context of Governance Exchanges

Specific context of the interactions—actors, their incentives, social mores, local situation, and processes—is also a material factor. This does not mean that the broad context and the policy environment can be ignored. Obviously the latter is material in providing a broad framework for the micro interactions between the government and the citizens, but there is a need to take account of the perceptions, biases, beliefs, and values of the interacting parties, as these are also material inputs for the outcomes of the interactions. To take an example, the processes for property registration have been simplified in most of the states in India. Generally the process has become discretion free and the transaction (deed registration) is concluded on the day of presentation. The practice of making payment of a percentage of the value as 'rent', however, continues because generally people have been led to believe that they may face a problem if they don't pay. This is partly re-enforced by the interest of property dealers, who handle a majority these transactions, to keep the registration authorities happy, as their dealings with officials are frequent and it is necessary for them to retain the goodwill of the Registrar. They are, in this case, the 'opinion leaders' for the public. In the case of reporting of births, the lack of attention to the context explains, as we shall see, the disproportionately large number of delayed and wasteful interactions. Cultural and situational factors have a bearing on the outcomes and why the problems continue, despite digitization of processes and elimination of discretion of officials.

The relevance of context has been wonderfully explained in *The Tipping Point.*[34] Gladwell refers to the inadequacy of 'dispositional', as compared to the 'contextual', explanations in explaining human behaviour, a conclusion strikingly illustrated by the Princeton University psychologists, John Darley and Daniel Batson in the 'Good Samaritan' Study. What influenced individual behaviour, to help an injured person on the road was not the sermon given, but whether or not the subject was in a 'rush' (a state induced by the experimenter). *Indianomics*[35] and *Nudge*[36] provide two interesting examples of context: in the former case, effectiveness of the 'Final Mile' poster intended to deter citizens from crossing the railway line in Mumbai, and in the latter, the progressively close spaced stripes painted on the Lake Shore Drive, Chicago, to give the car drivers a sensation of increasing speed and so to reduce it. The latter 'nudge' is for the driver on the road, the former for persons crossing the rail track. Most of the governments seek to do the opposite, with rules instructing agents on what the citizens should do, rather than understanding the behaviour and incentives of citizens.

Governance needs to be viewed in terms of systems, processes, and mechanisms of interaction with citizens. A shift in focus from macro to micro interactions of government agents —with individuals and groups—may be useful. There is a need to seek meaning and assess attributes, actions, and outcomes at the point of interaction within the unique situations and context of specific exchanges and services. Governance may need to be viewed, not in terms of internal processes and systems or as an agglomeration of attributes—of transparency, fairness, responsiveness, et cetera—but in terms of processes of interaction and exchange and their outcomes within the specific and unique context of different sectors and services. The dimensions of objectives, priorities, incentives, and needs of the stakeholders and the institutional frame for each service need to be examined within the specific micro context comprising the totality of factors—material incentives, rules and regulations, structure of the organization, et cetera. Examining micro level interactions within their unique context may be a more productive route to improving governance practices and help develop, if not worthwhile 'theories' and scientific 'theorems', at least working, (to use the innovative term of Hawkins) 'theoroms'[37] of good governance.

Formal Institutions and Rules: The Hidden Hand

One important aspect of public governance is the universality of formal and written codes, rules and institutions for all interactions, macro or micro—unlike economic and social areas of interaction, which may be subject to informal rules, practices, and customs. Institutions and rules, especially political, economic, and social institutions have been studied in great detail. Not much information however is available regarding the formal 'street level' or 'operational' rules of interaction (mostly involuntary) between government agencies and private actors, and how they shape and affect incentives of the parties concerned and outcomes of interaction. The only work which appeared somewhat relevant is by Elinor Ostrom.[38] She has identified seven broad types of rules (position rules, boundary rules, scope rules, authority rules, aggregation rules, information rules and pay off rules) 'that operate configurationally to affect the structure of an action situation'. Formal rules address most of these issues in the situations of governance interaction and can cumulatively impact incentives and outcomes. Pay off rules may, for example, be effective for outsourced services, whereas in the case of direct delivery by an official, there is no pay off, and therefore the aberrations in the government agents' behaviour that we see.

Douglass North[39] defines institutions as 'rules of the game which create environment for cooperative solutions to complex exchange, reducing uncertainty'; institutions impose 'constraints on human behaviour, define the choice and opportunity sets of the agents/organizations, and structure and define incentives'. Organizations and agents adopt a profit optimizing strategy within the set of given institutions and thus 'institutions shape human interaction and structure incentives in human exchange—political, social and economic'. Unlike economic markets, which do not have elaborate rules, and the 'invisible hand' supposedly is the benevolent deity, here the 'hidden hand' of the bureaucrat drafting the rules is vital.

One advantage (or problem) in public governance is that everything must be backed by a rule, even though it may be for something as macabre and horrible as the Holocaust. Starting from the 1935 Nuremberg Rally's proclamation, prohibiting not only marriage but even extra marital sexual intercourse between the Jews and citizens of German blood,[40] whole ethnic groups were declared 'not worth living', opening the route to gas chambers. It is difficult for the state institutions to function in the absence of rules—noble or perverse. In public governance, rule design would appear to be a part of the problem as well as the solution. Complex and centralizedsystems need rules to ensure coordinated actions, and typical 'command and control' systems, as in the case of the Nazi Germany, need them much more. In India, in any case, formal rules dominate the play in the arena of public governance. Starting from the formal laws passed by the legislators and the rules laying down procedures and systems, rule-making culminates in the issue of administrative instructions issued by the governments for the guidance of a large number of front desk and delivery agents for each service/programme/transaction. Visible rules guide and determine the nature and impact of public services. Informal practices are mostly a response to the formal rules as we shall see and are being integrated in the rules (as best practices) or censured (as bad practices) by the issue of instructions.

The codes, rules, and instructions, whether discretionary or SOP (Standard Operating Procedures) based, also define the trajectory of the action and behaviour of the government agents, and to a greater extent, than in the case of the citizens and private parties to the governance exchanges and interactions. Sometimes, as stressed by Ludwig von Mises,[41] these rules constrain the nuances of discretion and thus define the dominant frame of action by agents—the frame of 'rule compliance rather than results'. And this implies a lot of activities which may have little link with the results, as in the TV serial 'Yes Minister', where the hospital has a building but no beds, nurses or patients, and the full complement of administrative staff is busy making work for each other! The present elaborate structure of rules, whether about interaction, conduct of government agents, boundary conditions, accountability, or pay offs (incentives), however, makes it rather difficult to distinguish the 'signals', the reality, from 'noise' ('signal is the truth, noise distracts us from truth'[42]). Micro rules, whether process-oriented or outcome-oriented, play a key role in governance exchanges. The bureaucratic logic of rule-making, may however, in practice result in process-oriented rules in the areas where initiative may be required (purchase of goods and services) and outcome oriented rules, where process orientation, in the absence of clear outcomes, may be a better option (health, education).

Transaction Costs in Public Governance

Citizen-government interactions are governed by the rules made by the State. In a way, the transactions can be viewed as civil contracts governed by the appropriate administrative law. TCE (Transaction Cost Economics) provides a framework for this purpose. Williamson[43] refers to TCE having adopted the purposive perspective of John R. Commons in naming a unit of analysis: 'The ultimate unit of activity... must contain in itself the three principles of conflict, mutuality, and order. This unit is a transaction. Not only does transaction cost economics concur that the transaction is the basic unit of analysis, but it views governance as the means by which to infuse order, thereby to mitigate conflict and realize mutual gains.' In public governance, however, unlike economic exchanges, the government agent is one of the parties to the transaction and there is no 'invisible hand' to impose order. The void created by absence of prices (as indicative of the optimization of utility of the two parties) is filled, in the case of governance interactions, by transaction costs.

In the economic exchanges, parties to the transactions are private, and formal rules, if at all, are not very relevant, and mostly develop historically from the informal institutions devised among the buyers and sellers (for example the institution of credit notes in the city states of Italy[44]). These formal Institutions mainly regulate information, enforcement and risk among the private parties. Price is a material issue in the economic markets; there are transaction costs but these are mostly pass-through costs, and transactions are voluntary. Formal fees and costs being negligible in most of the government services, the transaction costs are important, unlike economic exchanges, which involve mostly 'pass through' transaction costs; these are estimated to have risen substantially, over time, from 25 per cent to about 45 per cent[45] of the national income. In the case of public governance exchanges, the transaction costs, rather than the formal costs of service, appear to be more material. Given that price is not a material factor in these services, transaction costs provide the frame for bargaining and settlement in most of the exchanges.

The area of governance we are concerned with is what Williamson[46] calls 'second order' institutions of governance. These are concerned however not only with the 'play of the game' as stipulated by him, but also the second order 'rules of (play of) the game'. Transaction costs in public governance are material for the citizen and the government, especially in the case of collective goods (ensuring for example universal vaccination, or that the TB patients do get the treatment and also continue the drug regime till cured). It appears appropriate to focus on the government-citizen exchange or transaction as the basic unit for the analysis and assessment of governance. The government-public interaction can be viewed broadly as an exchange in the 'market' for services. Service exchange is mostly involuntary; the supply (of services) is not restricted, and mostly there is no constraint of budget as in the case of economic preferences—apples and oranges are both available. Whether the government can or should do something to influence choices, is an issue covered later.

Transaction cost economics is concerned with the contractual arrangements and the costs of enforcement and information due to 'incomplete contracts'. In the case of government-citizen services, due to the involuntary nature of interactions, there is little problem of costs of information and enforcement and transaction costs are primarily about the opportunity *costs* of time and uncertainty in concluding the process of delivery for the service desired. Even in the case of crime or customer protection (against defective delivery), transaction costs appear to circumscribe or define the incentives of the non-government parties, though these are rarely taken into account by the government agencies.

Actors and Incentives

The rational agent model, supplemented by insights into market failure and the behaviour of 'humans', has been fairly satisfactory for exploring economic interactions. The interactions in public governance are more complex, and may need more attention to the 'humans' rather than the 'econs'. Material value is not always a dominant feature of the governance interactions in respect of public 'goods' and 'bads' (for example organ donation, a 'good' and crime, a 'bad'), involving as these do, not only social, but also moral and emotional levers of action. Incentives are linked to the opportunities and benefits obtained from a particular service, and therefore, can change if there is basic change in those assumptions. Students from the rural areas are assured admissions in colleges in some of the states in the US. The top 10 per cent of high school graduates for example may be assured admissions in the state universities, instead of simply being given marginal preference over urban area candidates. If this happens in India, the nature of demand for such certificates would change dramatically. Similarly, the benefit and utility of a ration card was very different at the time of rationing than what it is now.

Another relevant factor, affecting the incentives of parties, is the intensity and frequency of interaction between the official and the applicant. Some of the services are or should be one off transactions, completed in a single interaction—for example, an SC certificate required for admission in a medical college. In other cases, the transaction may be the starting point for further recurring interactions with the public authorities (applications for old age pension leading to sanction and monthly payments). Incentives in case of crime are at a different level, and evaluated differently by economists, sociologists, and psychologists. The structure of the demand side incentives can vary greatly depending on these factors, and in turn, influence the 'expression' of perverse incentives on the supply side. It seems necessary, therefore, to study specific public services and the nature of governance interactions in their micro context.

'Frame of Negative Experiences'

The marketplace for the governance interactions and the playing fields for the government-citizen exchange, are important from another perspective. Perceptive surveyors and analysts have remarked on certain peculiarly Indian traits, tendencies or whatever, which seem somehow to hold India back, in economic, political and social development. People sometimes wonder whether we are capable of the commitment required for decision-making. The speculation about the cultural constraints or genetic limitations is evidently misconceived. The energy and dynamism of the Indian 'diaspora' is in sharp contrast to the ennui and the lack of social capital of the Indian 'lebensraum'. The link may be what Deepak Chopra and Jim Clifton[47] describe as India's 'troubled state of mind', with 33 per cent employees 'actively disengaged', and with trillions of unsatisfactory interactions: 'Organic human development will not occur in India if the majority of everyday experiences are negative', and if 'every interaction with a bureaucrat brings expectations of obstacles, red tape and/or a bribe'. The moment to moment experiences matter cumulatively; experience of the micro 'street level' governance interactions can be lasting, especially as these are mostly involuntary. This negative frame can be addressed mainly by improving the quality of experience in the micro governance interactions. The experience of citizens at a public tap provided within 100 metres of walking distance as per policy, who spend hours waiting their turn, is as relevant as that of citizens who get the supply without any problem. Policies like the RTE Act focus on the 'missing children'— children not in school or the dropouts. But as in the case of the 'missing women', discussed earlier, what happens in the case of children wanting to be, or already in school, may be more relevant to understanding the problems of the former, as we shall see later.

Game Theory in Micro Governance

Prisoners' dilemma (PD) and game theory appear to have little applicability in public governance. This is mostly applied at the stage of designing the policy and the rules, where different lobbies may adopt this approach, cooperating or competing as their interests demand. The accused don't queue up to be 'approvers', for example, in the classic situation of the Police Department. Some do not trust the word of the police; others stick by the rules of 'no ratting'. Most of us do not make these rational calculations to arrive at the only viable strategy of confessing. Prisoners' Dilemma may not therefore hold in the 'human' situations. In fact, in the context of governance, the main protagonists practising the game theory appear to be the political parties, who are proposing ever more utopian solutions to out complete rivals in the game for political mileage. The game theory, despite attempts[48] to popularize it, is mainly for 'econs', whether prisoners or nuclear strategists. The 'expected utility hypothesis'—that decision-makers weigh the possible outcomes according to how likely they are—is not for humans. In real life situations, in fact, even 'econs' tend to act as 'humans'. Robert Axelrod[49] does hint at some possibilities for cooperative outcomes through changing the pay offs in areas like taxation where individuals don't have private incentives to cooperate, but may do so due to the possibility of being caught and sent to jail. These are not, however, typical PD situations.

Behavioural Economics and Governance

Studies of political economy have highlighted the 'agency' problem in governance—misalignment of the agents' incentives and interests with those of the principals, aggravated by lack of information about the agents' actions, which is a typical problem in large organizations. Another problem is 'public choice', which reinforces the self-interest driven behaviour of a rational agent, but results in public policy failure. The 'Leviathan' State is torn apart by its (proximate) principals as well as the agents, and even the proponents of state control need to take note of these factors; such problems, however, are rarely taken note of, while framing expectations about, and evaluating the results of government policies. Behavioural economics and of course experimental psychology would, in the context of incentives, actors and exchange mechanisms, appear to be especially relevant. The incentives defining government-public interactions may not be always economic, as in the area of crime, despite the popularity of the application of economic analysis to such areas. Behavioural economics has added to our understanding of economic markets and exchanges, through integration of the values, goals and emotions of parties into the frame of rational responses by the *homo economicus*; its contribution, however, was not so much to demonstrate the well known 'affective' influences on the economic choices, but to point to the 'cognitive heuristics', 'biases', and 'illusions' which affect decision-making of human beings, even in areas not involving emotions.

Most of the government-private interactions involve economic incentives, as some utility is involved. Economics has been and is useful in these areas even though its practical use has been mostly confined to areas like auctions by government (of airwaves for example). Even the diehard neoclassical economists recognize the non-material character of incentives. Friedman[50] accepts goals, values, et cetera also as incentives which need to be taken note of by the economists. Crime for example has been dealt within a frame of cost benefit analysis for devising rules for the scale of punishment. Criminals however may not always respond as 'econs,' as will be seen, and these are the areas where behavioural economics may be helpful in understanding how the game is played.

'Heuristics and Biases'

Psycho-physical and behavioural peculiarities of human beings —not only 'affective' but cognitive 'heuristics and biases'—may thus need to be kept in view while designing the rules and institutions of interaction and exchange. The role of the two selves ('automatic' and 'deliberative')—System I and System II—is material. System II is rational but lazy and mostly takes the easy way out, by mostly endorsing the intuitive System I.[51] Rationality is of course affected by emotions but also by 'systematic errors in the thinking of normal people—traced to design of the machinery of cognition rather than corruption of thought by emotion'.[52] Antonio Damasio[53] points out that our economic decisions are not guided by pure rationality and are significantly influenced by powerful biases—'biases relating to gender, race, manners, accents, attire; the setting of the interaction brings its own set of biases linked to familiarity and design'. Thaler and Sunstein[54] refer to System I as 'automatic system'—'uncontrolled, effortless, associative, fast, unconscious, skilled' and System II as 'reflective system'—'controlled, effortful, deductive, slow, self-aware, and rule-following'. Kahneman and Tversky stipulate[55] that the rational agents may not always be driven by forces of self-interest and material incentives; they sometimes spontaneously make choices, take decisions and undertake activities which may not be in their real interest. Preferences are not fixed, and are subject to reversal, depending on 'framing' and other factors, and the expected utility function does not show 'invariance', as modelled by the economists. Some of the factors affecting choice and judgment are 'availability', 'representativeness', 'anchoring', 'risk avoidance for loss but risk appetite for gain', 'overconfidence' in one's abilities, 'myopia' (obverse of the 'availability' heuristic), 'status quo bias', et cetera. It has been demonstrated that economic and logical reasoning does not come naturally to *Homo sapiens* who are dominated by System I rather than System II. One counter-intuitive finding is the limited power of punishment and rewards—incentives and disincentives—which tend to be dispensed on the basis of chance and luck rather than performance.[56]

'Nudges' and 'Default Rules'

The purpose of invoking behavioural economics in understanding public governance is to see whether this can help governments design better rules of interaction through what Thaler calls 'nudges'—small changes in framing rules and situations, 'choice architecture', building in 'defaults' while offering choices, enriching rather than complicating processes through providing appropriate details to encourage voluntary compliance, and so on. *Poor Economics*[57] and *Nudge*[58] provide a number of examples—magic of 'free' (free bed nets), financial world (default options for savings). These insights may be even more relevant for the government 'agents' rather than the private parties to public governance interactions. *Indianomics* seeks to explain political, social and individual choices in terms of game theory and behavioural economics—'optimal stopping problem', 'moral hazard' (in the output of a house maid) and 'negativity bias'.

The problem with these very sound findings is that they have little predictability in the specific situations of individual decision-making, which may be determined by one or the other 'dominant' factor depending on the context. It is not that every autorickshaw driver avoids eye contact with the prospective passenger in Mumbai, to take one example from this book. That depends on his specific situation, where he is headed, whether he has made enough money, his first impression of the passenger, and so on. That is the reason to focus on the specific situations of interaction in their local and micro context. Since the book *Nudge*[59] came out, governments have been fascinated by the concept and have initiated such approaches in the realm of government-citizen interactions. The UK is reported to be doing something about the default option for donation of organs. The US government has issued a set of instructions regarding the format and presentation of regulations[60]—flexible approach, default rules, disclosures in place of mandates and bans, 'look back' on existing Laws, as in the 2012 Regulatory Plan. Despite a number of such initiatives, the approach is yet to be, to use a term popular with social scientists, 'mainstreamed' in public governance. It would appear that we tend to operate in a typical 'bureaucratic' frame of designing rules when working in the government, even while wholeheartedly supporting the softer approaches in a different 'frame' adopted at the seminars and conferences. Behavioural economics appears to provide an answer, something similar to the experience of Taleb,[61] who found that the bankers and stockbrokers while fully agreeing with him on the relevance of the 'black swans', went back to their desks and went on merrily applying the same quantitative models ['portfolio theory', 'VAR' (value at risk) and all] as before! Most of the interactions involving the government agents and private parties are in the backdrop of the economic and material interests of the parties and a microeconomic frame may be generally appropriate for analysis—demand, supply and utility to the party, transaction costs (rather than prices), imperfect transactions, delay, and corruption. In complex interactions—protective regulations/ crime—even economists find it difficult to adopt a consistent economic frame. Kahneman has adequately illustrated this in the trick questions administered on 'probability' to the statisticians themselves.

One problem in applying the lessons and findings of behavioural economics is that it is difficult to find, in the non-experimental situations, the unique mantra or amalgam, which will help achieve the objectives of public policy. Even experts are liable, outside the laboratory situations, to make mistakes: 'Humans somehow fail to recognize situations outside the context in which they learn about them.'[62] That is the reason for a focus on the specific context and situations of governance interactions so as to find a 'fit' if possible. In a way, the application is easier, as it only needs reframing the written rules of the game. The problems of a simplistic application of 'nudges' to affect behaviour however are indicated by Matteo M. Galizzi:[63] 'more remains to be done by experimental and behavioural scientists who wish to inform the design of more effective health policies to curb the dramatic burden of risky behaviours (overeating, smoking, excessive alcohol consumption, and a sedentary lifestyle). The main problem is "internalities"—costs that people impose on themselves but don't sufficiently take into account in their decisions.' What works may not be evident. This is another reason for looking into the specific situations and context of governance interactions.

The Framework: Incentives, Context and 'Rules of the Game'

The paradigm of governance, as in use today among the political and economic leadership—academic or otherwise— tends to be defined in terms of the macro institutions, policies and perspectives, though some at least of the academics do seem to value 'interactive governance' at the 'street level'; the prescriptions however translate back to the macro concerns—corruption or the Basel Accord for the norms of capital adequacy to address the Bankers' incentives, et cetera. There is little of relevance to the 'raw' fish or vegetable market exchanges between the parties concerned which may not necessarily tread the path designed by the macro institutions, due to the problems of information, enforcement and incompatible incentives. Meaningful public governance would therefore appear to need a different framework with focus on micro rules and institutions appropriate to incentives, behaviour and human frailties of citizens as well as the agents.

'Default Rules' for Default Behaviour

The principle of having 'default rules', for example, appears to have great applicability to the governance interactions which involve activities generally perceived to be in public interest, unlike economic exchanges which we have 'discovered', following Adam Smith, to be in the public or social interest. In the simple interactions, what we call alpha services for example, the default rule at present, based an implicit assumption of bad faith on the part of the public, is to question, check and verify each document and fact—whether through affidavits or field verification by the officials, or police verification of the applicants for passports and new entrants to government service. The example of the 'default' rules given by Thaler[64] in respect of the defined contribution saving plans under 401 (k), to address the problem of procrastination among the employee beneficiaries, provides an apt illustration. Employees were being asked to choose one of the many bewildering options, (the liberal cafeteria approach) which many of us fail to do or delay; instead, they also have now the 'default' option such as savings plans which are carefully determined in consultation with experts and which become automatically applicable, *in case no choice is exercised/intimation not provided to employers.* Defined contribution plans like the 401(k) in the US are in employees' interest, as the employers have to match the contribution (of course up to a defined limit of the salary), but 30 per cent of employees still do not enrol! Introduction of a default rule for automatic enrolment, *unless an employee opts out*, was helpful to the 'human' employees. Governments, employers, and clubs resort to such default rules occasionally—asking the employees to donate a part of salary or a specified amount for a particular cause, and billing them on the basis of the assumed consent, in case no response is received. The area of organ donation provides an example of the default rule (you are a donor if you don't opt out) as indicated later.

Every citizen obviously is not the 'noble savage' of Rousseau's world but political society is based on the assumption of socially acceptable behaviour on the part of the majority; social conditioning, if not the genetic evolution of the *Homo sapiens*, generally ensures this. This is the assumption behind the jurisprudence principle 'presumed innocent until proved guilty'. Deviant behaviour is considered exceptional by the society and various measures are devised to prevent, control, and punish in such cases. We need therefore to incorporate the 'default rules' in the case of governance exchanges and the public services, to bring them in line with the 'default' mode of (good) human behaviour. In the case of release, on parole, of convicts for example, the default rules could provide specific exceptions (persons convicted of repeated/heinous crimes) instead of the erratic and discretionary processes and decisions, based on the uninformed testimony of the probation officers or the NGOs and ill informed and whimsical decision-making; I read somewhere of a study which found that the decisions of judges on parole cases depended on whether the case came up before lunch (mostly rejections), or after lunch (mostly grant of parole), based on the bliss of a full stomach!

It may be appropriate to study the formal 'rules of the game' —the institutions for interaction—in the micro context of various services and exchanges, offered by or expected from the government. The context is what Williamson calls 'play of the game'. The specific micro exchanges and structures need to be examined, keeping in view the role played by the formal rules and institutions, transaction costs to parties, the complexity of incentives, limitations on rationality and the cognitive biases the parties bring to the table. Governance is, in a way, a social interaction, defined by the specific rules, which influence how different actors interact in different situations and circumstances. There is a tendency to ignore the human actors on the two sides of the interaction, treat them as atomistic citizens and assume uniform responses, ignoring the complexity of incentives—material as well as emotional, social, and moral. Behavioural insights are likely to be much more relevant for governance exchanges, involving as these do more than a 'felicific calculus' relevant to the economic interactions.

It is difficult to separate 'good governance' from 'good government'; the latter is obviously important and that is where the socioeconomic underpinnings of the basic laws and governance structures come in. On the other hand, it is possible to have good 'government' even in the Leviathan States, at least in some areas say of education and health as in China, and probity as in Singapore and Hong Kong. We shall construe governance as a process for achieving the objectives a good government should have—whether in education or health or addressing poverty and so on. To that extent, therefore, the macro institutions do become relevant. Fortunately, it is very rare today even for the rogue states not to proclaim objectives and policies very similar to those of the 'good governments'. Every nation is queuing up for signing the Human Rights declaration or the International Convention on Corruption. In any case, the context being limited to India here, there is little problem. India is a pluralistic democracy, with all the panoply of the 'rule of law' and progressive statutes and rules, covering all major areas of governance interaction. An analysis of the micro governance exchanges and the rules governing them—whether in the basic administrative services or in the police-accused/victim dealings, may be more useful even in assessing the effectiveness of macro institutions.

The government can be considered as a hypothetical corporation, producing diverse goods and services, with the shareholders being the *exclusive* customers. Obviously the policies and prices will be laid out in the Boardroom, but the shareholders can easily judge corporate governance as customers, and not necessarily by attending the AGM. It will be helpful if we give attention to the primary stakeholders of the country and the state—the citizens and their concerns, and to 'operational governance' at the level of interaction with citizens rather than to the policymakers and the 'hangers on', more interested in the boardroom intrigues. Our focus needs to be on how governance is played out in the context of specific interactions for various public services, as distinguished from governance in 'policy', which involves a limited number of in house actors and outside professionals, with the public acting as the 'guinea pig'. We need to focus, to borrow the term from evolutionary biology, on 'extinction' (failure) rather than 'survival' (success), and on the specific environment and context of governance interactions, and tease out governance from the political and economic beliefs and values. The essence lies in applying the economic approach and the insights, which the economics of market failure and behavioural economics have provided, to governance transactions similar to economic exchanges, and in the case of other services and interactions, such as crime prevention, structuring the analysis and solutions around the incentives of 'humans'—incentives which may not be necessarily physical or monetary, but are drivers of behaviour all the same. We need to study public governance, not in the Board rooms and meetings but on the playing fields of public services, exchanges and markets, in which interactions of the government agents and the citizens take place. There is need to factor in the transaction costs rather than (market clearing) prices, the formal rules which condition the behaviour of parties and determine the outcomes of interaction rather than the informal institutions, and the incentives, motives, dispositions and biases of the players—the citizens and the government agents involved—rather than our expectations and beliefs.

4

Governance Markets: Taxonomy of Public Services

The previous chapter has attempted to tease out the unique dimensions of context specific micro interactions and exchanges between the State/government and its agencies on one side, and the citizens/corporations/legal entities on the other. The core of governance lies in these micro level transactions in different public services and the State needs to justify its existence to its principals, the public, primarily in the latter's capacity as customers and clients, in their myriad exchanges and 'encounters' (including fake ones with the police) and only secondarily as voters, and not to the other countries or in relation to them, whether for getting encomiums or aid or investment. Micro public governance is about these interactions and exchanges, public services, and regulations. The problems of a focus on macro policy divorced from the micro context are illustrated by an article,[1] which is perfect in defining the importance of the context and the incentives of parties to governance interactions—legislators, the executive, and citizens. What is to be done, however, in view of 'both handed' options and alternatives is not clear. Thus, as mentioned later, if the attendance of nurses or schoolteachers is not affected by civil society monitoring or supervisors (short of their having the 'god particle' in them, which is mostly missing; they are also 'human'), what is the government department to do? It is necessary, therefore, to look into and understand the public service exchanges and markets, the 'genotype' as well as the 'phenotype', in their unique context and situation.

The problems of macro governance, macro institutions and

models, and the need for a shift of focus to the micro institutions and exchanges, have been indicated in the previous sections. One manifestation of the obsession with macro level governance and policy is the debate on Track I (growth) of Jagdish Bhagwati vs Track II (welfare) of Amartya Sen, a New Gujarat versus a 'New Bihar'.[2] The terms of the debate, posing the two respected economists and their philosophy as bipolar, are of course an over simplification. One has only to go through Sen's writings for example to see that he is as much aware as any other (economist?) of the relevance of economic growth and development. One needs instead to see how such policies unfold in the government-private interactions. Privatization in Russia was a macro policy: how it got translated in terms of the plunder of State assets through the sale of individual assets is the story of interest for micro governance. Micro governance is 'street level' interaction, in Lipsky's[3] idiom. He refers to the public services involving street level bureaucracies such as schools, police, welfare officials, lower courts: 'interactions with street level bureaucracies are places where citizens experience directly the government they have implicitly constructed'; how 'work responses of street level bureaucracy combine with values and agency pronouncements to add up to what the public ultimately experience as agency performance'.[4] The advantage of this approach appears to be that it does not demand omnibus solutions even in broad sectors like health or education, but seeks to locate the source of outcomes in the detailed context of each specific interaction. 'Public policy is not best understood as made in legislatures or top floor suites of high ranking administrators and one should add the crowded front offices and daily encounters between the public and the agent'.[5]

Ignoring for the moment the now extinct model of socialism, which superseded all markets, both political and economic, broadly governments leave it to the economic markets to provide for the citizens' material needs and concern themselves mainly with providing civic and basic services – water, power, physical and social infrastructure, social security and welfare, apart from the basic political and economic institutions for the administration of justice and property rights. The complexity of the government-citizen exchanges and interactions may not be as vast as of the economic exchanges, but there is tremendous diversity. There has not been, to my knowledge, any comprehensive listing or classification thereof, partly for the reasons indicated; specific governance markets or exchanges do not form part of the research agenda, except as 'case studies' relevant to macro policy or as 'second cousins' to the implementation of policy. The most comprehensive list we could find is provided by Kenworthy,[6] in the context of the assistance the government provides to the poor through such services. Countries like India have a baggage consisting both of 'right' and 'left' regulations—the former mostly choice inhibiting and the latter mostly a product of the welfare State. Thus, while the overall trend of punishment for the criminal offences is liberal —focus on the rehabilitation of convicted criminals and death penalty in the 'rarest of rare' cases—the government in India found it difficult to go against the popular demand that the offence of rape be punished by death penalty; an uneasy compromise has been struck. The laws on sex trafficking especially demonstrate the ambivalence between the notion of public order and the sanctity of private choice, as will be seen.

The 'Tree' of Public Services

The range of interactions is vast, and citizen initiative and behaviour is based on their needs, desires, and obligations, and influenced by the political, social, and economic policies and institutions as well as the micro rules of interaction. While the service specific context and structure of incentives continue to be important, it may be possible to group these services based on their design and processes. The 'tree' of services and exchanges is similar to the tree of evolution—each species is unique, with some shared genes depending on the course of evolution. The only difference is that, here, 'nurture' is all and everything can be redesigned in the petri dish of rules!

At the risk of adding to the cauldron of the alphabet soup, and considering the difficulty of finding eponymous symbols, we have chosen to adopt the common Greek letters for classification of these services. The inspiration, thanks to Ridley,[7] was provided by Aldous Huxley. The *Brave New World* has a hatchery where human beings are reared for different capabilities and functions—alphas, betas, and so on. The only difference is that the listing here is in the order of the need, intensity, and quantum of use by the 'everyman', the *aam admi*, the John Does who, in Huxley's world, are the epsilons, the dregs of society. The services are arranged in the order of their importance and relevance to the ordinary citizens.

Governance interactions can be voluntary—purchase and sale of goods and services, as in the economic markets, and it may be possible in such cases to address 'governance failure' through the use of economic models. Most of the governance interactions however are involuntary and prices for most of the services are nominal and not relevant for incentives. What is an exception for the economic framework—monopoly of supply—is the normal frame for public governance. On the other hand, the exchanges are similar to the economic transactions at least for the citizens; material interests of the citizens are the main drivers of the governance interactions and transactions.

The public-private interactions and exchanges cover a vast area—contingent and need based services used by most of the households, economic and social infrastructure, public goods, social regulations, resource transfers/welfare services mostly for the disadvantaged and the poor, but also for the rich albeit for 'noble public purposes' like boosting growth, exports, and employment, and fiscal regulations and taxes. It will be presumptuous to try and capture the diversity and range of the government citizen interactions even in respect of the core government and State functions, let alone activities of the vastly expanded but self-professedly benevolent 'Leviathan'. It needs no emphasis that the classifications attempted are like the colours in the spectrum of light—we have the broad categories and tens of individual services but they form a continuum. The incentives, structures and rules of interaction underpinning the character and shades of different services are like the wall paints listed in a catalogue; the shades constitute a part of the primary colours, but remain unique.

Alpha Contingent Services

Alpha plus services deal with the contingent, need based documentation services and are merely the enablers and gateways for social and economic opportunities (identity card, passport, domicile certificate, ration card, the UID). They have no direct relationship to any functional activity and are, if one may use the term, fungible like money. A residence certificate, as also a ration card, may be used for a number of purposes. These have a contingent character—some of the citizens may need and/or use them, others never or rarely. Generally, the government or its agencies are not the interested parties in respect of these interactions. These services are prerequisites for availing of specified opportunities but the delivery of services has no direct relationship to economic or other benefits, as there may be other barriers for availing of the benefits under the public policy (for example, in the case of admission to educational institutions, one needs to qualify academically and compete for admissions even though one belongs to an SC category and has such a certificate); the criteria may be more liberal but one still has to compete.

Alpha minus services cover one time documentation—permissions and approvals—required for social and economic activities, under regulations imposed mostly in the interest of securing orderly social functioning within local communities and among *citizens* (such as driving licence and building approvals), that is, not directly in the interest of the State but of the community. These basic and need-based civic and similar services are made available (through statutes or administrative sanctions) to the citizens by the appropriate governing jurisdictions—mostly the local governments all over the world, but in India, also by the state governments. We won't need rules for driving left or right in a jurisdiction with just two cars but such rules are essential when masses of vehicles are moving on the roads; before the rule for a licence for driving, all that was required was to send a flag bearer ahead to warn people of the approaching vehicle! Alpha minus services may also require some element of physical interaction—driving test/vehicle test for fitness/inspections of construction activity et cetera.

Transactions, such as initial approvals for the use of civic amenities, like water supply and power, are also included. Buildings and zonal by-laws ensure that neighbourhoods do not have to suffer from a lack of aesthetics, light and air. A city may not be livable if people are left to do whatever they want in respect of the houses they live in, and the shops they operate; driving has to be safe for the pedestrians and other drivers, hence the need for a licence. Alpha minus services mostly impose restrictions and sanctions in the interest of orderly functioning of communities and the regulations are in a way preventive, designed to eliminate the possibility of negative impact or costs imposed by individual actions. The distinction, as compared to public goods and 'bads', is that the third party is generally identifiable and not the public at large. These alpha-minus services do not provide options, choices or alternatives to the users unlike alpha plus services. An SC candidate has a choice—he/she can always compete in the open quota. Obtaining satisfaction or exercising a particular alpha minus service, preference or choice—having water supply, sewerage, electricity connection, or driving a car—requires going through the specific regulatory gateways. Of course, if I want build a college in the wilderness and live like a hermit, I may not need these, or may be land use permission is still necessary!

Civic services are in the same group but are repetitive in nature (deposit of payment for water and electricity supply—a regular and repeated process) and may be sometimes viewed as more of a problem than say obtaining a driving licence. Many years back, under the 'licence—permit raj', it was common in some states, for the electricity department officials to hold up the electricity bills so that bribes could be extorted through the threat of disconnection on account of non-payment of a bill, not even delivered to the consumer! These services, however, are now generally satisfactory, partly because of the supply side fiscal interests and are sometimes outsourced. Computerization has also helped. These have, especially now, with increasing privatization, outsourcing and regulatory controls on pricing et cetera, taken on the character of commercial transactions and are ex-cluded from consideration; there is now little difference whether a utility is a public one or operated by a service provider.

In the alpha plus services, the end product delivered is a document, generally enabling, unlike alpha minus services, which are sector-specific and authorize a particular consumption or utility or activity by the private actors. The two groups of alpha services do not involve material and physical exchange and are mostly concluded with paper/document delivery. The importance of such services to the citizens will be obvious from the fact that in Punjab with a population of over 28 million, 8 million applications are filed every year, more than one for each household. They form a significant portion of the focus on citizen charters and even the proposed law on citizen charters referred earlier, makes these services the main focus. These basic contingent services affect large masses of citizens, impose heavy and completely unnecessary transaction costs on applicants as we shall see, and are a sad commentary on the quality of 'interactive governance'.

Beta Services: Economic and Social Regulations

The Beta regulations are concerned with regulating (mostly) voluntary economic and social exchanges and interactions among private parties—corporates or individuals—and addressing the issue of impact on one of the parties to the interaction. Unlike the civil law, where all parties are equal and any party can be the first mover for redress, these regulations are based on certain value assumptions—say in favour of the tenants in the case of Rent Control Laws or the customers in the case of exchange of goods and services. Beta regulations address the exchange problems not only of the identifiable parties to a transaction, but also of others who are involuntarily brought into the ambit of an activity. The regulations for economic transactions, beta plus services, deal with the consequences of economic interactions (labour laws, tenancy laws, et cetera) and may sometimes involve extensive and continuous enforcement. The sanctions are (mostly) financial/ economic and compoundable. As in the case of labour laws, physical sanctions may be provided sometimes as a deterrent, but are rarely invoked in practice.

The beta minus regulations are concerned with social interactions and their adverse impact on the vulnerable individuals and groups—children, women, persons challenged in some way as per social perceptions where some private parties are in a position to have interaction with them, exploit them, and impose consequences not considered socially desirable such as dowry laws, sex trafficking, child abuse laws, and so on. Basically, the protective social regulations seek to regulate the social as differentiated from the economic interactions, and protect the interest of parties to the mostly voluntary interactions and exchanges. The regulations are based on certain social and moral assumptions and values—for example, the assumption that women are generally the aggrieved parties in dowry cases. These assumptions are a function of policy and not questioned here. The issue is what rules and systems the government should have, to ensure that the objectives are fulfilled. Some of these social regulations may reflect some debatable and ambiguous moral concerns of the policymakers depending on the 'conventional wisdom' and morality of the times. Most of 'victimless' crimes under special and local laws are covered under the beta minus regulations—prostitution, gambling, and narcotics et cetera. The logic for treating these as a category apart from 'crime' is the relative character of the values underpinning such regulations and the fact that the regulations don't depend primarily on sanctions and punishments but also seek to promote the interests of the 'underdog' through pro active policies—for example, through Women Commissions, Advisory Committees, and Rescue Homes for the Immoral Traffic victims. The government is an active participant, directly or through a regulatory agency, in the beta regulations, whether for protection or for sanctions.

Alpha services involve *ex-ante* approvals and permissions for certain activities, whereas the beta regulations come into play *ex post*—after the activity is undertaken. Consequently, they involve continuous interaction between the state agents and one or both the parties (the perpetrators of injury or the party aggrieved) in the social and economic exchanges. The regulations control the character of the private contracts in respect of the liability for actions by defining the boundaries of the social and economic activities. Out of court settlements are feasible and may even be done in practice. For example, if a labour law is violated affecting the interest of an employee, the matter may be settled mutually if both parties feel they will gain. The main feature of the beta regulations in India is that by and large the regulations do not simply define the standards and obligations of the economic and social agents, a necessity for smooth functioning of markets; they go beyond this to set up agencies for enforcement ('a labour inspector shall have the right of entering the premises at all reasonable times', et cetera), and thus, assume a direct responsibility for ensuring those standards. As will be indicated, this may also be necessary in the case of delta and gamma regulations—a purchaser of medicine cannot assess the quality of a drug by using it, but surely nobody can be fooled by under-weighment or by an electrical appliance which delivers shocks instead of heat.

Delta and Gamma Services: Public Goods and 'Bads'

The delta and gamma services relate to public 'goods' and 'bads' respectively—positive and toxic/negative spillovers for parties, some of whom may not be identifiable or who may not even be bothered. Public goods are generally described as non-rival and non-excludable. There are only a few goods that approximate the ideal—probably defence and air, and may be streetlights locally. Some of these—'toll' goods (highways, TV transmission) —have some mechanisms for exclusion (through tolls/coded transmission). These thus become non-rival but excludable. On the other side are the collective goods like a village well, or the classic 'pasture' of Hayden ('Tragedy of the Commons'), which, however, are not infinite in supply. The value of the public goods to the users keeps on changing. Water may become an acute problem years from now, but the reference point for this value is the present state of availability. It is debatable whether education is a public good (Milton Friedman had some doubt, as indicated later), but going by the 'conventional wisdom', this area, as also preventive healthcare, is included as a delta service. Crime against person and property is generally 'non-compoundable' and these regulations are a class apart, one of the main *raison d'etre* for the State, and are classified as gamma services.

Omega Services for the Poor

The Omega services comprise material and financial benefits provided by the State to its citizens—social security, pensions, food for the poor—as well as for promoting economic activities —for example, tax rebates for industries to help job creation, et cetera. These have become increasingly important and consume more and more of State resources: 'welfare' for the poor and a 'stimulus' for the rich. Citizen interaction involves complex and extended regulations and activities, covering the corporations and individuals and probably causing 'burn out' (as some feel) of the taxpayers' money at both ends of the candle.

Alpha services are mainly about screening processes for eligibility, and in some cases, for entitlement (such as to drive a car or build a house) and the consumption/use of economic and social goods. Beta regulations address the impact of economic and social activities, mostly on the parties to an exchange, but sometimes, also on third parties. Delta regulations and interactions concern public 'goods' areas—infrastructure for the public at large, as well as generally socially desirable 'goods' (such as education), which are supposed to promote welfare beyond the measurable benefit to individuals. Gamma regulatory services comprise economic or social activities adversely affecting second or third parties, as also those having adverse impact on society at large, as in the case of crime/ pollution. This toxic category needs to be distinguished from public 'goods', such as infrastructure and education, which are 'positive economic goods' that 'yield services with cost to men, irrespective of whether or not one is willing to bear the cost'. Gamma interactions are concerned with the 'negative economic goods' which 'yield disservice and man is willing, able and required to expend resources getting rid of the disservice'.[8] Here, the regulatory objective is to prevent harm not only to the specific third parties but also to the public at large. For example, one argument for the government regulations for pesticides may be to prevent the adverse impact on food production, even though the impact is through actions involving bilateral interaction; similar is the case with the drug regulations; in their absence, public health may be jeopardized, even though the effect is on individuals. 'Victimless' crimes, despite some externalities, have been considered beta services as the value structure is context specific, which accounts for the very different ways in which countries choose to address, say, prostitution or narcotic drugs or emigration issues, whereas crime as such, in relation to violation of basic personal and property rights, is treated similarly.

The main omissions are taxation, which involves government as a party, not as referee or regulator, and the commercial functions of the State—purchase/sale of goods and services—which it may be more appropriate to leave to economic analysis. The latter is discussed in the context of corruption, mainly with a view to completing the picture of governance interactions, even though, considering the limited clientele taxation involves in India, we may, to complete the score, describe taxation as an Epsilon service.

PART II

ALPHA 'CONTINGENT' SERVICES

Alpha plus services are basic administrative services, which, in India, constitute the bulk of governance interactions. Most of the advanced countries may not even be having many of these, as their data bases have citizen profiles, identity, and socioeconomic details, whereas in India, neither the government nor the citizens themselves have such documentation, and hence, the large number of service requests. Examples are affidavits, residence, area and income certificates, all relating to the socioeconomic profile and identity of citizens. These services are likely to get phased out in India, especially with the universalization of the UID. Alpha minus services (such as driving licences, approvals for new water, power, sewerage connections, new construction) are mostly civic services provided by the local governing jurisdictions. The problem of delivery in these services is mostly high transaction costs and the solution seems to be to accept the stipulations made by the citizens. 'Default rules' for self-selection in respect of these services seems to be the most practical strategy, though with some variations depending on the context, as indicated later for different public services.

5

Registration of Births and Deaths: 'From Cradle to Grave'

The institution of registration of births and deaths is governed by the Births and Deaths Registration Act of 1886. The objective of the law was to have a record of these events for gathering demographic data of relevance to government for administrative purposes as well as for socioeconomic policy. This data was necessary for determining the resources required for health, education et cetera, apart from the need to administer property and personal rights. The law and the rules have a simple structure. The health department set-up available at the district level was used for the management of various activities, whereas at the village level, which was the only other available administrative sub-district unit at that time, the role for recording was given to the village *chowkidar*, who was responsible for reporting to the local SHO (Station House Officer) in respect of various activities relating to crime and law and order. The family concerned was made responsible as the 'notifier' for reporting the events of births and deaths. For the urban areas, the responsibility for implementation was given to the municipal committees. The act and rules provided for reporting and recording of events by the family/health institutions, and the village *chowkidar* or the municipal office. The rules also contained a provision for the transfer of all records, after one year, to the Civil Surgeon who was declared the District Registrar. The law provides for a simple system of reporting within 21 days, recording with payment of late fee up to one month, recording with the permission of the District Registrar in cases of delay up to one year, and in cases of delay beyond one year, provision of an affidavit by the family and approval thereof by a Magistrate. There is now a ban on such events being recorded if reported after a gap of 15 years. The basic rules have broadly remained unchanged over time, except that there have been changes in the powers vested in different officials.

The rate of recording as a proportion of the actual events (of births and deaths) has been tardy. The registration of births picked up in the 1980s mainly due to its requirement for services like issue of a passport and admissions in educational institutions. No assessment has been made in Punjab of the percentage of registration of births as compared to estimates thereof, but the view of the officials who were interviewed in this connection was that the recording rate is over 98 per cent. Births are mostly reported, but due to various problems, may not be registered immediately and getting the certificate is still a problem. So far as the reporting and recording of deaths is concerned, in the case of adults, percentage of reporting has increased mainly due to the need for the death certificates to settle issues of inheritance, et cetera. However, deaths of infants mostly still go unrecorded for the same reason. Whatever the available data, it is rarely used for estimating infant deaths, for which there is absolute dependence on the Sample Registration System (SRS). The formats for reporting deaths do provide for information to be given on factors such as age, sex, cause of death, et cetera, but none of these are used for compiling data or analysis and India therefore lacks reliable profiles of common and endemic diseases. What is available is guesswork based on samples, surveys, and opinions, all subject to the 'Law of Small Numbers'. In fact, in Punjab, the data about deaths is only compiled from the information provided by the government hospitals, which is meaningless and can even distort or give wrong direction to policy interventions as the hospital deaths (and that too only in the government hospitals), as a percentage of the total, are negligible.

The processes and systems of reporting, recording, and certification of events are sub-optimal due to the compounding of the disincentives on the supply and the demand side. A village functionary is at hand to record births/deaths immediately, but the family has no incentive at that time to make a report. And negative incentives on the supply side (Panchayat Secretary/fees) as indicated later, add to these problems. The incentive for the family or the child arises a few years later in cases of births—for admission in school, for other required documentation like the passport (an important activity in Punjab). These incentives are reflected in the high transaction costs (on procuring 'fake' documentation for certification or the long waiting time due to the discontinuous process flow) imposed on the applicants. Utility is a prerequisite for effective demand. A person needing a passport will be willing enough to pay his way through the rules and official structures; the usual transaction costs would not affect his 'consumer surplus.' The principle of a market-clearing price for such transactions is therefore inappropriate, as the formal price (fees plus documentation costs) is negligible. The consumer utility is not a relevant framework for designing policy in this area.

Ideology Trumps Reality

Some changes made in the rules appear to be based on 'ideology' and 'ignorance' of ground realities (the two 'I's of *Poor Economics*, the third being inertia[1]). One example is the institution of the Local Registrar. Earlier, it was the village *chowkidar* in Punjab, but later on the Panchayat Secretary performed the function (this has, however, changed recently). The then ideology of 1960s dictated that the rural local government institutions should be made responsible for all matters involving the villagers. The decision ignored some important facts. Firstly, the Panchayat Secretary has no office or fixed place of work, at least in Punjab, and no place for keeping even the panchayat records. One Panchayat Secretary may be handling more than one village panchayat. The panchayat jurisdictions tend to change over time and one village can even have two panchayats with more than one Panchayat Secretary responsible for different wards in the same village, thus creating problems of multiple registers even for the same village. Even where the families provide the intimation, the registers do not get completed in time. The Panchayat Secretary, moreover, has little functional commitment or orientation to this duty and considers the duty as an imposition.

The field situation in Punjab is that records are not handed over to successors at the time of transfers (which are frequent) and all in all, it is a big mess when, at the time of transfer of the records after one year, these have to be got completed by the District Registrar. The silo functioning of the departments means that there is little coordination and cooperation between the district health office and the Panchayat Secretary who is responsible to a different hierarchy of officials. Due to these problems, an overwhelming percentage of the applications are filed simultaneously for registration and for certificates, much later than required in routine and only when a certificate is needed. Though there is much 'back slapping' for the panchayat staff having been given the responsibility to handle this function, the system has grave limitations, as the local registrars keep records for only one year, whereas most of the requests are made later, when the records rest in the District Registrar's office. In the era of extensive population mobility and digitization, decentralization thus may not be very efficient – even from the perspective of citizens. Foreign countries and other states may not even accept the village level officials' authentication. The rules are made in complete ignorance of ground realities and the 'status quo bias' ensures that the same continue.

Rules and incentives; The 'Green House' Effect

A similar problem, though for different reasons, arises in the institution of the 'notifier'. Presently, the 'notifier' is the family. The issue is whether the family would expend time and effort to notify the event of birth in the family. Most of the poor families may not have any incentive to report deaths or even births, as they have no plans for education, no assets, and consequently, no problems with issues of dispute of property, et cetera. This is especially true of infant deaths. In the case of births, the problem is the human tendency to discount possible future benefits, which may impose small costs in the present due to 'temporal inconsistency'. One tends to procrastinate in respect of actions that may provide benefits only in the remote future – a problem noticed in regard to the difficulty of making savings in the present. The present costs loom larger than the future benefits. The rules thus seem to neglect not only the disposition, capacity, and resources of the government agencies, but also the motives and incentives of the families – in this case, the fact that people look at short term costs and tend to ignore the long term advantage. The fact that the certificate may be needed for a child in the remote future may not be sufficient to make the head of family take the trouble of filling the form and approaching the local registrar. This is similar to the attitude of parents who, due to this problem, don't educate their children, even though this may create much more earning potential for the children when they grow up.

Due to the problems indicated regarding the institution of the local registrar, these behavioural constraints are transformed into major disincentives, given the problems of an unwilling Panchayat Secretary, a tortuous route for recording births if delayed beyond 21 days, with extra fee and formalities, with the result that most of the applications for registration are made only when a certificate is needed by the person/family. The rule structure becomes a sort of 'green house' needing excessive energy inputs when ordinary sunlight will do.

Cycle of High Transaction Costs

The fees—late fee and certificate fee—are nominal, but the related costs are high. In the first place, even timely recording is not free of these costs, as the subsequent processes of getting a copy of the record and a certificate are tricky. The application, even if made in time, may not necessarily result in an entry being made or a copy of the record being provided, at least under the present dispensation where the Panchayat Secretary is the Local Registrar. Secondly, in most cases, the name of the new born would not be entered, even if reported in time, since the naming ceremony is much later; in the case of some states it is held as late as six months after birth. The Hindu families mostly do the naming ceremony of the child one month or more after birth. They would have to file another application for adding the name in the register even for cases reported in time. The appropriate strategy, even for a family, which is sensitive to the relevance of the law, is to wait for reporting till a certificate is needed. If the law provided say a 6 month period for initial registration, there would be little problem and much less work all around, handling delayed cases and separate applications for intimation and name entry. Thirdly, the late fee is nominal, but the system of deposit of fees is complex and mostly avoided by village officials with little experience of or interest in account-keeping of this nature, and both parties may prefer to postpone reporting/recording during this period. Fourthly, the process of approval in the case of events reported after one month is tortuous and can mean repeated queries and visits on the 'progress' of the case, as these need approval of the district registrar. The rules require registration of births within one month; applications filed after this period need to be referred to the District Registrar for approval so far as the rural areas are concerned. The latter is located at the District Headquarters and there is no normal business relationship between the Panchayat Secretary and the District Registrar. These rules add to the problems for families who have little incentives to report in the first place.

An affidavit is to be sworn in before the Magistrate for cases after one year of the event. This means, apart from typing, stamps, and related fees, a visit by the applicant along with a person to identify the applicant and may involve a day—all told, around Rs. 500 for a simple service, which need not cost anything under a simpler regime of rules. All these costs no doubt add to the GDP, but like earnings from crime, are better avoided. In cases where the application is delayed by more than one year, this problem is further compounded by the informal practice, probably peculiar to Punjab, of asking for a certificate/endorsement from the hospital/midwife/sarpanch/*lambardar* about the fact of birth. Thus, if a home delivery has taken place without a midwife's assistance or the midwife has moved or is not available and/or the sarpanch is unwilling to certify, a family has to 'manage' bogus certification/endorsement, even though the law does not require this. The practice was started only because some cases of issue of wrong certificates came to notice. It is like banning alcohol sales because there are traffic accidents due to drunk driving. Transaction costs in such cases, even without corruption, can be really high.

High transaction costs in low demand cases can be a barrier to access and in high demand cases, for corruption. This is precisely the result of the brew of rules and practice under this law. In fact, what the rules do is to turn a low demand service into a high demand service (when a certificate is needed) and transfer minor transaction costs into high cost bribery.

Right Incentives, Wrong Targets

There is another 'progressive' provision introduced in the 1980s, which bars recording of births 15 years after the event. This is a classic case of visiting the sins of parents on their children. Parents are to be blamed for the negligence in reporting, but the child will be punished by being denied a passport and for all other matters for which a certificate is the prerequisite. And he or she can do pretty little by the time he/she is old enough to appreciate its importance. It is in practice causing substantial hardships and ignores ground realities—ignorance and illiteracy, apart from lack of incentives, on the part of parents, for timely registration of births. It appears irrational as the party affected—the child—is denied the opportunity to act on his/her incentives, and in fact, may have the incentive to 'game' the system (in case this is needed by a grown up child after 15 years)! The 'game' strategy employed in such cases to register the birth somehow cannot be ascertained. Probably the records get manufactured; this is easy as there is no digitization at present and manual records are subject to manipulation.

Designing Incentive Compatible Rules

Most of these issues and problems can be resolved by an incentive and capacity compatible design of the processes and structures for implementation, without any change in the basic law or even the rules in some cases. The ASHA (Accredited Social Health Associate) and the ANM (Auxiliary Nurse Cum Midwife) have specific jurisdictions, and their functioning and territoriality is not subject to the electoral politics and the process of delimitation of the Panchayat jurisdictions. They are specifically responsible for the monitoring of births and maternal and infant mortality; they even get incentives for improving the percentage (40 per cent in Punjab at the moment) of institutional deliveries. These functionaries, therefore, are ideally equipped to ensure 100 per cent recording and to cover the blind spots such as infant mortality, and this can be easily done by notifying ASHA as the notifier and the ANM as the local registrar. This will also achieve the objective of having reliable data on infant and maternal mortality. This practice was adopted in Tamil Nadu as mentioned later with good results. One advantage is that these functionaries are within a single hierarchical structure (of the health department) headed by the CMO (Chief Medical Officer), the district head of the Health Department, who is the Registrar, and thus, the arrangement will eliminate most of the problems of compilation of records, logistics and coordination.

Reporting Protocols

The incentive structure of the citizens implies that they would file the applications for certificates only when needed especially in view of the difficulty of having to keep a certificate in safe custody for years if obtained immediately, in view of the fact many families don't even have a proper place for the safekeeping of papers. The process of reporting can be simplified by extending the period of three weeks or one month to perhaps six months—with no late fee or the need for higher level approvals. And instances of delay beyond one year could perhaps be recorded (without undue formality or red tape) on the basis of an affidavit as required by law (or better yet, a self-declaration) in order to encourage universal reporting.

Death Registers: Formats and Rules

The states need to explore this 'window' for easy acquisition of universal data to orient public policy and resources accordingly; this is not being done at present. At present, the broad categories in the form prescribed for recording deaths are natural causes, suicides, and accidents, whereas there is no classification of morbidity attributable to particular diseases. The formats can be designed to take cognizance of diseases (for example, cancer, water borne diseases, a list that could be modified from time to time to reflect those diseases that are a cause of worry) in the context of Punjab; a possible classification of causes of death could be: (i) accidents/crime; (ii) suicides; (iii) death due to specified diseases namely (a) cancer; (b) water borne diseases (both relevant for Punjab); (c) diseases other than those listed for (a) and (b). Thus, the total number of classifications would be six and not difficult to specify for laypersons entering the data. The advantage of this approach would be that: (a) the State Government will have ready information on the major parameters for MMR (Maternal Mortality Rate), IMR (Infant Mortality Rate), and deaths due to diseases that need to be monitored, and (b) the policy interventions can be devised accordingly without having to depend on periodical surveys, which may not be very reliable for this purpose. The data can be digitized at micro and macro levels so that the status in respect of major indicators (IMR, MMR, morbidity due to particular diseases) can be calculated and local and context-specific interventions designed. This information, once available in the village abstract, as prescribed in the rules, can be used for getting the local/district/regional picture in regard to IMR, MMR, and deaths due to various diseases for which critical and reliable data of incidence is not available.

Rules and Incentives

It would thus appear that:

(a) The rules (mostly) and practices (occasionally) discourage rather than encourage recording events of births and deaths in time;

(b) A number of problems—the institutions, processes, and incentive structures especially of the 'notifier' family, detachment or even a negative disposition of the local registrar, problematic logistics and processes for delayed registration (as per the law or administrative practice), informal practice of endorsement from midwife/sarpanch leading to high transaction costs or bribery, and the (ignored) cultural context—adversely affect the objectives of the law.

The service is designed for universal coverage, there is no exclusion, and the state agencies are responsible for designing of micro rules and their implementation. There are no vested interests responsible for a biased design of rules, as for example, in the procurement of public goods and services. The rules, however, are not compatible with the incentives of the families or of officials. In fact, the rules seem to be designed not to achieve but rather to defeat the very objectives they seek to fulfill. It would appear that it is the formal institutions and rules which are the source of most of the imperfections in the public agent—citizen interactions, and not the implementation agents or the cutting edge processes and protocols, usually the scapegoats for inappropriate outcomes—delayed recording, troublesome registration/certificates, levy of fees with unnecessary and ancillary problems of accounting. The usual solutions of creating incentives for the Panchayat Secretary or organizing capacity enhancement programmes, solutions which keep everybody happy, are obviously sub-optimal. The orthogonal relationship between the rules and incentives of the parties—officials as well as the clients—is a distinct feature of these regulations. Registration of these events is a public service in which there is no exclusion and there is little incentive for filing a wrong application or even getting a wrong certificate. Further, considering the diversity of staff (thousands of local registrars in one state) anybody with moderate resources can procure a wrong certificate, if he or she sets her mind to it. One need not be a 'Jackal', the professional assassin hired to kill De Gaulle, who manufactures a fake identity through this process.[2] The additional safeguards of late fee, approval, third party certification, therefore, are hardly deterrents for those determined enough, but act as irritants and add to the transaction costs for the applicants.

6

Verification of Caste Certificates: A 'Cascade' of Ignorance

Unlike birth and death registration, which is an example of a service of moderate utility for the mass of applicants, the SC (Scheduled Caste) certificate (and similar other certificates such as Backward Class/Other Backward Castes) represent somewhat higher order services in the sense that the certificate is a prerequisite or a necessary condition but not sufficient for providing the facilities and concessions for which it is obtained. The SC/Caste certificates are required for availing of scholarships, admissions in the technical schools/colleges against quotas reserved for the category concerned, and most importantly, government employment. Admissions in the professional medical colleges are especially valued. Simple procurement of a certificate is not sufficient, as most of the entitlements and concessions require additional criteria to be fulfilled. In the case of admissions to professional institutions, it can be a lower cut off in a qualifying examination and for government employment, an income criterion for the exclusion of the 'creamy layer'. The utility of an SC certificate, therefore, is more substantial than in the case of area certificates, but is not directly derived from the certificate itself.

Most of such services are not backed by any statutory rules; administrative instructions are issued from time to time by the executive. In the case of the SC certificates, instructions require an application form, an affidavit, and verification by the elected and/or government officials. For some years, possibly due to reasons given earlier (such as prevalent ideology), the legislators were authorized to issue the SC certificates in Punjab, but the practice was subsequently discontinued.

Verification Rituals

The process of verification is different for the urban and the rural areas. For the urban area residents, verification by an elected public official, such as a Municipal Councillor (MC), is sufficient. The rural area residents suffer from double jeopardy as verification is done by the sarpanch (an elected public official heading the village panchayat), or the *lambardar* (an official appointed by the government through a quasi judicial process, for a specific block of agricultural lands, *a 'patti'*, which may not be coterminous with the village boundary) and in addition, also by the revenue agency through its *patwari* (the village revenue official) and the *tehsildar*. The issue is, if the MC can be the sole agent for verification in the urban areas, then why not the counterpart sarpanch in the rural areas? There is no evidence that elected public officials in rural areas are less responsible than the MCs! Evidently, the process is just to complete the checking of the boxes by the authorities issuing the certificate and probably the practice started because initially there were no elected village officials (the election mechanisms were introduced in the late 1950s) and the verifying party in a village could only be the revenue official; the elected officials in the rural areas have been added later to the list rather than substituting the revenue officials as they should have, an example of incremental rule-making. The revenue agency in any case does not have information on the economic and social conditions of the families and is only concerned with the administration of lands, but this fact is conveniently ignored. A *patwari* deals with land records and is not expected to have information about the residence, caste or family size of the residents. The same is the case with the *lambardar,* who is only concerned with land revenue. Probably the village *chowkidar* would the better equipped to handle the query, but most of them may not be literate. Similarly the Sarpanch or the Municipal Councillor may generally have some information about the voters, but this is more likely to be general information about the caste and religious composition of the constituency rather than detailed knowledge of an individual's economic and social status. Thus, none of the verifying parties has access to information relevant to the application. Unless, therefore, these officials take the trouble to spend time and effort to acquire such information (this is unlikely as they have little incentive), they are likely to endorse the applications in good faith. At the most, some casual enquiries may be made if an official happens to be conscientious. The MC concerned, for example, may not even be representing the ward of the applicant, as there is no such requirement.

In the case of elected officials, the only incentive is provided by political and electoral considerations, which means that he/she cannot afford to refuse to endorse the application. If an application is to be endorsed, why would he/she spend time and effort to make enquiries? If factually correct, the applicants will only be annoyed by the delay; if incorrect, it will still be in his or her interest not to refuse to endorse for the same reasons. Public men, by nature of their position, which is dependent on the constituents' good will, can rarely afford to refuse on the ground of lack of personal knowledge, and verification by the public men is generally therefore a ritual without much relevance to the correctness of the stated facts. Thus, the strategy for the public official is to simply sign the application when approached by the applicant, a sort of 'Pascal's wager'; the winning strategy is to appear to believe in the authenticity of facts and sign!

Patwaris and *Kanungos*, who are concerned with land matters, do not have access to information regarding the caste status. The practice of verification by them, therefore, in any case, needs to be discontinued. There is little logic in making the process more onerous for the rural areas, just because revenue officials happen to be available there. In fact in a couple of states, the associations and unions of the revenue officials have protested against this extraneous duty on the ground that they don't have access to such information and have to go by hearsay and/or some elected official's word or report, and are therefore, unnecessarily held accountable for the lapses.

Transaction Costs

It would thus appear that neither the revenue staff nor the

elected officials have any incentive to expend resources on acquiring information about the applicant. The process of verification, therefore, is a ritual. The result of these seemingly innocuous procedures is that hundreds of government and elected officials handling thousands of applications spend umpteen hours and the applicants incur huge transaction costs in terms of time and money (which are being further compounded by the enthusiastic efforts indicated later) to get facts verified from persons—elected or otherwise—who have no information that has any bearing on the issue, and have no incentive either to gather such information. In the process, the applicant may have to incur an expenditure of Rs. 500–1000, assuming an opportunity cost of two days lost at Rs. 500, apart from the costs imposed on the verifying agencies and officials.

The process has been sometimes perverted by some government officers who have taken 'innovative' steps to pre-empt bogus reports based on informal bilateral settlement among the applicants and the revenue officials. Some district administrations in Punjab require that the applications be deposited by the applicant at the front desk (District Suvidha Centre), which receives the application and transmits it manually through the revenue hierarchy to the *patwari*. This is done in the hope that there will be no exchange of money and the verification will be objective and impersonal. In practice, this only adds further links in the chain of delivery, multiplying transaction cost for the applicants who have now to track the applications, arrange to meet the revenue officials at the appropriate time, and ensure quick response/report through some mutually satisfactory arrangement. Some other enthusiastic officials have started the 'innovative' practice of allotting code numbers to the MCs to ensure that they represent the constituent applicant's ward, thus making the whole process, in the garb of objective reporting, more tortuous still, without gaining any advantage in terms of increased authenticity of verification.

Linking Incentives and Liability

In most of these services, therefore, the process of verification appears completely misdirected; the process merely amounts to completing a formality, as the agents have neither information nor any incentives (or disincentives) to acquire that information. For the applicant, transaction costs translate into a simple alternative of negotiating them through bribery/speed money; and of course, higher the stakes (as in the case of employment and admission to preferred institutions), greater the incentive. Simpler alternatives of aligning incentives for compliance through the applicant's personal liability are likely to be more effective and self-enforcing. The wrongdoer is always identifiable—as the recipient of whatever benefit he or she has obtained—and the procedure is likely to be more of a deterrent against 'adverse selection'. And the pressure from competition for such concessions provides the market correctives. There have been cases where candidates from the SC category for admission to the MBBS, have not only complained against candidates admitted on the basis of bogus certificates but have also got relief from courts.

'Moral Hazard' of Self-selection

Generally, the justification given in defence of these verification processes is that there is no alternative and self-certification by the applicant will only lead to a 'moral hazard' and 'adverse selection'. So there is an affidavit, which itself costs much more than the service fee (in terms of related cost of drafting, attesting, et cetera), and also further cost of verification (especially in the rural areas as indicated). Ideally, since the MC/sarpanch are not the custodians of information about the applicant, nor do they have any structured means of checking the veracity of information, self-declarations should be adequate in most of the cases. In case the proposal of self-selection appears to be risky, a simpler, 'softer' solution to these problems appears to be available, which would impose nominal transaction costs and pin the responsibility on the applicant. One example of a simple solution is the process of passport verification, where verification by the police is based on reports by two persons in the neighbourhood. One may not always have access to the MC/sarpanch or may not be on good terms with them, but even a

'Mr. Bean'[1]—dropped from the sky without relatives, family, or friends—has to have neighbours. An applicant can easily produce known witnesses who endorse the facts given. Witnesses having some identification (voter card, UID, ration card et cetera) from the area/neighbourhood, would be an effective alternative to official verification. The process of verification by such witnesses can be refined—personal presence in case of more risk prone transactions and only written endorsement in case of others. This will enable the process of certification in such need-based services to be limited to a one-stop-one-visit transaction and eliminate transaction costs for both parties—the applicants and the officials. As mentioned in Chapter 3, the expected 'default' behaviour—truthful self reporting—in the case of these alpha interactions warrants appropriate 'default rules'.

7

Motor Vehicle Regulations: Rash or Negligent!

These regulations—mainly registration of motor vehicles, issue of driving licences, and annual fitness certificates for commercial vehicles—seek to address the problem of costs imposed on others by the drivers of motor vehicles. The purpose of registration of a vehicle is to identify its owner; the owner has to bear the liability for the harm caused to a third party, irrespective of who may have been the driver. The rules require the owner to produce sales documents containing the vehicle details—chassis and engine numbers—and proof of address; he or she is required to contact the designated transport department office for the deposit of papers and fees, and get the vehicle 'passed' after inspection of the vehicle by officials.

The present system of issue of the Registration Certificate (RC) in most states requires two to three separate visits—one for deposit of fees and documents, one for physical inspection (one or two days or a week are fixed for this purpose), and the third for getting the Registration Certificate, which concludes the interaction. These processes are being refined ostensibly to eliminate middlemen, but in practice, achieve the opposite result. A new system to streamline procedures resulted in further chaos in Haryana, according to a newspaper report.

Streamlining RC Delivery!

- One day required for getting the registration file, which takes about 4-5 hours.
- Another day for passing vehicle inspection, a full day job.
- 3rd day for collecting a token for delivery of the Registration Certificate.
- 4th day for collecting the Registration Certificate.

Source: *Dainik Bhaskar*, Chandigarh Edition 24 January 2012.

Owners can pay a lump sum tax on vehicles and the transaction costs incurred in the course of getting the registration certificate (in terms of time involved), which we estimate to be Rs.1000–2000, are therefore only a fraction of the road tax. No wonder the middlemen, who know the tricks, are in demand. They make their services available, if required, right when one takes delivery of a vehicle and will deliver the RC at one's home! Similar stages are involved for the issue of driving licences (which require deposit of an application, a driving test, and the issue of a licence) and 'fitness certificates' issued annually for the commercial vehicles. A driving test is conducted for the applicants' driving skills and physical inspection is prescribed for checking the roadworthiness of the commercial vehicles, before the issue of a fitness certificate. These three services—issue of registration certificate, driving licence, and fitness certificate—involve some amount of paperwork such as documentation, deposit of fees, et cetera. They also require physical interaction for the process of 'passing' the vehicle after inspection, testing the capability of the applicants to drive, and checking the roadworthiness of the vehicle. The processes relating to documentation have been or are being simplified. E-applications have been developed and the main interventions required now are minimizing the time spent in queues to just deposit papers. What the state governments also need to attend to, however, is simplification of processes in respect of (a) 'passing' of vehicles for granting the Registration Certificate, (b) annual inspections for certification of fitness of the commercial vehicles, and (c) testing of the driving skills for a driving licence.

Inspection of Vehicles: Issue of RC

The whole exercise of inspection and 'passing' of vehicles is a formality and everybody knows it. Officials know there is little risk involved if proper inspection is not done, at least of the new vehicles. The rules are, therefore, considered a formality even by them, and the opportunity for corruption lies only in expediting or delaying the process. Some of the states have, however, given powers to the authorized vehicle dealers to issue the RC (Registration Certificate) to the owners. The inspection for 'passing' a new vehicle is, in practice, a two-minute formality, but considering the number of vehicles, the transaction costs are high. Motor vehicles are standardized, sold only by the reputed manufacturers and the inspection would appear to be unnecessary. Assuming a sale of two crore vehicles in India annually and an average of eight hours waiting for vehicle 'passing', this means a loss of Rs. 600 crore in terms of opportunity costs. The dealers could be similarly authorized to issue the 'passing' certificate, thus saving substantial costs in terms of the time expended by the officials and the owners of vehicles.

Fitness Certificate

Similar options are available for the fitness certificates required to be issued for the commercial and goods vehicles every year. The authorized dealers who sell the vehicles have the best facilities for testing as well as for rectifying the defects, whereas it is expensive, due to the tremendous variety of vehicles that are now in the market, for the government departments to develop such facilities in-house. The current process consists simply of performing the pointless routines of inspection and checking, supplemented by speed money or whatever one may call it. Not only are the authorized dealers the best equipped to handle this task, they are also the most concerned and affected by the manufacturers' concern for reputation. Transferring this function to the dealers is unlikely to create perverse incentives for misuse, as the main business of the authorized dealers is sales, not repairs and certification. Competition among the numerous dealers is likely to ensure reliable certification; manufacturers have already created enough competition in this regard. Instead of adopting such simple solutions—even when the department does not have adequate resources in terms of facilities for checking—ambitious proposals for funding of the government owned and operated testing facilities are being contemplated in some states, ignoring the fact that the markets would provide the least expensive and efficient solution.

Driving Licences: Incentives for Testing Skills

It is not clear whether the grant of driving licences, without rigorous testing of the driving skills of the aspirants, has resulted in higher social costs in terms of accidents et cetera. Landsburg,[1] quotes a study bySam Peltzman, that the use of seat belts, padded dash boards, et cetera, did not reduce the number of accidents; there were fewer driver deaths but more accidents, and the number of pedestrian deaths increased. The somewhat surprising findings were sought to be explained by the change in the incentives of the drivers who could indulge in rash driving/speeding due to the apparent additional safety provided by the seat belt! We can hypothesize similarly that skilled drivers may cause more accidents; they are likely to be more confident as compared to novices, who may drive more carefully precisely because they are diffident! Probably the Indian experience is a giveaway; frequency and intensity of accidents do not appear to be a function of (lack of) driving skills, as most licences are in practice issued without any effective test of skills! A study of the Delhi transport department showed that the issue of a driving licence was correlated more with willingness to bribe, rather than driving skills.[2] This is not to say that a test of driving skills for the issue of driving licences is irrelevant, but only that, considering the incentives of various parties as indicated, outsourcing the job of conducting the driving test may be a socially efficient solution in the Indian context. And one need not forget the incentives of the applicants; surely they are also interested in their own safety and a car driver cannot be certain of escaping injury while merrily inflicting damage on others. That may explain the popularity of driving schools and the driving lessons they provide, even when applicants may be well aware that such lessons are irrelevant for obtaining a licence.

Incentives and Context

The solution suggested in the case of ensuring fitness of commercial vehicles—certification by authorized dealers—may not however work in the case of driving licences; outsourcing the task of testing skills to the private driving schools may not by itself be the desirable option. The perverse incentives and pay offs for certifying driving skills of candidates who may not really be qualified, would only get transferred to the authorized testing schools. The government, therefore, needs to create competitive conditions, rather than simply transferring the government monopoly to the private sector. In fact, a news item[3] shows the pitfalls of outsourcing the monopoly services; in Delhi, the certification for the fitness of commercial vehicles was outsourced to a single company, leading to allegations of misuse of official position in the selection of a single party. Monopolies, whether of the government or the private parties, are subject to similar problems. Context matters and simple outsourcing, a good solution in one case (such as the vehicle fitness certificate), may not work for another. Outsourcing this function to private parties, therefore, needs to be supported by close monitoring. Officials would be required to regulate and monitor only a limited number of entities which are authorized to recommend the issue of licences and the genuineness of certification can always be test checked. There may be some misuse by private organizations at the initial stage, but in due course, with competition, the parties that do not provide quality services will not be empanelled or approved and will go out of business, and the remaining parties will acquire, over time, stakes in their reputation.

Before concluding this chapter, it may be appropriate to mention the oddity of creditor-friendly rules relating to hypothecation of vehicles in favour of the institutions providing loans for purchase of motor vehicles. Owners are not estopped from selling immovable property (even if mortgaged) and incur only civil liabilities. In the case of motor vehicles, however, each hypothecation must be entered in the Registration Certificate and clearance from the lending agency obtained before sale by the owner. The procedure for release from mortgage, once the loan is repaid, is almost as rigorous and time consuming as for the issue of a new Registration Certificate. And all these rules are in aid of the creditor, one of the parties in a private transaction! If an owner wants to sell the vehicle, but there is some dispute about the discharge of loan liability, he/she has to do the bidding of the creditor. There is little evidence in this case of 'market failure' which requires such regulations designed to favour the creditors. And it is claimed that India is a free market for economic transactions!

8

Civic Regulations for Buildings: Roof for Citizens

New construction—residential or commercial—involves substantial investment on the part of applicants. One would, once the finances are tied up, like to start building as soon as possible and complete it in the shortest possible time. The rules, therefore, giving power to officials to delay either the start or the completion of a building can lead to significant corruption. That is the reason respondents in the *Study on Urban Governance* in Punjab, referred earlier, consider it as the most corruption prone regulation. It does not matter whether the construction is for non-commercial use (residential buildings) or for profit (commercial and industrial buildings and structures).

A series of transactions is required under the building bylaws to complete the process and bring it to the final stage of getting permission to occupy. The first step is getting the plan of the building approved. The plan has to be prepared by a private architect licenced or empanelled by the ULB (Urban Local Body). The plan is approved, after scrutiny of the plan by the building/civil engineer and/or the architect, who are expected to ensure compliance with the rules and standards of safety/design/zonal restrictions, et cetera. In some cases, a field visit by officials may be mandated before the construction proceeds beyond the plinth level. Once the construction is completed, approval is required for issue of a Completion Certificate, which again requires a visit by the concerned officials to ensure that the building is as per the plan and conforms to the bylaws. Once the Completion Certificate is issued, another application for an Occupation Certificate is required in Punjab, which is given after the water supply and sewerage connections (two independent transactions involving different departments) are sanctioned. The whole process thus involves three to four specific stages, each involving a number of processes and clearances by the ULB. There are additional requirements for commercial buildings, such as a 'no objection' in advance from other government departments, namely, for scheduled road clearance, power, sanitation, environment, water supply, et cetera. The bylaws are mostly uniform across the ULBs in Punjab and even extend to controls over planning of internal spaces for residences, which otherwise are not relevant from the point of view of safety, zoning, et cetera. Minimum dimensions of bathrooms for example are specified in the bylaws of the ULBs!

Negotiating the Maze of Rules

Some of the bylaws are so opaque or complicated that, given the propensity of staff to interpret them differently, the architects resolve the problems during 'negotiations'. Architects' fees for preparing plans, et cetera, mostly include informal payments to be made to the authorities. Corporate entities generally find this convenient, rather than manufacturing bogus vouchers for accounts/audit purposes. The quantum of informal payments depends on the potential for invoking of regulatory restrictions to delay approvals (for example, for nursing homes and hospitals that have more complex regulations, all in the interest of the local community). The process of transfer of payments is smoothened and effectuated by middleman or even middle-level employees.

Rules do require response/approval within specified time limits—for example, 30 days are provided for residential buildings—but this is subject to the applicant complying with all the formalities. Considering the complexity and ambiguity of rules, this is a tough nut to crack. The building bylaws are complex, have diverse objectives of public interest—aesthetics, light and air, safety of buildings, safety of users of commercial buildings, et cetera—and it is always possible to point out some omission to keep the approval pending. Simplification of rules, therefore, is unlikely in case of construction of structures and buildings; rather the complexity and diversity of regulations is likely to increase to take account of developing concerns about safety (earth quake proofing in earth quake prone zones), environmental compliance (now extended to major commercial buildings, as well as industry and even residences regarding rain harvesting, solar panels). Given that there is little likelihood of deregulation, one has to think of innovative ways to incentivise the two parties. The only feasible option now is the 'under the table' payment to avoid delay and multiple objections. The amount of corruption involved can go up to one per cent of the project/construction cost and may be higher in the case of commercial buildings, which are subject to more stringent regulations.

Citizen Incentives

A person investing in a building will like to complete and start using the structure as soon as possible. Considering the returns, short cuts—through contacts or corruption—which expedite the process or reduce the delay, could very well be the rational strategy. The costs of delay in this situation transcend from innocuous transaction costs of time to real cost of 'sunk' capital. The second set of incentives of customers/clients concerns compliance with the regulations. Safety regulations in respect of structural soundness (generally certified by structural engineers) are likely to be willingly compiled with, except in case of builders of multi-storey apartment blocks, who may pocket the sale proceeds and disappear after transferring the property to individual owners. There is little premium in constructing unsafe buildings if the owners are to live in them. Similarly, use of internal spaces will be optimized according to one's preferences and the danger or harm to the community in case of noncompliance may not be worth the regulatory ink or print. This is also true of architectural designs. The architect has no incentive to design a building in violation of the rules—for reasons similar to what has been stated in case of the users—and in fact, more so, as his/her professional reputation can be compromised. In any case, substantive changes can be made without any problem later, with or without the architect, by the user. The officials know this and the processes only result in providing them incentives to make money. The whole process of compliance with rules, with tough scrutiny of plans and inspections, is a purposeless charade and a huge social waste, which entails substantial transaction costs for the official agency as well as the users.

What the local councils should be bothered about is issues like zoning, open spaces, and the number of floors, since these are regulations for the public good, ensuring aesthetically pleasing and harmonious fronts and adequate light and air for neighbours. In case of water supply and sewerage connections, especially in case of the former, the objective is to ensure that the water quantities are not appropriated disproportionately, particularly where metering is not perfect or water supply is limited. If compliance is left to consumers, there may be incentives for misuse, as the return on violations can be high; but even in case of these regulations, the design of the enforcement process, namely, paper scrutiny and the pre-occupation inspection, is hardly sufficient for ensuring compliance. Simple options for bypassing the regulations are available, and in fact, are being used. The authorities make a visit and issue whatever authorization for occupation they have to issue. The user simply waits for this process to be over and then does whatever he/she likes—cover open spaces, install a higher capacity water line or boosters for pumping up water, and of course, make any internal changes, which in any case, cannot be easily noticed. More than 80 per cent of the houses in Chandigarh and Panchkula appear to have carried out these modifications after the occupation certificates were issued. The only other time the 'net' closes in again, is when the owner has to get an NOC (no objection certificate) for sale, and this is again smoothened out through informal payments.

It would appear that in respect of the major objectives of the building regulations—safety, air, light and aesthetics—all that the different stages of processing and evaluation provided as part of regulations do, is to complete the paper formalities All concerned know fully well that there is no way of ensuring long-term compliance. In fact, the only victims in this process are the 'turtles' caught unwittingly in the fishing nets—honest citizens making honest mistakes in construction and having to pay compounding fees officially, or in case of non-compoundable violations, bribes unofficially. Some 'fishing boats' have been reported to be hauling up more turtles than fish; similar is the case with the building bylaws. The levy of penalty appears to be in inverse proportion to the gravity of violations; graver violations are settled 'out of court'!

Agency Incentives

Coming to the incentives on the enforcement side, even dedicated officials know the reality as outlined above, that their scrutiny and inspection is illusory. Even if they were to ensure compliance at the time of inspection, there is no way that long-term compliance can be ensured. Some officials may, on this account, be a little lax in scrutiny but there is a strong incentive for the large majority to make trouble free money in the process. 'Rational expectations' may or may not work in the capital markets but are very appropriate here. In any case, it can always be claimed by an inspecting official that the construction was regulation compliant and violations were made later, that is, after inspection, and there is no way to check. So far as the structural safety of buildings is concerned, only a structural engineer knows whether the design and construction is sound; it is impossible for the user to know about the safety of design. This anomaly—holding the owner liable rather than the engineer or other professional—has been mentioned later in Chapter 11 in connection with the issue of approval of industrial structures.

Aligning Incentives

The problem in case of these building regulations is making the rules compatible with the incentives of owners as well as officials. Safety is in the interest of owners themselves whereas compliance with the zonal and frontage regulations—public goods—is in the professional interest of architects. Probably the regulations should place the onus for compliance on the third parties (builders/structural engineers/architects) who have the appropriate information and professional incentives. The builder, rather than the owner, is likely to be more aware of structural defects, but the present rules turn the process upside down by making the owner liable for safety. Needless to say, the regulatory staff can and should ensure proper enforcement in the case of apartment blocks and other buildings, where the owners have no long-term stakes, don't bear the consequences, and therefore, have incentives to economize on safety measures. Unfortunately that is precisely the area where rigorous inspection is the least likely—all a matter of incentives!

Most of the building regulations can be left to self-enforcement, as it is impossible to have information on compliance, and in any case, it is (except in case of 'build and disappear' entrepreneurs mentioned above) in the applicants' own interest to comply. Regarding the public interest regulations affecting neighbourhoods, affected neighbours are the appropriate 'self selected' parties for signalling violations and enforcing compliance. In fact such complaints are mostly the basis for action by authorities even now. The structure of the building regulations, therefore (a) ignores the incentives of architects and builders, (b) imposes some unrealistic obligations which are likely to be violated (for example, use of inner space), (c) ignores the problem of 'information asymmetry' of the enforcement staff who cannot observe the activities relating to construction, and thus encourages all concerned to 'game' the system.

The problem of accidents—fire, explosions, and poisonous fumes (as in the Union Carbide case in Bhopal)—is different. These can sometime happen due to a very human cognitive problem—'disaster myopia'—rather than inadequate technical measures for safety. The example[1] by Loretta Napoleoni regarding the fire incident at Zhili in Shenzhen, China, which caused the death of 135 workers in the year 1993, is pertinent. The owners hoped the 'black swan' event would not occur in their factory, all the factories being in the same circumstances of being noncompliant! The key is making the consequences costly for the owner (only US$ 5000 compensation per worker was provided in China). This issue is addressed later.

It is easy to design incentive compatible and self-regulatory rules: a driver knows that driving without having any skills can be unsafe for him/her also; a homeowner is unlikely to build a house that will collapse. Violations of some of the regulations would also impact other parties who can always complain or seek compensation and/or compromise at a point that is optimum for both parties,[2] once the rules and penalties are clear. Enforcement will be easier through third party, neighbours' referral/complaints (in case of regulations for light and air) rather than one time certification of compliance by the authorities. The local authorities need to make clear rules and withdraw, leaving it to parties to settle and come into the picture only if this does not happen.

9

Transparency: The Market for Information

Information is the equivalent of an alpha male in public services; unlike most of these, the interaction can be voluntary and demand driven or a one-way street, as in the case of mandated disclosures. Akerlof[1] demonstrates the critical role of information in the functioning of economic markets through the analogy of 'lemons' traded in the 'used car market' and how the 'used car market' can collapse due to asymmetry of information among sellers and buyers. Other major areas of market failure have subsequently been explored, such as the insurance and job markets. Markets have developed corrective systems—rating agencies, grading for perishable foods, et cetera—but these may not by themselves eliminate market failure. Devising suitable institutions to create a level playing field in respect of information, therefore, is one area where even the committed free marketeers concede that the State has a role to play, rather than hoping for the market mechanisms to do so. Information is a critical input for productive exchanges in the governance market for obvious reasons; there is little else available by way of mediation mechanisms. Fortunately, the supply of information in the governance markets is not constrained by competitive pressures or vested interests, as in the case of sellers in the economic 'used car market'. The State's role in addressing this problem in the area of its own activities appears, however, to have been neglected. The issue has generally been addressed on a moral plane to ensure 'freedom of receiving information' rather than ensuring free flow and 'imparting' of information in the government's possession. This moral basis is provided by Article 19 of the Universal Declaration of Rights: 'Everyone has the right to freedom of opinion and expression; this right includes freedom to hold opinions without interference and to seek, *receive* and *impart information* and ideas through any media and regardless of frontiers'.[2] This moral stance has been the basis of freedom of information laws passed by a large number of countries. While these laws provide detailed rules, processes and mechanisms for providing information which is sought, the obligation of the government agencies in respect of information to be 'imparted' by the government gets a somewhat casual treatment under an implicit assumption that this is secondary to supply of information when demanded. This is so despite a large volume of information required to be voluntarily disclosed under the RTI Act in India, as we hope to show. Transparency is more than simply making information, activities and policies open and needs to include not simply freedom of the public to seek and impart information but an obligation on the part of the state agencies to provide information to citizens they may require, but may not be aware or vocal about, for enjoying and consuming the state products and services and for socially productive interaction with the government agencies. Information is a necessary pre condition for avoiding governance failure, as in the economic markets. Information is 'like air, a pre condition for other things to happen'.[3]

Access to information is the gateway for various services, activities and outputs provided by the public authorities and a precondition not only for efficient interaction but also for good governance attributes especially participation and predictability. Effective participation is not possible unless the citizens are well informed and predictability may remain a mere slogan, if actions of the public servants are enveloped in secrecy. Information, especially when volunteered, however, has to be delivered in appropriate 'bytes' and packages, suitably designed to address the needs of citizens and other public and private entities. The Federal Government in the US under the guidance of Cass Sunstein has provided a good example[4]. Surely a government should first be able to do a good job in respect of its own information sets, if it is to be credibly aggressive (at least in democratic countries which believe in active interventionist policies) in intervening similarly in the economic markets.

Right to Information in India

The Right To Information Act (RTI) is now the main institution in India for delivery of information—voluntary or on demand —to all the stakeholders. There are provisions for supply of information to citizens on request, on payment of a modest fee, appointment of the PIOs (public information officers) and Assistant Public Information Officers (APIO's) by each PA (public authority) to receive applications on their behalf and appointment of appellate officers. The State/the Central Information Commission is the final authority for complaints and appeals. The act also provides that every public authority should take steps to provide as much information as possible *suo motu* to the public so as to minimize occasions the latter have to file applications requesting for information. The RTI provisions for *suo motu* display of information [Section 4 (i) (b)] appear to be comprehensive and cover major areas of citizen demand and interest, including participatory governance; information on the functioning of committees, councils, and boards of the public authorities, and information on the arrangements made for consultation with the members of the public on policy, formulation, and implementation, are required to be provided. In addition, the RTI Act provides for mandatory display of information on staffing, remuneration, budget, concessions and subsidies, statutes, rules, bylaws and instructions, and norms and standards adopted by the departments and the PAs.

The RTI law in India does not contain any reference, as in case of the UK, to routine information on the public services provided by the concerned officials and agencies. In the UK Act, this is defined to be the duty of the concerned departments. The UK law on Freedom of Information[5] specifies that the concerned officials will continue to provide information on services provided by them to citizens and the RTI law in the UK therefore excludes such services from its purview. The law in Thailand[6] is directed more at macro issues of policymaking, contracts, et cetera; Thailand is more concerned about State capture through the manipulation of the State regulatory mechanisms and the focus there is on transparency in the formulation and finalization of major policies, procurement, and contracts. Individual citizens and their information issues in respect of basic services are not the core focus, as the cutting edge service delivery systems are viewed to be satisfactory. On the other hand, the South African law[7] focuses on the common man's issues by providing specifically that the government agency should display the list of services they provide and the service standards thereof. In India also, this area is important as is clear from a proposal favoured by the CSOs (Civil Society Organisations) as well as the government for a law on citizen charters referred earlier, which mandates the disclosure of service standards, grievance systems, et cetera. Citizen charters are generally not displayed under the RTI Act; the relevant clause is, at least for bureaucrats, comfortably vague. It refers to 'norms' that obviously cover standards of service, but these standards and norms are rarely disclosed under the RTI. Some other problems with the micro rules for mandated disclosure have been detailed in a monograph[8] on the RTI Act I wrote some years ago.

Lazy Systems of Information Delivery

There appears to be substantial deficit in information transfer and exchange, whether for routine governance interactions or mandatory disclosure practices and even for demand-driven supply of information. The RTI Act does not appear to have effectively addressed this problem. In the first place, the departments do not display information about the services they handle, let alone information about the processes and service standards. Such information is mostly available only on the websites of the Single Window District Suvidha Centres in Punjab for example, but rarely made available by the agencies and departments. The studies done by the Institute for Development and Communication (IDC) referred earlier indicate acute information deficit among the citizens regarding the 'how' and 'what' of various services. In the case of water supply in the urban areas of Punjab for example, 68 per cent of respondents were not even aware of complaint systems or where and how a complaint may be filed. Furthermore, 73 per cent of respondents were unaware of the procedure for accessing most of the need-based services. In the rural areas, 82 per cent of the Below Poverty Line (BPL) families were even unaware of procedures for getting a BPL card. The respondents were also ignorant of the grievance redress mechanisms, if any, regarding the selection/issue of cards. Only five per cent were aware of the RTI Act itself. The agencies responsible for various services, as also those for mandatory information disclosure fail to provide basic and 'minimum needs' information required by the public.

Mandatory Disclosure of Information

The Punjab government has a specific website for display of the RTI information for the departments.[9] Information on most of the 17 counts of mandatory disclosures is, however, missing. In the case of departments that have disclosed information with respect to the 17 items covered under Section 4 (1) (b) of Act, the information given is incomplete, sketchy, or irrelevant. Abundant information is available on routine aspects, such as pay scales, staff details and duties of staff; but information on the vital bits of information, for example, norms adopted by the department, lists of recipients of concessions, subsidies, authorizations, and meaningful budget details, are mostly missing. Similar is the case with information required to be disclosed regarding public participatory mechanisms. Most of the other states fare no better in this regard, if their websites are any indication. Interestingly, in Punjab, most of the departmental websites do not provide the RTI information; it is placed on a common website and is mostly outdated, the 'champion' of a common platform having departed long back! The site for e-tendering is not open to the public, as it should be. One needs a code, which probably only the parties concerned are provided. Simple information on service standards or even services is missing. In the case of old age pensions in Punjab, the yearly totals are not updated beyond 2006 by the department concerned. The Delhi government citizen charter does not give time schedules for services.

Section 4 (1) (b) of the RTI Act requires specified information to be disclosed and placed in the public domain by the PAs. This covers information relevant for the need-based and regulatory services (norms of supply of services) as well as collective goods (budget, participation mechanisms). Examination of the websites of various departments indicates the divergence between law and practice. For example, in the case of the budget, some Municipal Committees provide information on budget items classified as per their whims, and that too, only monthly figures. Very few PAs provide actual expenditure figures, as required under law. In the case of pensions, subsidies, and concessions, lists of the beneficiaries are not displayed as required. No information is provided for the purchase of goods, services, and contracts by the public authorities. Information about the pay scales, directory of officers, and their duties is provided, but that is of little interest to citizens in general.

The areas of information which interest citizens, apart from alpha services, relate to executive decisions and actions by the public agents and entities, especially in areas where some amount of discretion is involved, for example, allotment/use of public lands, grant of subsidies, pensions, purchase of goods and services, procedures and processes for various services and programmes affecting citizens and employees, capital expenditure including that on goods and services and the details of recipients/beneficiaries under various schemes, programmes and plans, et cetera. An evaluation made by the Punjab Governance Reforms Commission (PGRC) in 2011, with which I was associated, showed that requests for information are mainly regarding these issues, thus probably accounting for the relatively large number of complaints/appeals in such cases. While therefore the overall scheme of mandatory disclosure is comprehensive, ambiguity in the rules and formats of disclosure of information, on budget, expenditure, norms, and standards of service, et cetera, provide scope to the agencies to do as they please. This may be due to incompetence or inattention rather than conscious manipulation, but the result is the same. We need to call in the services of a Cass Sunstein, as the US Federal Goverment did!

Responses to Demand for Information

Official responses to public requests for information fare no better. The handling of requests for information is beset with problems of delays and transaction costs. A survey was conducted by the PGRC and was based on (a) information available in 200 case files decided by the Punjab Information Commission, regarding the time factor involved at the different stages of delivery of information and the nature of information asked for and (b) interviews of 50 applicants who had filed appeals with the Information Commission and were contacted on 'first come' basis. Respondents in the second set were interviewed regarding the transaction costs incurred by them in terms of time, number of visits, travelling and typing costs, et cetera. Major issues that interested the public, as assessed from the 200 randomly selected case files, were about public and private lands, their use and allotment (25.5 per cent), corruption, complaints, enquiries (17 per cent), personnel matters (19 per cent), and financial issues (13 per cent). In the case of 50 respondents interviewed in detail, personnel matters accounted for 38 per cent, corruption 22 per cent, and land 26 per cent of the total number of requests for information. There may be some overlap in terms of classification of information – for example, information relating to public lands and their use appears to involve issues of corruption and misuse of discretion. The same is the case with personnel and financial issues that may overlap with corruption and complaints. Broadly, it can be stated that the bulk of requests relate to issues of misuse of authority, corruption in relation to personnel, financial matters, allotment/lease/(mis)use of public lands, and in the case of private property, availability and accessibility of revenue records. Cases relating to public property (especially lands), corruption and related complaints, and personnel matters appear to constitute over 80 per cent of the information requests.

Most of the requests can be easily anticipated and appear to be broadly covered under the provisions for disclosure of information as indicated above; the reason appears to be a lack of 'details' in the rules for disclosure of information to be provided, leaving it open for official discretion. Only one of the 50 applicants got information within the prescribed period of 30 days. In 20 per cent of the cases, information was supplied within a period of 46 to 90 days. Most of the applicants chose not to approach the appellate authorities and filed complaints directly with the SIC (State Information Commission). Only 24 per cent of the 200 applicants filed appeals to the appellate authorities, and even in these cases, a majority (over 50 per cent) got a response from the appellate officer, much after the prescribed period (within 46 to 90 days), which also apparently did not satisfy them. Disposal of requests and complaints at the SIC level was some what better than at the PIO level: as many as 39 per cent cases involved only one hearing, 28 per cent two hearings, and the balance, three or more hearings.

High Transaction Costs

Disproportionate transaction costs, in terms of time and money, were incurred by the applicants at the PIO level. About 62 per cent of the cases involved three or more visits, whereas ideally, the supply of information should be concluded within, at the most, two visits (if not one)—one for request for information and one for delivery of information. At the SIC level, the performance was much better, as 72 per cent of the cases involved only two hearings. The survey also assessed the time taken (number of hours) on account of visits by the applicant. About 32 per cent of the 50 applicants interviewed spent 15 hours and above at the PIO level and the average number of hours was twenty nine.

The average of costs covering all the stages in the 50 cases is Rs. 22 (fees), Rs. 124 (typing), and Rs. 1518 (travel). At the PIO level alone, the average cost is Rs. 11.80 (fees), Rs. 91 (drafting), and Rs. 243 (travel). Expenditure on travel at the PIO level varies from a minimum of Rs. 80 to a maximum of Rs. 2500. The average incidence of transaction costs is Rs. 335 as against only Rs. 11.80 as fees – the direct cost of information as prescribed. At the SIC level, the average cost is Rs. 124 (typing), Rs. 1391 (travel). The minimum cost for travel is Rs. 100 and the maximum Rs. 5000. *Transaction costs can be thus 30 times the official price (fees) for obtaining information.* These would be much more —perhaps 100 times the fee—if one adds the opportunity cost of time. The PIO system is evidently dysfunctional and imposes disproportionate costs on citizens who may not have enough money or influence to delegate the activities involved in personal visits for filing applications and collecting information.

It appears that information service is one area where even the letter of the rules is vitiated due to inappropriate practices by the departments and the RTI authorities (the PIO's). The culprit, however, appears to be the structure of the rules of disclosure, especially their ambiguity, and also appointment, as the PIOs, of officials the least equipped to perform the function, given the hierarchical structure of government agencies. The system imposes disproportionate transaction costs when accessed through the RTI, mostly due to the mismatch between the custodians of information and the suppliers of information (PIOs). In a way, the PIOs are government nominated middlemen, but unlike the private markets, they add only to citizens' transaction costs. No amount of training or capacity building and sensitization is going to help in the absence of appropriate rules, institutions and models for simple display of information. One result is that it is mostly the skilled and resourceful government officials, apart from some dedicated NGOs, who have appropriated the opportunity and the resources made available by the law.

It appears that the departmental structures, the RTI legislation for mandatory disclosure, and the designated systems for the supply of information have not been able to address major information problems of citizens. Not only that, very high transaction costs for information are imposed on citizens wanting information, which in the first place is required to be openly available. The problem is that the process of information delivery is not a 'transactional' service, as in the case of other alpha services where remote single windows can be good alternatives; it is 'interactional', requires application of mind in identifying the sources of information, and organizing that information. Moreover, the PIOs need to have sufficient maturity to be able to screen the applications to see whether the information should be given or denied. On the other hand, these parallel and inefficient institutions for the supply of information cut across the accountability structures of the department. To be effective, the PIOs must have access to the information asked for and the resources and authority required to collect the information. In the context of the organization of state departments where generally the district heads have reasonable seniority, authority, and control over the information available within the district, it would be appropriate to declare only the district heads as the PIOs in respect of all departments. The Police department follows this system—SSPs as PIOs—and has addressed satisfactorily a huge number of applications primarily for this reason.

Sanctions and Fines: A Mismatch of Incentives

Punishment in terms of the threat of fines is unlikely to resolve the problem. It is mostly suffered by officials who are the PIOs but who don't have control over that information. One can imagine, to take Adam Smith's example, the PIO as the person who is responsible for fixing the pinhead, being given the responsibility instead of the foreman or 'undertaker' (to use Smith's terminology for the entrepreneur) to provide information in respect of all the 18 separate activities.

The main problem causing delay in supply of information, as ascertained in discussions with PIOs, is a simple one. It is not a problem of incentives. They face the consequences of delay —fines—despite their best efforts. Rules for appointing PIOs are the problem. PIOs do not have ready access to information and resources, which are spread out in the departments across various branches and officials. The solution appears to be a simple one – to fix responsibility for supply of information on the officials who control the information resources (such as head of department/district head, et cetera). These problems could be easily addressed if the Chief Executives were to hear the appeals instead of an army of officials spread across the department who have little suitability for the appellate role, except that they happen to be the next senior in line, but face the same problem of lack of access to sources of information.

Designing 'Sticky' Modules for Disclosure

Mandatory disclosure of information can be made more productive by elaborating the scheme of the information sets to be displayed. What is needed is a system making it less costly and more convenient for the officials to supply information to the public. This can be done by fleshing out the sketchy outline of mandated information as indicated so that the officials know what exactly is required of them. Rules could provide budget expenses, for example, to be displayed in the following format:

Information Disclosure 'Module': Budget and Expenditure under Section 4(1)(b)

1 Budget items/schemes	2 Estimates current year	3 Actuals previous year
Total budget of the department/ agency		
Total staff salaries and staff related expenditure		
Total non staff budget (capital) (Rs.)		
Details of non staff expenditure (all items more than Rs.10 lakhs)		
(a) Capital		
(i)		
(ii)		
(b) Revenue		
(i)		
(ii)		

Similarly, information on purchase of goods and services

and contracts could be prescribed by the rules to be displayed in the following format:

Information Disclosure 'Module'— Contracts/Purchases

Description of purchase/ contract	Estimated cost	Details of bidders and price quoted	Contract price and party selected	Date of final payment

Note: (i) Information must be displayed on the website up to six months from the date of final payment.
(ii) Information must be displayed within one month of the award of the contract of purchase and updated monthly.

Such 'modular' rules and checklists are likely to 'stick' and will chart a clear line of action for disclosure of information by the officials responsible. It is difficult to devise appropriate material incentives for officials putting up information for public display and one way to boost compliance may be to remove ambiguity by preparing modules[10] in which information may be provided by officials, rather than leaving it to their competence, imagination, or empathy with citizens' needs. Officials will find it easy to comply and cooperate if formats and modules for display are designed in the rules; at present, departments do not know what exactly is expected of them in respect of the information specifics to be displayed. The RTI rules provide a laid back and lazy solution to the disclosure of information, leaving it to the departments to understand the spirit and make proper display, thus invoking the 'least effort principle' of System II of the collective cognitive system of the department.

What we have in view while suggesting such protocols is not inconspicuous 'priming' or 'the subtle influences (which) can increase the ease with which certain information comes to mind'[11] but something more in the nature of 'channel factors' defined as 'small influences that could either facilitate or prohibit certain behaviours'.[12] Such visible priming in this case is required not for the public, but for the government agents responsible for displaying information. What better way to 'prime' bureaucrats than the rules they themselves swear by!

'Jumping Genes' of Information Delivery Systems

The human genome carries a lot of genetic stuff that has no function for the development of the organism, though it is good at copying itself. Some of these are 'jumping genes, which disrupt the functioning of working genes and mess them up.[13] It won't be an exaggeration to describe the present role of the PIOs similarly—they have little contribution to make for the RTI in their extant official capacity, but by virtue of the 'forced error' of defective rule-making, they need to jump from one holder of information to the next. It seems the governments specialize in artificially developing these 'jumping genes'. The proposed Public Grievances Redressal Bill seeks to continue in the same vein, by nominating an official, who may not have the authority, to be responsible for addressing complaints, thus creating another disruptive clone by design. What is more, unlike the human genome, governance structures are unlikely to find ways to suppress them or control the (unintended) damage they cause. There is a need to design appropriate rules for display of information and eliminate the distance between the locus for compliance and punishment. The information delivery structure of the RTI Act itself creates asymmetries in functionality. It is like a heart patient being asked compulsorily to report to a PHC first for reference to the appropriate hospital. The 'ideology' that information to citizens should be available at the doorstep, seems to be the culprit.

The rules of the RTI for mandatory disclosure don't address the problem of unevenness of information and add to asymmetry in the government data and information sets. Only a skillful operator can, like the expert mentioned earlier in case of the 'used car market', negotiate the gap. It is common knowledge that the main users of the RTI Act are the government officials themselves, estimated to account for around 50 per cent of the work load, though, when the monograph, referred above, was written, I was apprehensive they may even monopolize the RTI window. Most of the citizens don't have enough motivation, knowledge, or resources; and in the circumstances, only 'sticky' algorithms, protocols, or 'checklists', or whatever you like to call them, for disclosing information, are likely to help the public. The government agents need to a) be 'nudged' through 'modules', 'channels' and 'sticky' protocols for the information sets mandated for disclosure (for example, budget, goods and services purchase, citizen charters), and b) avoid the 'jumping genes' problem by integrating resources and functions in the case of the PIOs/Appellate officials.

10

Alpha Services: Aligning Incentives and Institutions

It may appear that disproportionate space has been devoted to these contingent services, considering their ephemeral character in the march of public governance. Most of these are almost autonomous in societies with more organized governance systems—the issuance of passports for instance, which generally should not require any public verification at all, once you have identity as a citizen. Hopefully, with the universalisation of the UID now under way and a national database for crime records, these administrative and social vetting and verification processes will be done away with. These are, however, important to the Indian citizens today, as the public discourse shows; the draft Public Grievances Redressal Bill covers mainly these services.

The framework of economic exchange, which may be relevant for some areas—of property crimes, or contracts with the government—may not be appropriate for the vast range of these essentially administrative services. The cost effective route to overcoming the problems indicated, appears to be zero transaction costs, self-regulation, and addressing the risk of misuse through *ex post* measures. There is need to frame rules that are aligned with and sensitive to the (mild) incentive problems both of government agents and the citizens and removing irritants such as banning birth entry after 15 years of the event. One needs to shift from the framework of 'gatekeeping' by the government officials to that of service delivery/approval as the routine 'default' option, with discretion limited to *ex post* investigation and action. The simple recipe for efficient and corruption free delivery appears to be minimizing the transaction costs. Suitable changes in the rules and procedures can be made, as indicated earlier, to provide an almost perfect 'fit' between the objectives and the incentives of both parties—citizens and the public agencies—to the exchanges.

One is tempted to claim that the rules of verification demean the *aam aadmi* and are based on the colonial legacy of distrust; adding ideological flavour or fervor to rules may, however, not resolve the problem. The need-based services, involving as they do a large number of citizens, need particular attention because, unlike repeated transactions, the demand pressure for improvement is missing—customers need the service only once in a while, whenever the need arises. People find shortcuts to obtain the alpha services, whether through corruption or by incurring high transaction costs. Corruption is in a way the obverse of the transaction costs. Citizen and user dissatisfaction in respect of these services can only be observed directly—when they are in a queue. As Ariely[1] remarks, people don't carry long term memories of the minor irritants which are not frequent and only remember the intensity and the end points of experience rather than the duration—pleasant or otherwise.

Information, Self-selection, and 'Moral Hazard'

Some of these services require information that is private and held personally. The government agents are in no position to verify such information, and as seen, none of the verifying agencies would be able to do so with confidence. So why not depend on information provided by citizens? Citizens continue to be liable and have little incentives for misuse. In any case, a reasonably determined person facing substantial gain or loss, can easily game the system by producing appropriate witnesses and documents. The demand for the alpha services may come down over time, with more and more people acquiring identity documents under the UID programme. That identity, however, will not be of much use if the information supplied by the citizens is not accepted and instead made subject to official endorsement and certification. In cases like the residence certificate, there is little incentive to apply for a false certificate. In the case of caste and similar certificates that are more valuable, the competition is likely to provide a more effective solution to misuse. If a false SC certificate is used to procure admission in a medical college for example, the candidates excluded have and can question the same successfully. There is little problem therefore of 'moral hazard' or 'adverse selection' in the case of alpha services.

Transaction Costs and Corruption

One problem is the substantial costs citizens as well as the government agents have to bear in the process of applying for and obtaining the documents. These transaction costs—especially opportunity costs of time— are substantial. A wage earner may have to forego 2-3 days' earnings just to get one of the simplest certificates (say of residence). Bribery/middlemen become more feasible alternatives. It is difficult to estimate these transaction costs but extrapolating the data collected for Punjab —over 80 lac Alpha transactions as per data compiled by the Suvidha Centres and the Punjab Commission on Right to Service —it would appear that over 30 per cent of the population of India is making use of such services, thus incurring (40 crores x Rs. 500) Rs. 20,000 crores of transaction costs annually. This is without counting the costs incurred, in terms of time and paperwork by the public officials. The costs of bribery, Rs. 2000 crores, estimated by a Study[2] in India, are immaterial in comparison. Corruption is less of a problem in these services than the transaction costs, including the opportunity costs of time spent in obtaining the services. The middlemen who expedite the process, and maybe even save some transaction costs, may have a role after all!

The assumption of distrust behind the tortuous processes and procedures may or may not be justified but it is quite clear that the systems are almost always unable to screen such exceptions even while imposing substantial time and transaction costs on the overwhelming majority of the compliant and truthful citizens. As in the case of crime, effective deterrents in terms of penalties for misuse appear to be the only weapons (even though not very effective) against the determined risk takers; ritualistic verification processes are unlikely to work. The risk of misuse is not controlled by letter of the law and the rules but by motivations and incentives and how these are affected by the former.

Gatekeeping by the Government Agencies

These services involve only moderate utility and the gatekeeper role of the public officials needs to be deemphasised. These transactions need to be viewed as facilitative rather than restrictive and what Bimal Jalan calls 'self-certification'[3] should be the norm. This approach is similar to what the Customs Department does for the passengers' baggage. Passenger declarations are accepted in routine, in fact not even read. Similarly the Income Tax department accepts declarations of income at face value. It is puzzling that for innocuous Alpha activities involving minimal risk, and given the difficulties of filtering out bad cases, the verification procedures continue, whereas these have been abandoned in the areas involving substantial incentives for risky behaviour—smuggling of contraband and disclosure of income.

Context and Rules

Context for alpha exchanges and transactions appears to be the major relevant factor in designing micro level rules and instructions for the particular services—rules which build on the incentive possibilities of the actors on the demand side (lack of incentives to misuse in most of the cases) and lack of information on the supply side. The rules and processes illustrate all the major problems created mainly by the formal rules, rather than informal practices—high transaction costs, low incentive compatibility, difficult compliance standards—resulting in governance failure. There is a need to examine various rules and institutions in order to eliminate, redesign, exterminate, and simplify them. The solution lies not in making more integrative and comprehensive legislation that compounds the problem of the attention span of the legislators, the officials and the public but to look into the specific rules in terms of their impact on the quality of services. The enforcement mechanisms and rules need to be rooted in the specific context of a particular service, keeping in view the parties, their gains, losses, and incentives. What is okay for vehicle fitness and residential buildings may not be the solution for driving licences and high rise apartments to be sold out by a builder, as shown earlier.

In the case of alpha services, formal rules provide another interesting perspective on incentives. Relaxation of rules is a common practice in the internal management of governments. Whether it is induction of sportsmen (for example the Olympic medal winners) into government jobs (in addition to the sports quota which is mainly for middle level jobs) or the appointment of a DG Police who has been charge-sheeted in a criminal case, or even minor areas like the grant of advance from the provident fund, the rules tend to be casually relaxed. The rules requiring immediate registration of an FIR are also ignored by the police, on the plea that some vetting of a complaint is necessary; this happens in spite of the law, which has been reinforced by the courts, requiring immediate registration of the FIR. We have, however, yet to see any evidence of rule relaxation in the case of an applicant needing a birth certificate who does not fulfill any condition or in the case of an application for construction where some routine certification is missing. The less rules matter, the more the focus on rigid compliance. The Chandigarh Transport Department insists on personal presence or an authority letter, even for a simple transaction like handing over of the Registration Certificate! Officials can and do wink at these omissions, though there is some cost to be paid! That appears to be one reason the bribes for the registration of sale and purchase of property continue, even in Karnataka, which was a leader in eliminating discretion and ensuring registration on the day of presentation of documents. A report mentions Rs. 25 lakhs to be the price for securing posting as a sub-registrar.[4]

'Default' Rules for Officials

These services are necessary but not sufficient for social or economic utility, and have only a moderate consumer surplus.

The services are demand driven, without any limitations on supply, are not subject to competing pressures/possibility of exclusion/discrimination, and do not present incentive problems. The need here is to provide 'default' rules (automatic approval and issue) as a policy for the front desk government agents, in place of gatekeeping and checking. The default option of service delivery on the basis of self-certified compliance can be moderated by checking samples for detailed investigation (as in the scrutiny of income tax returns or customs check for passengers) or overall evaluation periodically (such as assessing the number of Caste Certificates issued vis-à-vis estimates, et cetera). As indicated, the more competitive the advantage a service confers, the more the likelihood that a third party will signal the misuse. What we require is the discontinuation of the rules and practices which provide that the government agent should 'satisfy' himself or herself about the eligibility and qualifications of the citizen for that particular service or facility – be it a ration card or an income certificate or the certificate for the fitness of a vehicle. That process needs to be substituted by the approval or issue of a service as a 'default' rule. There is minimal risk in these noncompetitive services, mainly due to the self-interest of the citizens. The other parties will always be looking over the shoulder, in case of services that provide competitive advantage, such as education/employment in case of income certificates, BPL entitlement, et cetera. Simple self-certification processes, with marginally improved complaint redress systems, and *ex post* misuse identification mechanisms, will save tremendous transaction costs to the citizens as well as to the government.

The social institutions in today's post-Leviathan phase are predicated on the assumption of 'good conduct' of citizens. Citizens are no longer shadowed by the police to prevent crimes; gatekeepers are, however, placed at every step in these areas of innocuous choice. Self-regulation, a focus on *ex post* detection of misuse and discontinuation of the verification processes, which are decoupled from or even tangential to the incentives of the concerned parties, would appear to be the appropriate alternatives to the present rigidity of the agency-centric rules.

In the case of services where self-certification may lead to a situation of 'moral hazard', a system of third party regulation, not confined to public officials, may address the incentives of the citizens, as indicated in the case of construction approvals (architects), driving skills (authorised driving training schools), and vehicle fitness (recognized service stations). The supply of alpha services is not limited and prices not material; the demand is easily satisfied, except in limited cases where persons are not eligible. The procedures, by their very nature, cannot however be rigorous enough to screen out such cases, nor can penalties be severe enough to provide effective deterrence. The obvious course is to accept self-declarations of eligibility and focus on *ex post* rather than *ex ante* measures.

PART III

Beta Services: Social And Economic Regulations

These regulations cover bilateral interactions among citizens in social and economic areas, and address the adverse impact or externalities of the actions of one of the parties on the second or a third party. The economic regulations, beta plus services, covered here are labour (health, welfare, and wages) and fertilizers quality control. Beta minus services are concerned with social interactions (emigration laws, sex trafficking), which are mostly 'victimless crimes'. These provide scope for 'governance without government' and adoption of the market mechanisms for self-enforcement of 'rights' and harnessing incentives of the actors involved.

11

Labour Laws: Regulation 'In Excess of Situation'

Labour laws cover a major area of the Indian economy—production relations and economic exchanges between the entrepreneur and the worker. As explained in Chapter 4, these Beta plus regulations envisage an interventionist third party role for the government agency and its officials. The role of the government agencies can be executive (enforcing minimum wages, inspecting premises for ensuring compliance) or quasi-judicial (adjudication systems provided under the Industrial Disputes Act). There are about forty Central and State laws and a couple of hundred rules and notifications directed at ensuring the safety, health, and economic and social security of the labour employed in the manufacturing and service sectors, extending from the minimum wage regulations for preventing exploitation of labour to health and welfare of labour—for example, a crèche for the children of the female labour. Labour laws are mostly legislated by Parliament; amendments by the states mostly concern trade union related issues. The rules, however, are notified by the State governments.

As usual, the debate about the desirability of these regulations tends to be bipolar. On the one hand, the neoclassical school advocates minimal regulation and a market approach, and it is expected that market competition will bring about the desired outcomes; on the other hand are the advocates of tougher laws and strict enforcement. Popular opinion, reflected in an article[1], is to rationalize labour laws and reduce their complexity and overlap, rather than abolishing them. It is proposed to show, through an analysis of these laws with reference to the State of Punjab, that the focus on policy and basic statutes (what and whether to regulate) is somewhat misplaced. State Governments would be well advised instead to attend to the details of operational and micro rules and processes which are within their domain and which may sometimes generate perverse incentives and be more of problem in bringing about the desired outcomes.

The Punjab government has traditionally taken the lead in promoting industry, especially the small-scale industry, through provision of infrastructure and incentives and creating a proper climate for investment. The thrust of the latest government policy is on minimizing government controls and improving the ease of doing business, apart from material incentives provided for specific sectors. A number of steps for improving competitiveness of the industry (easy credit, debt relief, concessions to sick small-scale units) and for infrastructure development (industrial parks, communications) have been taken. There has, however, been little change in the regulatory regime even though the 'licence permit raj' has officially been abandoned. Initiatives such as self-regulation introduced on an experimental basis in the 1990s have had a quiet burial; in fact, I could not locate, despite efforts, even a copy of the scheme.

Labour regulations broadly consist of three sets. One of these, and the starting point of most of the regulations, is the safety and well-being of workers and employees in factories and production units. These are meant to address the adverse impact of production processes on the workers, as profit, the main driver of industrial activity, may sometimes become a 'juggernaut' for the workers' welfare. Most of the regulations cover only the organized sector—defined in India as having 10 or 20 employees (depending on the objective of a particular statute)—and deal with labour safety and welfare especially of women and children and the work environment. The Factories Act 1948 is a comprehensive legislation that covers these aspects and defines safety, equipment standards, and design parameters to ensure that adequate air and hygienic environment is provided, and workers are protected from physical harm through safety measures in respect of equipment, machinery, or noxious substances. The laws go to the extent of even providing spittoons (a sanitation 'initiative') for workers, apart from designated plans for toilets and provision of drinking water. The minimum wage regulations seek to prevent economic exploitation of labour. In a way, these two laws seek to address the first two of Maslow's hierarchy of needs—physiological and economic. There are separate laws for the protection of contract labour, women, and children. The regulations are best examined with reference to the major laws, their objectives, rules and practices of enforcement, the incentives of parties, and the costs imposed by the regulations.

Minimum Wages Act

The Minimum Wages Act, 1948, provides for fixing of minimum wages by the state government in respect of: (a) employees covered in employments specified in Part-1 or 2 Schedule (Part-1 covers mostly employment in mining, rice mills, tobacco, oil mills, local authorities, et cetera, whereas Part-2 covers employment in agriculture); (b) any employment added by the state government through a notification, under the powers given as per Section 27. The state government is competent under Section 26 to provide exemptions and exceptions in cases where it is of the opinion that is not necessary for any reason to fix the wages. Apart from the obligation to pay the minimum rate of wages, the employers are also required to maintain various registers and records—annual returns, register of wages, et cetera. Penalty for paying less than the fixed rate of wages is imprisonment up to six months or fine up to Rs. 500, and for other violations, only a fine upto Rs. 500. The Punjab Government has been fixing minimum wages through notifications covering practically all categories of employment. The operational rules which specify minimum wages through annual notifications—which we have defined as micro institutions—appear to be designed to raise rather than resolve the implementation problems. The notification used to run into 60 pages and the department claims to have simplified it now by reducing it to 20 pages of close print. It seeks to (a) specify the wages for the large labour market consisting of unskilled, semi-skilled, and highly-skilled labour, which also includes the engineers, (b) attempts to define, under a somewhat shaky assumption of perfect information, the nuances for example of the piece rates of brick kiln workers on the one hand and tailors on the other, and (c) lays down the vertical mobility standards (a semi-skilled employee must be placed in skilled category after five years of employment!). Even assuming the necessity of defining minimum wages, surely the government could do so for the entry level unskilled and skilled labour, and leave it to the market and the competition for skills to do the rest, including vertical mobility of labour. If tailors are more in demand than security guards, they will be paid more. All told, the annual notification is a first rate recipe for raising disputes, rather than a mechanism to settle them. Most of the cases filed under the law relate not to the denial of basic wages, but disputes about the match between the designations (there are about 100 listed in the notification) and the specific pay levels.

The basic contradiction in the Act is that if the implementation is successful, it may tend to make some industries non-competitive; units not bound to comply or not complying with the regulations may be at a competitive advantage. It can also restrict opportunities for employment of new entrants, who may be prepared to and may even deserve lower wages (due to lack of skills/experience), and thus, add to the pool of the unemployed. This aspect has been adequately analysed by economists. Friedman remarks with reference to the USA:[2] 'we regard the minimum wage rate as one of the most, if not the most anti-black laws on the statute books', (one of the consequences being, for example, that the unemployment rate for black teenagers was double that of white teenagers). Leaving aside the economic issue and whether the law is responsible for restricting employment—the unemployed may prefer lower wages to their present status of being unemployed—or for preventing a race to the bottom due to unlimited supply of labour, there are some other major problems apart from those indicated above, affecting compliance and enforcement.

In the process of specifying wages for a large number (about one hundred) of categories the government tends to lose focus on the critical areas—wages for the vulnerable sections of labour —women labour and labour in the traditionally exploited sectors such as roads' construction and brick kilns, which in any case have separate economic and social security regulations (for bonded labour, construction workers). A little more concern for the logical proposition of Occam's razor would be more productive and enable a practical regime of oversight.

The law appears to have incentivized the employers, not to provide the minimum wages as intended, but to find economical short-cuts. Shadow labour is engaged but not brought on the official records. Industry estimates of such labour are 30 to 50 per cent in the small and medium organized sector in Punjab. The narrative below provided during an interview, indicates the irony of the situation. If the employer does not show the labour on the rolls, she need incur neither the minimum wages nor the transaction costs of maintaining records.

Incentives for 'shadow' labour:
Labour Commissioner visits a factory

A Labour Commissioner accompanied by a friend happened to stop by at an industrial unit run by the friend's relative. The identity of the Labour Commissioner was disclosed at the gate. As they entered the factory, they noticed a large number of people rushing out of the factory gate. On enquiry, the owner, now assured that it was not an official inspection, confided that the labour leaving the premises were workers not shown on the rolls.

In conditions of prevalent unemployment, labour may willingly agree to this arrangement especially since, while they do get wages even below the minimum specified, they don't have to make the contributions (EPF, health insurance) applicable to registered labour. And these contributions can hurt even labour on minimum wages; very few of the employees allow their contributions to accumulate to levels adequate for providing the security these are meant for; the rate of pension is rather low. In any case, the EPF records were in such a mess till recently that, given a choice, labour would prefer cash or deposit in individual bank accounts. The Act was designed to address the problem of excessive supply leading to starvation wages. The result has been simply to push out labour into the informal/shadow area of economic activities for all categories of labour, including the skilled, who could otherwise compete in the labour market for wages, above the basic wage fixed for unskilled labour. The informal institution of 'shadow' labour restores the equilibrium in the labour markets, based on informal wages, which match effective supply and demand.

Labour Health and Welfare: The Factories Act

This Central Act provides for the health and safety of the workers in the factories and is applicable to the units employing 10 workers (factories with power) or 20 workers (factories without power). Section 6 provides that specific industries, as the State Government may decide, should be subject to the following:

(a) Simple submission of the factory plans (no approval required);
(b) Prior approval of plans before commencement of the operations;
(c) Licencing and registration.

Section 6 - Approval, Licensing and Registration of Factories

(1) The State Government may make rules:

a. requiring for the purposes of this Act, the submission of plans of any class or description of factories to the Chief Inspector or the State Government;
   (i) requiring the previous permission in writing of the State Government or the Chief Inspector to be obtained for the site on which the factory is to be situated and for the construction or extension of any factory or class or description of factories;
b. requiring for the purpose of considering applications for the permission the submission of plans and specifications;
c. prescribing the nature of such plans and specifications and by whom they shall be certified;
d. requiring the registration and licensing of factories, or any class or description of factories and prescribing the fees payable for such registration and licensing and for the renewal of licences;
e. requiring that no licence shall be granted or renewed unless the notice specified in Section 7 has been given;

Evidently, the intention of lawmakers was to make these provisions applicable to specific groups of industries, which may require submission of plans/prior approval of those plans and which the state government considers to be in public interest to so regulate. Surprisingly, however, no attention has been paid to this fine distinction and, as a result, the Factories Act and Rules have been indiscriminately extended in Punjab to all the units that are covered under the definition of 'factory', instead of specifying the limited classes of factories that may be covered. The Department has in fact proceeded to grant exemptions from registration/licencing, et cetera, to some of the industries whereas the Act requires the Government to specify the (presumably limited) industrial units which may need to be regulated through the submission of plans, approvals thereof, licencing and registration! Thus all the units in Punjab, barring a small exception, are required to file the applications for approval, submit the plans and obtain licences under the provisions of Section 6, before the production processes are initiated. All additions and alterations are also covered.

Rule 3 of the Punjab Factories Act

The State Government or the Chief Inspector may require, for the purposes of the Act, submission of plans of any factory which was either in existence on the date of the commencement of the Act or which had not been constructed or extended since then. Such plans shall be drawn to scale showing.

(a) the site of the factory and immediate surrounding including adjacent buildings and other structures, roads, drains, et cetera;
(b) the plan, elevation and necessary cross sections of the factory building indicating all relevant details relating to natural lighting, ventilation and means of escape in case of fire, and the position of the plant and machinery, aisles and passage ways, and;
(c) such other particulars as the State Government or the Chief Inspector, as the case may be, require.

3-A Approval of Plans

(1) No building shall be constructed or used as a factory unless plans in respect of such building are approved by the Chief Inspector.
(2) No additions/alterations or extensions in the existing factory building shall be made unless plans in respect of such additions, alterations or extensions are approved by the Chief Inspector.

The licence-permit raj continues in Punjab even though the Government of India has abrogated the much criticized Industries Development & Regulation Act, and this practice continues not because of the main statute but the micro rules notified by the state government.

Licencing is technically an alpha service, an irritant resolved easily through informal customary payments. Even the Labour Department considers it a formality, but has to keep the papers shuttling for 2-3 months to demonstrate the application of mind for a purposeless and illegal formality. Except for the units engaged in rudimentary manufacturing, the officials may not even be qualified to scrutinize the plans and the process of approval is superfluous in any case for the drug or the food industry which needs a licence under the elaborate procedures of the Drugs and Cosmetics/Food Acts.

Incentives of the owners and the department have of course beautifully and seamlessly adjusted to this senseless regulation; the delay is not fatal, it only means the owner having to file one additional copy of the plans—and the approval is easily negotiated. In addition, the units generating hazardous substances need specific clearances under this law and the duplicative process continues, despite the elaborate pollution control laws and the specific authorities set up for this specific purpose.

Some of the regulations under the Factories Act provide an almost perfect illustration of the premise that sometimes, the problem is not with the basic statutes but the 'operational' micro rules. The provisions of the Act (Section 13) regarding temperature control are not very bothersome. Industry is expected to maintain temperatures, so as to ensure safety and health of workers—temperature to be 'kept low as far as practicable'. Flexibility is provided to the 'inspectors' to direct a unit to make appropriate provisions, in cases where the arrangements for the control of temperature may be considered unsatisfactory. The Punjab rules (Rule 19A), however, impose their own definition of what the temperature in any factory should be and seek to impose uniform norms across different industries. The rules lead to a situation where very few units are in a position to comply with the rigid specifications, and thus provide discretion for selective enforcement. Similar is the case with the statutory provisions regarding 'spittoons' (Section 20); Rule 53 of Punjab Rules goes to be extent of specifying details of two different types of spittoons to be maintained!

Indian Boilers Act

The Indian Boilers Act provides for the inspection and certification of boilers by the factory inspectors. It is understood that an amendment is likely to be or has been made permitting third party certification. The ritual of the annual certification of boilers by the government inspectors, however, continues. The current practice is wasteful, imposes unnecessary costs not only on the unit but also the department. In any case, the owners continue to be liable for any consequences arising out of accidents/malfunctioning. It is in the interest of owners to ensure boiler safety, as continued production is a function of smooth operations. The appropriate course may be to accept the certification by the Boiler manufactures or by qualified persons approved by their associations (the UK law has similar provisions), and to harness the incentives of owners to attend to the safety of equipment, by escalating the cost of damage to parties affected by accidents/explosion—labour and others. As indicated in case of laws relating to vehicle fitness/ roadworthiness, the disincentive of being saddled with huge compensation costs would be an effective deterrent, at least in the case of economic agents who are driven primarily by considerations of saving costs and maximizing profits. And the insurance markets are there to adjust the premiums accordingly. These wondrous markets can be harnessed to deliver the state objectives and ensure that costs of damage, in case of accidents, are borne by the parties liable, that is, the owners. In any case, as mentioned elsewhere, accidents can happen and do. No sensible owner plans to have an accident.

Standing Orders (Rules) Act 1946

This Act requires the Industrial units to draft their own rules for employment and deployment of labour. It applies to the units having 100 or more workers. In Punjab, this has been applied, it is understood, even to units having 20 or more workers. It seems from the Labour Department's reports that over 9000 establishments in Punjab are still required to get the standing orders approved but only about 1300 units have got this done! The fact is that it is difficult to secure approval of the department. The Standing Orders are approved by the department only if they reflect almost in totality the model provisions. Most of the Industry as well as the department are aware of the difficulties of getting approval. In one case in my personal knowledge, the process continued for a number of years till the industrial establishment discovered the solution—adopt the model provisions! And no need to bother about enforcement—everybody knows it is a formality. The 'heuristic and bias' of the enforcing department is simply having the rules approved!

Regulatory Burden: Registers and Returns

One common aspect of most of these regulations is the elaborate forms, registers and returns, to be maintained by employers under various laws. The idea seems to be to make it easy for the labour department to get the information and enforce the law, even though a situation of violation can rarely be observed or detected through this paper activity. The returns need not reflect practice. Even the tax officers find it difficult to detect evasion simply by a scrutiny of the returns, despite financial procedures and audit certificates and have to depend on random checks. A list of these forms and returns for the labour laws was compiled with great difficulty with help of the industry in Punjab. The records, forms and returns for two of the laws are listed below. The volume of duplicate/repetitive information required for the same units of labour in the same establishment —separate for example for bonus, for gratuity, for maternity benefit Act and so on – is mind boggling.

Forms/Registers/ReturnsPunjab Maternity Benefit Act, 1961		
S.No.	*Description*	*Form Nos.*
1.	Muster Roll	Form 'A'
2.	Notice u/s 6 of the Maternity benefit Act, 1961	Form 'B'
3.	Certification by Medical Practitioner	Form 'C'
4.	Certification by Mid wife	Form 'D'
5.	Certification by Medical practitioner on expiry of patient	Form 'E'
6.	Application from woman employee claiming benefit under maternity Act	Form 'F'
7.	Appeal to competent authority for non payment of maternity benefits by the employer	Form 'G'
8.	Complaint to Inspector for non payment of maternity benefits by the employer	Form 'H'
9.	Complaint to Inspector by legal representative for non payment of maternity benefits by the employer	Form 'I'
10.	Rejection of the order of the Inspector for payment of maternity benefits by the employer	Form 'J'
11.	Annual return for the year ending on the 31 December....	Form 'L'
12.	Employment, dismissal, payment of hours, et cetera, of woman for the year ending 31 December....	Form 'M'
13.	Details of payment made during the year ending 31 December	Form 'N'
14.	Prosecution during the year ending 31 December...	Form 'O'

Maintenance of records is by itself does not guarantee that the wages for example will be paid as per law or maternity benefits or bonus will be given. The records can be manufactured when required, as is mostly being done at present. These regulations seem designed precisely to encourage perverse incentives on the part of the employers. The cost of maintaining these registers in terms of time and labour may be stupendous, sometimes exceeding even the benefits to labour as in case of Maternity Benefit Act. This apart, there is the factor of inconvenience to employees, mostly illiterate, having to fill up the forms to get some routine benefits, and the cost of monitoring compliance of such superfluous rituals by the officials.

Registers and Returns The Punjab Shops and Commercial Establishment Act, 1958

S. No.	*Description*	*Form Nos.*
1.	Intimation under Section 10 (2)(i) of the Punjab Shops and Commercial Establishment Act, 1958	Form A
2.	Intimation under Section 10 (2)(i) of the Punjab Shops and Commercial Establishment Act, 1958	Form B
3.	Register of Employees	Form C
4.	Register of Wages of Employees	Form D
5.	Register of Deductions	Form E
6.	Statement for Registration of Establishment under Section 13 of the Punjab Shops and Commercial Establishment Act, 1958	Form F
7.	Form of change in respect of information contained in statement required by Sub-section (4) of section 13 of The Punjab Shops and Commercial Establishment Act, 1958 Form G	
8.	Registration of Establishment required under Section 13 (2)(i) of the Punjab Shops and Commercial Establishment Act, 1958	Form H
9.	Certification by Competent Medical Authority	Form I
10.	Boarding Register for the Women Employees (Arrival)	
11.	Boarding Register for the Women Employees (Departure)	
12.	Movement Register (Departure)	
13.	Movement Register (Arrival)	
14.	Movement Register (Common)	
15.	List of Women Employees Employed in the Establishment	
16.	Record Register of Women Employees Working in the Establishment	

The employers have adjusted to these problems of compliance in various ways by shifting a substantial percentage of labour off the rolls, as indicated earlier, and by avoiding these costs through the much less costly 'rents' to the inspecting staff. So far as the government agency is concerned, the penalties being low and compoundable (Rs. 500 is the fine), the best strategy is to confine the enforcement to 'record maintenance' and to promote compounding as the main element of enforcement, which of course also suits the employers.

Regulatory Burden: High Transaction Costs

The main complaint of the Industry is the high costs imposed by the Labour regulations, for example through the minimum wage laws which make it less competitive, as mentioned above. What matters also are the incidental, transaction costs of regulations, in addition to the costs of regulatory compliance which even the industry tends to ignore. It is the tiny and micro sector which is most affected by the transaction costs of negotiating through the maze of regulations. For example, a twenty five KW power connection may entail, in terms of time, manpower resources and informal payments, disproportionately higher costs than a 2 MW connection. Micro enterprises are rarely able to pass these costs through the market whereas major projects and companies may be better equipped to do so (one can recall the education and training component in the Enron Project in Maharashtra!). This sector may also be subject to more harassment by the officials, being unable to make pre-emptive payments to the regulatory staff, cash strapped as most of them are due to the low debt-equity ratio. In the highly competitive industries, control over transaction costs becomes the key to survival as the profit margins are thin. If transaction costs are, for example, five per cent of the investment, the company which is able to reduce these substantially will have a competitive advantage to that extent. The bigger units with their scale advantage not only have lower transaction costs but are also able to reduce the impact. The volume of transaction costs and the prescribed fees (for approvals, licencing, et cetera) as well as 'shadow' (under the table) costs is not insignificant. It is difficult to get accurate estimates of the latter, but from discussions and informal feedback, it appears that these are rather high especially for small/micro units. It is to be noted that these have to be funded outside the approved project costs, from cash resources of the entrepreneurs thus adding to the liquidity problems.

Starting a Business Transaction Costs for Rs. 30 lakhs Investment		
Formal costs/fees – approval, registration licence, etc.	1% of investment	Fees prescribed for approvals, registration/licencing, Central and State—all agencies.
*One time transaction costs	2-3% of investment	'Under the table' payments for getting approvals, etc.
*Transaction costs during operations are additional: maintaining records: 25-50% of administrative staff costs/10% of fixed costs; 10-15% of owner's time in case of small industry.		

Source: Interviews and Observations.

This estimate does not include the opportunity costs of time spent on approvals, et cetera.

Incentive Compatibility of Regulations

There can be some debate on the laws and their relevance, which are issues of economic and social policy. Much can be said on both sides. Even without questioning the basic legislation, however the issue is whether the 'mechanisms of governance' —the institutions, rules, and processes—are appropriate for achieving the objectives and whether these substantial transaction costs are justified. Probably some attention to the incentives of various parties—the government agency, employers, labour—may indicate the direction for change.

Incentives of Owners

The entrepreneur has an incentive to properly design and commission the factory and carry out the activities required for production. Architects and technical consultants are engaged and loans from funding institutions tied up. Apart from the owners, the other stakeholders are also interested in ensuring that the factories are technically sound and capable of delivering the desired outputs. This is especially the case where multi-institutional financiers are involved. Thus, there are a number of third parties (financiers and promoters and even professional consultants) who are looking over the shoulder, as their reputation and money is at stake, apart from that of the owner himself/herself. Regulatory enforcement for the construction and installation of a production unit is being ensured by the third parties as for example is done by the auditors, whose reports are accepted in routine by the Income Tax Department. A practice similar to the Labour Department approving the designs and plans of the production units will be for the tax department to appoint their own auditors! In the case of minimum wages, the incentive for the owner is competition for productive labour; if one pays less than the market wages, he/ she will lose experienced workers to others.

Second, there are severe criminal and civil consequences of negligence or a violation of laws, which the entrepreneurs have to face in any case despite various *ex ante* approvals/ permissions and inspections prescribed from time to time under the labour regulations. Industry cannot afford, therefore, to jettison safety and health issues even if the State withdraws from the actual oversight of regulations, so long as the State continues to make the regulations pragmatic and generally acceptable and is prepared to enforce them when called upon to do so. The fact is that no amount of oversight by the State authority for boiler safety, for example, can ensure that an accident will not take place. Owners in that case will not be excused just because they got the equipment inspected by the department and got all the clearances. On the other hand, no entrepreneur would plan the installation of inferior boilers or neglect their safety, not only because the owner continues to be responsible under the law but also because it is in his own interest to ensure the safety of the plant and the workforce. Arson in owned premises is of course dealt with as a crime.

The laws may need to be reviewed from this perspective keeping in view the incentives/disincentives for the owners and the 'agency' problems in oversight and enforcement. The implementation thus can be made more effective through self-regulation even within the frame of the statutes, rather than going by radical neoliberal solutions which recommend abolishing the regulations altogether.

Incentives of Labour and the Regulators

The enforcement agency lacks the information on violations and therefore even if willing, is unable to enforce the law. It knows that the laws are ineffective, impractical and difficult to implement. 'Rents' are therefore the only sensible strategy for them and the easy way to extract modest rents is to focus on records and returns rather than substantive compliance. This also suits the industry as it is happy to avoid the major costs of compliance not only of the substantive laws but also of record maintenance, which both the parties know, are not relevant. The implementation and enforcement is bound to be sclerotic. Most labour regulations are therefore mostly on paper; the regulators need information which is difficult and costly to access, and imposes substantial costs on both parties. The regulations therefore are likely to be circumvented by the limited number of determined violators who wish to avoid direct costs —minimum wages, proper plans, and construction as per law. The only result is extraction, may be modest, of 'rents' by the inspectors, with occasional case being filed for technical violations (non maintenance of forms and records), which suits the industry (low penalty) and keeps the regulatory clock ticking, a feeling that the regulations are being enforced. A charade of compliance is enacted around the regulations, by the Industry and the enforcers. Minimum wages are not actually paid, as the workers are not taken on rolls. Compounding is done for minor violations—non maintenance of records—where it is cheaper to pay the penalty rather than incur the costs of record maintenance. Licences/plans are approved, with some 'speed money', generally within a period of three months and without much scrutiny, which in any case is not practicable, even if it were possible, given the limited expertise and the resources available with the department.

Limitations of the 'Stick'

One has to take note of a distinct feature of such regulations. The statutes' basic weapon is stick or punishment. There is no scope for reward as the 'best practice' is what is prescribed as the 'minimum' acceptable. Costs of compliance are multiple and complex and the obligations for compliance are extended over time as well as space. Even assuming the objectives of the laws and regulations to be valid, good governance would consist of making voluntary compliance easier and relatively cost less, taking account of the incentives, the structure of the wage markets, especially as monitoring is not only impossible but even unnecessary. The design of rules by, for example, prescribing stiff penalties for damage to third parties may be adequate to bring about the outcomes of safety, health, et cetera. Clear rules of liability for damage, with enforcement being required only in case of a grievance—in fact this is the principle behind the Industrial Disputes Act, which sets up a forum where unresolved disputes between the employer and labour can be settled—may be more productive.

Bibek Debroy[3] provides enough examples of the unnecessary, inadequate or defective rules which we could do without—rules about the location of spittoons, white washing, manual rather than digital recordkeeping, sand buckets instead of fire extinguishers, et cetera. Some other examples, such as the Standing Orders (Rules) Act have been mentioned. Such regulations point to the salience of context, which should determine the nature of interventions. This also shows that the mechanisms of governance (self regulation in this case) are context specific. In fact, it may be better, in the case of some of these regulations, to consider a 'zero-based' approach and jettison the dubious baggage of regulations rather than making them simpler—an approach advocated by Milton Friedman.[4] The areas ripe for this treatment appear to be the Shops and Establishments Act/Standing Orders, but till they continue (one needs to take note of 'path dependence' and the 'status quo bias'), the agency can have more efficient enforcement, by acting on the triggers and signals provided by the aggrieved party, that is, labour. Surely, if labour is provided compensation for the loss of some right by the employer and is happy, there is hardly any need for the government agency to be the conscience keeper.

There is an interesting contrast between the enforcement of the laws on crime and on labour. The police have the powers to take suo motu cognizance in serious crimes—they don't need any complaint. In practice, however, it is very rare for the police to register an FIR *suo motu*—whether a murder or a car accident, they look for a complainant. In case of labour laws, most of the enforcement shows a reverse pattern—almost all the violations, mostly minor violations of maintaining registers and so on, are recorded and prosecuted (or compounded) based on the 'initiative' of the inspectors rather than the workers, the affected party. The contrast is a fitting commentary on incentives. Labour presumably have or will arrive at mutually beneficial arrangements—'shadow' labour working below the minimum wages, or getting more overtime pay than prescribed for longer hours than permitted, et cetera. Incentives of the regulatory staff push them to conduct the irritating inspections and visits even in the absence of any information about the violation of laws. The labour markets will and have found optimizing solutions, and the department is an unnecessary and unwelcome intervener, in the eyes not only of entrepreneur but also labour. Regulations may be justified in the case of protective legislation such as for bonded labour, where the latter is not a free agent, but surely not for the organized labour in the twenty-first century. Incidentally, the changes suggested can lead to tremendous improvement on the ease of doing business, especially in starting a business and the steps proposed would easily eliminate three to six months delay for industry without having to change the basic laws, but only by modifying 'operational' governance—abandoning the self-propelled inspection regime, and encouraging bilateral negotiations and settlement between labour and industry.

Arm's Length Governance

The regulations under various laws are generally meant to tackle the problem of externalities—some related to the third parties, that is, the public/environment, whereas others (most of the labour regulations taken up here) are directed at the safety and welfare of the employees. It is well settled that such issues can be best settled through bilateral negotiations so long as the parties (in the case of industry, the owner and the labour) can be clearly defined.[5] The rights and obligations of the two sides, of course, have to be clearly and unambiguously defined. The third party (the State in the case of labour regulations) will rarely have enough information to effectively intervene and bring about an efficient result. Labour may prefer working overtime beyond the weekly limits, if paid adequately; or prefer cash payment in place of a crèche for children. Enforcement of these regulations, therefore, can be left to the parties concerned and intervention by the State made only in case of complaints/ disputes. The 'choice architecture' or 'frame' for labour regulations would thus consist of:

(a) Arm's length governance through self regulation; withdrawal from direct regulation through maintenance of registers and forms; these are not functional and encourage perverse incentives;
(b) Encouraging labour-employer bargaining, within the frame of legal rights;
(c) Intervention only in case of disputes;
(d) Abrogation of disfunctional legislation and controls: Standing Orders, Shops and Establishment Act, licencing and approval of plans (Factories Act); these add only costs without any social benefits.

One needs to harness the second party (labour) interests and nurture their incentives, to trigger/signal violations of safety, health and economic regulations for labour and let the interested third parties enforce compliance with the safety, structural and technical regulations during construction and operations. In Rome, the builders faced the risk of bridge collapse—they were the first to be asked to spend time under the bridge; as Taleb[6] notes, the builder rather than the owner is more aware of the structural defects but the present rules turn the process upside down by making the owner liable for building safety. Reduction of the ancillary cost of regulations— maintenance of registers and accounts which are very high for the entrepreneur, is another area. As remarked[7], 'forms and registers are a declaration of innocence—no company or employer will use these registers to admit wrong doing and so no government officer will read them'.

12

Fertilizers' Quality: Neglect of Incentives

The Fertilizers Control Order 1985 provides for the registration of manufacturers, importers, dealers and packers; it also provides for standards/quality specifications, defines the standards and norms for fertilizers and their enforcement through the Fertilizer Inspectors and other staff. Prima facie, the regulations appear to have some logic. It is not easy for the consumers to ascertain the quality of fertilizers at the point of purchase. As in the case of use of a particular drug, the result can only be inferred later in terms of the impact on crop production. The sampling process, the major tool of enforcement, may be adequate for assessing the quantum of the problem (assuming the samples are really random, which is rarely the case) but not necessarily for ensuring quality. One has also to take note of the motivation of suppliers, incentives of the inspectors and the nature of trade (economical and easy to fake 'packing'). The present system does not appear to provide adequate incentives for farmers. Enforcement agencies don't appear to have any system to elicit information from the consumers or the whistle blowers. The trade bears only a negligible statistical risk in view of large number of retailers, seasonal turnover, the practice of storing fertilizers at multiple and undeclared locations, difficulty in visual detection of adulteration, ease of 'faking' and so on. The regulators thus face difficult problems in ensuring quality.

The Market Solution

One view usually advocated by the free marketeers in such

cases, is to leave the quality aspects to be addressed by the market forces. It is hoped that quality manufacturers will build their reputation in due course while the 'fly by night' operators are likely to close shop. This may not, however, work in India, considering the lack of political support for this initiative and the presence of a large number of suppliers, unlike some other countries where a limited number of mega corporations dominate the market and are thus easier to regulate. A presentation by the *Trade*, 'Fertilizer Quality Control in India April 2011',[1] advocates better testing facilities, more realistic standards, and maintaining a distinction between substandard and adulterated fertilizers for penalty/prosecution. Bibek Debroy andLaveesh Bhandari[2] demonstrate, by the analysis of data regarding sample results, that even in the case of two of the most adulteration prone fertilizers—zinc and micro nutrients —deviations for most of the adulterated samples are marginal. According to them, the regulations need to be reviewed so as to isolate the cases of deliberate adulteration from those due to involuntary deficiencies, storage, technical problems, et cetera. They propose that the regulations should be used in a discretionary manner and marginal variations treated leniently and subjected only to cautionary administrative action rather than prosecution. Considering the problem of proving intentions, it is suggested by the authors that government could consider allowing compounding in cases where the variation from standards is not more than say 10 per cent. Even in cases where the department proceeds to prosecute the dealers, they advocate imposition of fines rather than imprisonment; this will, they feel, help create congruence between the level of misdemeanour and incentives.

The problem with this approach is that the very structure of rules which now shapes the incentives of the manufacturers and suppliers will, if changed/restructured, modify the incentives of both parties accordingly; the 'rational expectations' hypothesis of Lucas applies here as well. As Harford explains,[3] in connection with a myth regarding inflation boosting employment, the 'Phillips curve' was believed to have established a positive correlation between inflation and employment and was popular among the economists as a basis for government intervention, for boosting employment; the 'rational expectations' hypothesis proved this to be erroneous; actors modify their behaviour according to their expectations of any particular policy. At present, the dealer can either choose to negotiate the 'fine' informally or be prepared to go to jail sometimes, apart from the cost of defending the case, which itself may high. Violations by the trade follow the structure of sanctions, something similar to what happens in case of the labour laws; most of the cases filed are for minor violations, with penalties of Rs. 500 or so, and are happily compounded. A similar situation may emerge in the case of fertilizers regulations, if these were to provide the options suggested, as the expectations of the trade and the enforcers are also likely to change.

Most of the US states do require licencing for manufacture and sale but distinguish substandard from adulterated fertilizers. Mostly the laws there provide for penalties proportionate to the percentage of variation from the laid down standards. Even though prosecution is provided, it is rarely resorted to and the laws generally provide discretion to the authorities to take adinistrative action[4] instead. In India, this thin line is not defined. Discretion is not available or not resorted to, due to the culture of distrust of officials and risk aversion. The safest course for the government agents is the file prosecutions in cases where informal deals cannot be struck or are too risky. The result is that suppliers don't look to customers for survival as in a competitive market. On the other hand, the risks for the suppliers of substandard fertilizers are negligible and always negotiable; the scale of prosecution and conviction is asymmetrical to the quality of fertilizers and convictions are mostly a matter of accident, rather than design, as the samples are taken on an ad hoc basis, where the sampling is not due to bias or information; the trade, however, provides little scope for the two contingencies.

What needs to be seen is whether the quality problems—for example, the problem of substandard fertilizers (excess moisture, et cetera), if treated differently under law, will provide the right set of incentives or only add to the attractiveness of the option of informal settlement by the two parties, the government agent and the supplier. One major problem is that we may tend to view such violations (as compared to say threats and problems which endanger human health as in case of adulterated drugs/adulteration of milk with urea) from a different perspective. There are a number of moving films and books (for example, Rachel Carson's *Silent Spring*) covering spurious drugs and the use of pesticides but rarely any on the harm caused by spurious fertilizers; human beings tend to view problems such as fertilizer quality as more of an economic offence even though the farmer mortgaging his land for purchase of fertilizer, which turns out to be spurious, may have ultimately put his life at stake. This may be one reason why unlike drugs, where knowledgeable people estimate adulteration to be not more than five to ten per cent in India at present, here the estimate are as high as thirty per cent in case of micro nutrients and fertilizers mixtures; experts feel however that there is little problem in case of urea and phosphates.

One reason, as in crime, is that only some of individuals indulge in adulteration for various reasons. Others may consider the activity too risky or may have moral and social compunctions in undertaking activities injurious to society. One may be selfish for material gains but may also be rational enough to take account of the possible risks, aided in this process by moral and social beliefs. Sometimes, there is a tendency to profit out of a criminal antisocial activity but this may not be confined to more than 10 to 15 per cent of dealers. Some would produce substandard stuff that does not inflict substantial harm, and may be rationalize this activity by blaming the competition or illegal demands from officials.

Designing Incentive Compatible Rules

The core function of an enforcement agency is, therefore, to identify the minority through encouraging whistle blowers, the public and the consumers, keeping information confidential and offering rewards. This is done in routine by the customs and tax authorities, as in the absence of information, it is almost impossible—say through a random check of consignments—to identify the culprit and the harmful cargo. In fertilizers, the enforcement strategy is exactly the reverse: go to the market, pick up samples right and left and hope for the best! There is of course a need to provide for differential treatment in the case of the substandard as against spurious/adulterated fertilizers; treat homicide on a different footing from a simple injury or picking the pocket and let, to take an analogy, the criminal faces of the adulterators of milk with urea stand out in a crowd of numerous venders diluting milk with water, rather than treating every dealer, irrespective of the degree of violation, as a criminal which is currently the default mode of the rules of enforcement. Adam Smith highlighted not only the self interest behind the actions of human beings but also the 'other regarding' dimension. 'Nature, when she formed man for society endowed him with an original desire to please, and an original aversion to offend his brethren. She taught him to feel pleasure in their favourable, and pain in their unfavourable regard'.[5] This somewhat under- emphasized feature of humanity ensures that only a few engage in socially destructive 'self regarding' behaviour. Officials on the other hand find it easy to show performance without worthwhile results, by engaging with or rather alienating the mass of suppliers, making it easy for the criminal few to merge in the crowd.

The structure of the rules and control systems implies that the gains from selling spurious fertilizers are certain whereas the loss due to sanctions is uncertain and can be avoided given the low social value attached to quality fertilizers compared to quality drugs. There is, therefore, a case for bringing such legislation in the domain of consumer rights, in view of the structure of incentives, organizational culture and other factors mentioned. Adding to staff, as suggested by Debroy et al., picking up more & more samples in shops and manufacturing premises, strengthening labs, and similar resource oriented solutions may not work. Given the incentives for informal settlement, more of staff is only likely to lead to accumulation of perverse incentives, in the context of a single line monopoly agency for enforcement, and lack of competition, if one may say, among the agency officials. Creation of overlapping jurisdictions for officials to encourage competition, though frequently advocated by the academics, is cleverly avoided on spurious pretexts of wastage and duplication of resources.

Random testing of fertilizers samples may not be enough. In case of drugs for example, if there are 1000 major drugs to control and 10 per cent possibility of adulteration, the chance of detection of adulteration is one per cent. Add the numbers of dealers and the probability can go beyond the zone of feasible control; probability mathematics will show that even random sampling can only indicate the broad spread of adulteration but can never be an effective deterrent, the possibility of detection being small, especially if you add on identical products put on the market by a large number of suppliers. One major difference from drugs is that the farmer always comes to know about the quality, may be after the crop is harvested, whereas a consumer of drugs may never know and information-based enforcement thus can be the key in case of fertilizers. One possible solution, therefore, is to have a general surveillance through a proper system of random sampling of fertilizers manufactured and marketed, and ensuring quick response systems for complaints, as information is the main problem in enforcement. The sampling can be more intense for items which are expensive, generally prone to adulteration, and provide substantial returns (micro nutrients, zinc). Second, the focus needs to be on purposive samples wherever any complaint is received from a customer or a whistleblower and on setting in place an organized system for carrying out this task fairly and objectively by defining the boundaries between the official receiver of information and the agent acting on the information. This is what the crime agencies do in routine. Information-based enforcement is the key and the route lies through incentivizing the whistleblowers and purchasers of fertilizers, and providing for compensation to buyers through fines recovered from suppliers and so on. In case a sample, taken on the complaint of a consumer is found adulterated, the fine can be passed on to the aggrieved party as in some of the states in the US. This will not only incentivize all the parties, but also eliminate perverse incentives of the officials, who may at present be able to trade, to their benefit, the threat of prosecution.

Customer and Agency Incentives

The rule and institutional design would thus consist of developing market systems for incentives of consumers through the provision of compensation, and of suppliers through constant exposure to public/farmer scrutiny (by providing information on quality and test results), and elimination of 'self regarding' actions by the government agents. Whether drugs or fertilizers or pesticides, experience of even the professionals, let alone the trade, clearly shows that random sampling and prosecution of suppliers/manufactures are not really deterrents; in the case of fertilizers and pesticides, enforcement is mostly luck of the draw, even assuming lack of bias—positive or negative—on the part of enforcers. They just don't have the information. Then there is the issue of perverse incentives or lack thereof. There is a well known through undocumented instance in Punjab of a highly connected pesticide manufacturer who was known not only for adulteration but the equivalent of the adage commonly used for milk in an apocryphal story ('This is not milk adulterated with water but water adulterated with milk', a plea offered by an accused in defence!). No officer would visit his factory and the manufacturer would nominate the Chief Pesticide Officer of the State! In the Indian conditions, it may be wise to abdicate the impossible responsibility assumed by the government, based on a policy of direct intervention, in case of economic activities such as fertilizers and pesticides, and instead activate and utilize the second party triggers—parties to the transaction like farmers who have the incentives and can and do approach appropriate authorities This can be done by providing for compensation to them, apart from prosecution, something similar to the consumer protection laws, and possibly doing away with the elaborate system of licencing and limiting it to manufacturing. The officials responsible for the enforcement of economic offences are very unlikely, whether through random or purposive samples, to detect major violations. The onus of enforcement can be shifted to parties to the transaction as in case of economic and social activities which affect others but where human life and health is not involved. The only help required from the state may be a provision of quick and effective mechanisms for adjudicating on the supplier liability and providing compensation to the purchasers of fertilizers, as done in case of the various products and services under the Consumer Protection Laws.

13

Emigration Law: The Ban on Rational Behaviour

The Emigration Act 1983 provides for protection of Indian emigrants going abroad on 'work' visas—for work confined to basic unskilled and skilled levels; it excludes managerial and professional assignments. The legislation is meant for the 'protection' of such emigrants and the purpose is sought to be achieved through registration of the agents, the ECR (Emigration Clearance Required) for the defined categories and so on. Thus, an under-matriculate needs a clearance before proceeding abroad. An enthusiastic Punjab government has recently passed the 'Human Smuggling Act' which seeks to prevent 'forced emigration', by requiring the registration and licencing of the travel agents in Punjab—as if an agent in the business of smuggling and illegal emigration needs a licence to operate, or even needs to operate from the Punjab soil! Even when a government regulates gambling or prostitution, the illegal market is not completely prohibited; some choice is generally available for the citizens. For example, wine making without a licence for own consumption is permitted. In this case, the Punjab regulation seems totally illogical. Travel trade, which is not directly associated with illegal emigration but is only indirectly involved at one or two of the formal stages—issue of tickets and getting visas—is sought to be regulated to control private activities that are not in their official charter of duties. The point that there is little exploitation involved in the process and the trade is primarily demand driven, is also conveniently ignored.

Immigration controls are enforced by all the countries at

present. India and Pakistan seem, however, to be two of the few countries, may be not more than five in all, which have a legislation covering emigration even of the responsible and rational adults who constitute the demand. This demand pressure creates its own supply- unregistered agents, the suppliers, as has been repeatedly observed, starting from the US Prohibition of the 1920's. Only a few countries have emigration controls, mostly in South and South East Asia. Philippines for example, passed the law only in 1995[1] with the objective to reverse the old policy of encouraging emigration as a route to economic growth and sought to balance it with the rights and dignity of the FWOs (Filipino Workers Overseas). And it covers all the categories of employment, unlike India. Despite these differences, the regulation follows a similar trajectory—registration of recruiting agents, an agency to administer and so on. Nowhere is the system however, considered a success. Website stories and reports, including those by the government commissions are full of stories of problems of exploitation of the protected by the very agents created for this purpose. A blog[2] lists the well-known problems —exploitation of labour, et cetera. Another website of Human Rights Watch[3] reports abuse of female migrant domestic workers in Indonesia and Malaysia; it refers to the NGOs reporting that 'owners of suspended recruitment agencies in Indonesia, may set up new agencies, under different company names and partner configuration', thus defeating the very purpose of the regulation for registration of agents. The only successful intervention, if at all, appears to be in the Philippines, that too mostly in the area of promotional efforts. The reason is the care and attention devoted to the resource and help centres which have been setup in foreign countries, to look after the immigrants' problems. The regulations in the Philippines were expected to be abrogated within five years, but evidently continue—an example of the 'status quo' bias. All in all, therefore, emigration controls, especially focused on sanctions, as in India, are part of a story of naïve interventionism by the government, whereas the parties might have found more productive outcomes, if left to themselves.

The dimensions of emigration taking place in India in violation of law are not easily quantifiable. A UN study[4] has made an attempt to assess the dimensions in respect of states of Punjab and Haryana. Illegal emigration is estimated to be over 20000 per year. The report listed a number of factors—'push' and 'pull'—for the substantial number of aspirants wanting to emigrate; sub legal migration is also not considered a stigma. Most of the transactions, the study indicates, are taken up by unregistered sub agents or agents located outside India.

The emigration law does not appear equipped to address the objectives (even assuming the same to be desirable) if one considers the incentives of the parties involved.

Incentives of Foreign Employers

Consider the demand for the Indian emigrants, from the foreign employers. Instances of exploitation are kept under watch by the national and international NGOs. Exploitation of foreigners in any country is difficult and risky for the employers; there is little incentive now for the foreign employers, at least in the formal sector, to exploit the immigrant labour. Even Saudi Arabia, according to a recent report, has now passed a law covering the infamous but informal sector of domestic workers. In any case, as the Indian experience indicates, employers may find it easier to exploit the local labour. There is little labour shortage locally for plantations in the West Indies or for mining in Africa. Most of these high demand areas are now capital intensive, and are rarely able to employ even the available local labour. Moreover, there is no evidence of any preference among the foreign employers for recruits from India; other countries provide quicker and may be cheaper alternatives and the problem is lack of demand (from the foreign employers). Factors of logistics and geography, say for the Turkish workers for agriculture in Germany, or the Mexicans in the USA, play an important part. The commercially profitable area of exploitation of immigrants is human trafficking, mainly directed at children and women, citizens or foreigners, and this area is specifically regulated by most of the countries. Human traffickers are also hardly likely to approach the registered agents to meet their requirements—their activities will always be sub-legal. The irony implied in the emigration law in the face of the disinterested foreign employers will be obvious from the fact that there is not a single country that encourages emigration from India (or any other country for that matter). Even countries like Germany, which depend on Turkish emigrants for farm labour, rarely encourage this and are limiting the intake of the 'guest workers'. Outsiders may even be reluctant to hire labour from India (even in case they feel they can get workers at cheaper wages here) due to legal restrictions. Why would they not take housemaids say from Indonesia or Philippines, which do not have such restrictions? Indonesia has, on the other hand, plenty of regulations restricting emigration to Indonesia even of professionals!

Emigrant Incentives

The law creates perverse incentives for the aspirants seeking emigration on foreign jobs. An interesting website[5] of Pakistan indicates the dimensions of problems created and the (ingenious) solutions devised—bypass the law by taking a tourist visa and obtain the employment visa while in a foreign country; negotiate the problem of exiting as a tourist with bribery. If one goes abroad on a tourist visa from Pakistan and gets a job abroad, there is no problem except the risk of being detained at the airport on suspicion, which is easily sorted out. But the other aspirants must go through elaborate procedures and engage registered agents (to show that the work visa was obtained as per law) and thus secure stamping of the passport by the Protectorate. The Protectorate is there to test the nerve of all the 'aspirants', even those who can get an employment visa on their own steam. It does not compensate them or help in case of fraud or mistreatment, in return for the hassles of going through agents, getting approvals from the Protectorate and so on. Once abroad, whether one has emigrated through one route or the other, the Indian government hardly cares. The role of the Protectorate is just formal; it is not available if and when even a legal emigrant encounters a problem abroad. The net result is higher costs even for persons who through contacts may be able to negotiate directly, thus creating disincentives for foreign employers as well as the aspiring emigrants but a happy Protectorate staff whose real job seems to be enforcing immigration restrictions on behalf of the foreign countries in India!

The regulations ignore the much stronger incentives of the real exploiters, mostly in 'sex trafficking', an area which needs to be and is separately regulated; the emigration regulations only add to the transaction costs of a large number of genuine adult and responsible aspirants and of a limited number of genuine employers seeking to employ labour from India. Emigrants have strong incentives; other countries provide negative incentives through immigration laws; if the latter cannot stop them, Indian regulations surely will not!

Facilitators/Agents' Incentives

Consider on the other hand, incentives of the potential emigrants and agents. The demand for persons wanting to emigrate from India—the kind covered under the Act—is limited but the supply infinite. Even if an Indian can find a job abroad directly, he/she needs an intermediary agent, as the work visa is only recognized if obtained through the officially prescribed route. Registered agents thus create what economists call oligopolies. Investment is required in getting oneself registered. Registration as an agent also means being in a position to claim a premium 'economic rent' for the service. Like the parallel economy of black money, some of the unscrupulous registered agents may also operate at two levels—limited legal operations in case of legitimate employer principals and *bona fide* aspirants, and extensive sub legal operations for meeting the demand of irregular emigrants. In practice, one agent's registration number tends to be used as a name tag by the unregistered parties at the appropriate time—when the approval is required— and provides rents to the registered agents. The registered agents are like the mafia, who entered the laundry business in the US to make 'black' white, a visible front for the illegal 'tip of the iceberg' activities; only the formal aspect of clearance for legitimate employment is routed through them. Of course, this also adds to the costs incurred by individuals in routing such requests for clearance through the registered agents. Genuine users would fare much better in a competitive market of agents, who would survive by reputation and rates, rather than the fact whether they are registered or not. In practice, as reported during a discussion with an office bearer of the registered agents' association in Punjab, the agent only acts as a middleman for the emigration staff who pocket Rs. 10000 or so and coolly stamp the documents at the time of departure.

The comic aspect of the regulations will be obvious from the fact that the total emigration may not be more than 50000 to 75000 annually. Data is not available, but the trade estimates the Punjab figure to be around 5000 to 10000. The number of registered agents in India servicing potential emigrants is 1835. It does not appear that they can manage with legitimate business —handling an average of 20 or even 50 calls a year. This is a temptation for the registered agents to take up semi legal activities, like charging a fee for endorsing work visas, even if obtained directly or arranging bogus visas and so forth.

Regulatory Paradox in 'Victimless' Crimes

There are a number of problems with the enforcement of such laws which deal with 'victim less'[6] offences; as Rogers points out, when anything that anyone wants and is willing to pay for is made illegal, there is incentive for an illegal market, and if the activity does not impose substantial cost on others, making the activity illegal is irrational. It appears illogical to impose restraints on the adult individuals to emigrate, under the false notion of maintaining national dignity; whether it helps is a 'fundamentally unidentifiable question', and impossible to prove or refute. The regulations only add to the costs of emigration. Futility of the registration system is evident from the routine but futile appeals made by the Protectorate to the newspapers that they should, before accepting any advertisement from agents for publication, insist on the client providing the registration number issued by the Protectorate of Emigrants. That advice as usual is ignored by the highly competitive media because they have their own incentives. If newspaper 'A' refuses, newspaper 'B' will be the gainer.

Emigration Laws: A Case of 'Governance Failure'

The net result of this protective legislation is that it is forcing responsible citizens to make surreptitious and sub legal exits from India and try to enter foreign countries of their choice. It is not enough if I can get an employment visa through a contact that is cheaper for all concerned. Both parties must also expend additional resources on the Indian formalities. Philippines and Indonesia have a proactive rather than restrictive policy and are replacing Indians in major areas like maids/nursing. In the face of increasing competition, the law encourages aspiring emigrants to adopt devious methods leading to tragedies like Malta. There may be in fact more need for state level protectorates of emigrants to protect the interest of the vulnerable groups in India itself; the domestic fish workers who migrate from Kerala to Gujarat appear to provide a stronger case for intervention.[7]

The 'porous' policy in India thus produces perverse incentives for the prospective migrants to flout the law. We have long out grown slave trade, say to the sugar plantations in the West Indies, but insist on keeping on the statute books, the same legislation whereas the whole context is dramatically changed. This regulation is a typical case of 'governance failure' at the level of policy but visible only when we look into the governance exchanges among the involved parties—government, registered agents, unregistered agents and the customers. The regulation distorts the market, adding transaction costs for customers in negotiating with agents in an 'oligopoly' situation (limited number of agents; registration by definition limits competition). Emigrants have to bear the costs of security et cetera, imposed by government on registration agents who naturally transfer the same to clients. They face the further risk of detention at the Indian Airports (which practically no other country's emigrant faces, as they don't have such regressive laws) in addition to the risk of deportation from abroad. One needs to remember that there is, in most cases of adult males who constitute the bulk of supply, no element of trafficking, as in the slave trade from Africa to the Americas in the eighteenth and nineteenth centuries. Prospective and aspiring emigrants are adults, males, admittedly not alphas but epsilons, but making conscious choices. Women under 30 years of age also require specific clearance under law. This indeed is a puzzling provision. For a woman emigrant, maturity begins at the age of 30, not 18 when she votes, nor even 21 when she becomes an adult!

Given the foreign country (dis) Incentives for the Indian emigrants, strong incentives on part of the aspiring emigrants, and the 'policy ineffectiveness' of the regulatory system to address these incentives, it may be appropriate to abrogate the law and instead focus on informational and protective measures (funds for repatriation, et cetera) for the unfortunate emigrants who may face some difficulty in foreign countries. In case it appears difficult to wind up the staff, they can be usefully engaged in adjudicating disputes and complaints!

A 'Sunset' Law

Some academics[8] advocate the adoption of a comprehensive policy after discussion among all foreign and local stakeholders, a rather tall order in view of very different incentives of parties. V. Santhakumar[9] has hypothesized on the possible rationale for this legislation; the law cannot prevent what happens in a foreign country, whether or not the emigrant obtains clearances in India; the regulations should therefore, according to him, basically address the information deficit of the party emigrating, regarding the possible risks and problems which may be unknown to him/her. But this is no different from problems of internal migration—say from Bihar to Mumbai. Further, the Protectorate is hardly equipped to handle such information problems. In fact its information may even be worse than of emigrants; it has no resources and little desire to keep such information. In practice its main job is redefined as registration of agents and informally structured as putting stamps on documents—dubious or not—for a fee or consideration! It was probably justified when massive labour was required for plantations and mines, and was likely to be exploited. Today, there are increasing restrictions on immigration by different countries, and penalties on illegal immigrants are much harsher and are stronger disincentives than the punitive provisions of the emigration regulations. Emigrants have strong incentives, wanting to go out at any cost. Add to this, the inability of the Regulators either to acquire information about credible employers or indifference to what happens to emigrants, once they have put the stamp on their passports. There are no follow up protocols even for the emigrants who get all the clearances. The remark, 'Some laws become "scare crows" over time—criminals, like birds, build nests on them',[10] appears appropriate for this law. The only possible conclusion is that it is a useless law, except for prevention of trafficking of women and children and in any case has to be rewritten, if that be the objective. This is a regulation that should not have seen 'sunrise', let alone one whose 'sunset' has arrived.

14

Immoral Traffic (Prevention) Act: Regulating Public Morality

Suppression of Immoral Act of 1956, despite some amendments, has retained its basic features—harsh penalties for sex traffickers, pimps, and organizers, and provision of rescue homes and lenient probation terms for sex workers. The Act is primarily meant for protection of women; penalties are expected to reduce temptation by the unscrupulous to exploit them. There is some contradiction here as in that case, arrest and prosecution of women, who solicit privately, makes no sense; these are women who as, responsible individuals, make a conscious choice and can be left alone, to take the example of the prostitute Allie in *Super Freakonomics*, a 'shrewd entrepreneur who kept her overhead low, maintained quality control, learned to price discriminate and understood well the market forces of supply and demand'.[1] There are many who may be exploited, need help and rehabilitation, but may not want it, and instead seek vertical (rather than horizontal) mobility to move to the higher end 'escort services', as documented by Venkatesh.[2] Then there are the pimps and madams who need to be prosecuted. The law is unable to make these fine distinctions.

The problem is an old one—whether to accept the legitimacy of sex workers as professionals, if they choose it freely, without coercion. At present, the simple fact that two or more sex workers are occupying the same premises, leads to the presumption of a 'brothel'[3] and obviously even genuine cooperatives and partnerships among sex workers are barred! There is also the social stigma which makes even a single sex worker vulnerable and means that the police can do what it wants—an FIR can always be registered and the worker marched to the police station. No wonder, the law creates more dependence on pimps! As many stories and serials (for example, *Cops*, a Fox TV reality serial) show, most 'street walkers' may be doing so due to fear of violence by pimps/men friends and are not free agents, but a cop has to book them for soliciting even though personally convinced that is not the case (the police has its own SOP's as James Q Wilson[4] points out). Licencing of sex work has its own social, moral, and (above all) governance problems, especially the 'agency problem'. Solutions are difficult and governments tend to abhor vacuum in these regulatory areas and try to do a tight rope walk, such as prosecuting pimp 'businessmen' and 'managers' while tolerating cases of individual choice by women with focus on their rehabilitation and protection. In practice, they are unable to make the distinction and end up with booking, prosecution and re-induction after release, in the same set up, of the women prostitutes, rather than their rehabilitation. Most of the arrests in India are affected through 'bogus customers' and sex workers are arrested even without there being any evidence of pimping. The net result is the prosecution of women sex workers rather than 'pimps'. Academics have highlighted the confusion among policy makers in distinguishing between forced and voluntary prostitution and whether to recognize the sex workers' rights, while penalizing coercion or exploitation.[5] In practice, prohibition results in the oppression of sex workers; the state rarely enforces the law against traffickers, pimps, or clients, whereas women are in routine subject to arrest and incarceration.

Legitimating Sex Work

This regulation has a peculiar feature. Unlike other crimes, neither of the private parties to the transaction if asked may vote for the law; the law deals with crimes 'without victims'. It is a typical case of the whim of a majority imposing its views on a minority (or possibly even on a majority which is not given a chance to express its opinion). And the majority opinion is based on a shaky, moral perspective' of the negative externalities imposed by prostitution. The society or the (majority of) citizens or opinion leaders may consider the externalities (of moral damage) a substantial cost and hence such laws. Economic analysis indicates that these regulations only add to the costs both of supply and consumption and lead to social losses rather than gains. Tough laws only result in high prices and reduced supply and are economically inefficient. Legalization in fact, may result in a net increase in social gains.[6] In case an open market is allowed to function, competition will ensure consumer protection (for example, against being robbed by a prostitute) and prices will match demand. If the trade is illegal, the supply is reduced, there is less competition and information about the suppliers hard to come by. There is therefore a case for abrogation of these laws, as has been argued by Rogers.[7] In *SuperFreakonomics*,[8] the authors in their inimitable style, indicate why the pimps are valued by the prostitutes (for protection from arrest, better earnings, et cetera), analyse the structure of demand and supply and its effect on the prices charged. The case of Allie who voluntarily decided to go solo in the trade, could generally decide herself on the prices to be charged, and be more autonomous and independent, unlike the street walkers, is an interesting sidelight indirectly supporting choice; this is the professional freedom the sex workers demand but are denied in India.

'Agency' Problem

Regulation of such social activities illustrates a typical dilemma in case of the 'victimless crimes'. Demand is there and supply follows or, may be, Say's Law is applicable: supply creates its demand. Restrictions however only add to the costs of parties (cost of punishment, expenses of avoiding arrest) and raise prices as well as transaction costs. Add to that the principal agent problem brought out in *Super Freakonomics*;[9] policemen may choose to ignore the law due to 'freebies' made available. Then there is the issue of the distance of the principal from the 'agent' policeman in India. In the US, it is may be a county Police Chief; here the principal is the State and the district police chief is only one among a procession of 'agents' for enforcement!

The law thus appears to have little economic, social or moral rationale. It may be more appropriate to integrate the objectives of the law within sex trafficking offences and to target the organization employing (rather than the self employed) sex workers. The present law only adds to the transaction and business costs both the suppliers and the customers, apart from those of the state—adding to costs of enforcement, loss of taxes and so on. In view of the demand for the product and supply, whether legal or otherwise, even though at higher prices, mild regulations to address the problems of exploitation and public nuisance may be adequate.

Exploring Options

A ban on street soliciting may have some logic, even though it does not appear to work in the US; most of the arrested streetwalkers are back on streets again. There appears, however, little prospect of the law having any impact in improving the 'moral climate' of the country though there could be some arguments in favour of restrictions in public places. Sex workers and the voluntary agencies operating in the 'moral underground' face tremendous problems, even in the absence of statutes. A positive, promotional bias in law, which encourages sex workers to make choices to provide services in private, without having to depend on the madams and pimps for negotiating the maze of the present law, may be more appropriate. The stranglehold of the pimps and managers may disappear, if the rights of sex workers are recognized and their incentives are 'channelled' away from a dependence on pimps to self dependence, while retaining the law for the sex traffickers and the like. The definition of a 'brothel', for example, can be more liberal to permit voluntary association of three or four workers. The fact that most of this business is shifting on-line is an additional reason for abrogating unrealistic regulations. These regulations need to be redesigned to provide for the recognition of the sex workers' rights and choice, decriminalizing sex work, and canalizing the sex workers incentives to regulate and control pimps.

15

Beta Regulations: The Coaseian Alternative

Enforcement of Beta regulations depends primarily on the information provided by the parties to economic and social interactions. In the case of electrical equipment for example, where the standards of safety and efficiency are defined, it is not possible for the government agencies to make inspections and ensure compliance by a large number of manufactures/traders. The futility of direct state intervention in the case of Beta services appears to have been recognized in the legislation relating to consumer protection. Consumers are therefore expected to approach the quasi judicial forums regarding problems of proper service/quality under the Consumer Protection Act 1986 which is a weapon 'in the hands of consumers to fight against exploitation by traders, manufacturers and sellers and providers of services'.[1] A consumer can file a complaint to the Consumer Disputes Redressal Forums and Commissions—a three-tier structure—regarding 'defect in product, deficiency in service, unfair trade practices and excess price'.[2] Before the law came in force, the civil courts were the only forums for these disputes.

Most of the Beta regulations, however, seek to place the burden of enforcement on the government agencies. This is the case for the Weights & Measures Act (now the Metrology Act) whose provisions seem to defy logic. Instead of a self-enforcing regulation (enforcement only in case of complaints), the law requires a whole panoply of actions—registration of trade and industry and periodical certification of weights—which is not only impossible for over forty million[3] establishments in India but also unnecessary. Surely, the suppliers providing goods in deficient quantities won't survive for long in a competitive market. The elaborate rules for registration and periodical stamping of weights to certify accuracy (a pipe dream after so many years) are in fact simply incentives to business to save these transaction costs by the 'omerta' money (no action) to the enforcers, who are themselves faced with an impossible task.

The structure of incentives for the parties entering into contractual arrangements or even for third parties (accident victims in the case of vehicles, labour in the case of industry, ordinary citizens in the case of noise pollution affecting neighbours) may require interventions and 'nudges' different from those advocated for Alpha services. Ensuring compliance of these regulations need not necessarily be the responsibility of public agencies, as the parties affected are available, identifiable and very much willing to see to it that the 'dominant' party, say, an employer in the case of labour complaints, is called to account. What is needed is making the liability rules for damages socially acceptable, and incorporating these in the laws clearly so that the aggrieved party can enforce them in a way which is socially efficient and productive. The irony of public governance is that Beta services can easily have some form of self regulation but are subject to *inspector raj*; on the other hand, Delta Services, such as public goods like education and health, appear to need direct state investments, as Dreze and Sen point out,[4] but the government seems to rely more and more on the private sector through constraining rather than facilitative regulations, to deliver social outcomes, as indicated later.

Coaseian Alternative

Beta regulations seek to address the harm caused by one of the economic or social actors—individuals or firms—to others. A number of these involve human or material factors of production. As remarked by Ronald Coase,[5] 'if factors of production are thought of as rights, the right to do something which has a harmful effect (such as creation of smoke, noise and smells, et cetera) is also a factor of production'. Leaving aside the desirability of government regulation in these areas of economic activity, the relevance of his analysis lies in focusing on the 'reciprocal nature' of the spillovers which is very much the case for most of the Beta services—construction/building laws, health of labour, et cetera. Defining rights in such areas is mostly a value judgment. Coase quotes Frank H. Knight: 'problems of welfare economics must ultimately dissolve into a study of aesthetics and morals' but adds that 'all effects must be included, some positive, other negative, in reckoning the social net product of the marginal increment of any volume of resources turned into any use or place'. If labour, therefore, permits its right to health to be harmed by the employer, it is entitled to compensation, irrespective of whether the law provides for the owner to have the medical tests done and provide free treatment to labour.

Whatever the regulation, the key Coaseian message is that the parties concerned are likely to reach socially beneficial arrangements, provided the rights are clearly defined and they may not need 'court ordering'. Beta regulations seek to supplant market transactions by government enforcement—whether for maternity benefits, or overtime for labour or fertilizer quality—leaving little space for the two parties involved and/or affected, to arrive at mutually productive outcomes. There is need to emphasize that Beta services, unlike public goods, are about activities which affect identifiable parties and where the transaction costs of negotiation and enforcement are not material. Such services provide ideal conditions where regulations need to just define the rights and then leave it to the parties to arrive at socially productive outcomes—whether for minimum wages or unauthorized construction in the residential buildings affecting neighbours, and so on. Needless to say, protective regulations for children and other 'challenged' categories, described as Beta minus, would obviously not qualify.

Transaction costs incurred by an aggrieved party in the course of enforcement of rights also appear to matter and quite a bit is added due to involuntary interaction with the government agency in this process. In the case of identifiable parties—labour in the factories, neighbours in case of buildings

– Coase's solution would appear to be the most appropriate. These regulations are designed to address the adverse effects or spillovers, which concern identifiable parties and where, therefore, the private parties are capable of negotiating more efficient social outcomes. Regulations empowering or incentivising the affected party (for example, labour in case of factories), in place of the ill informed and ill motivated government agent, might be more productive and efficient for all concerned. Complaint systems do exist at present, but the laws in many cases do not provide for defining the liability or the compensation mechanisms. One wonders how different the enforcement scenario would be if, as in the case of the Consumer Protection Act, the affected parties are encouraged to negotiate or if necessary approach agencies, such as the Consumer Protection Forums/Commissions, rather than the officials.

Karl Popper (*The Open Society and its Enemies*), one of the architects of neoliberalism, is quoted by S. Jones[6] on the nature of regulatory interventions:

> 'the first is that of designing a legal framework of protective institutions (laws restricting the power of the owner of an animal or of a landowner, are an example). The second is that of empowering organs of the state to act—within certain limits—as they consider necessary for achieving the ends laid down by the rulers for the time being. We may describe the first procedure as 'institutional' or indirect intervention and the second as "personal" or "direct intervention". The use of discretionary power must generally increase the irrationality of the system'.

The problem is that the first set of 'institutional' interventions, which may otherwise be desirable, is mostly exercised through the second mode. This is understandable in case, for example, of the law on Prevention of Cruelty to Animals where animals cannot seek redress, or in the case of children and similar categories but the governments have extended the second mode of 'personal' or 'direct intervention' into areas of economic and social interaction where the affected parties, whether labour, adult emigrants, or sex workers, both men and women, could be left to decide whether they want to protect their health, or travel abroad on tourist visas, or carry on sex work, rather than giving discretion to the 'protectorate', the inspectorate, or the police to interpret, intrude, detain, and prosecute.

In the area of economic and social interactions (for example, labour laws, tenant protection, consumer protection against overcharging and deficiency of service), human behaviour is likely to be influenced by incentives which are material or which the parties can translate in material terms (such as health for extra cash in the case of labour). The state in these areas has only to define the rights of the resources of production and provide easy Alternative Dispute Resolution (ADR) mechanisms for the parties unable to reach an agreement. In the case of 'victimless' social regulations (for example, prostitution, emigration laws), governance failure is probably caused by the very regulations whose objective is to promote the somewhat debatable social values. Governments seek to achieve compromises, by promoting social values and punishing contrary behaviour. Such compromises are difficult to structure into rules. There is need for the governments, therefore, to shift to the promotional domain of advice, help and assistance rather than indulge in 'shoves'—of licensing, registration and sanctions—which only add to the transaction costs of the parties, without achieving the outcomes desired. The only gainers in the process are the regulatory agents and the police.

Mancur Olson, while emphasizing the role of government in enforcing contracts, protecting rights, and promoting social and economic interactions, dismisses attempts to extend the Coaseian theorem or 'bargain' to the sphere of politics where the factors of power and coercion are material, and considers it utopian to seek to apply the 'Coaseian bargain' to 'involuntary exchanges which characterize government activities and regulations'. One couldn't agree more, and the argument here is a plea for the Coaseian bargain to be given a chance in the case of voluntary private transactions and exchanges, without the government distorting incentives.

Market Mechanisms: The 'Invisible Foot' (of Distrust)

There is another dimension of State intervention which is

ignored at present but may be helpful in the case of the protective regulations. Lott Jr. in a section titled, 'How rent control killed the Kitty cat: Enforcing the law when everyone involved wants to break it',[7] refers to an incident in which a landlord refused to rent out an apartment to the author as he had a cat which was suffering from a disease, whereas the regulations prohibited keeping diseased pets; this was the case, even though the rent offered was more than the rent fixed under the Rent Control Law. The apprehension of the landlord was that the tenant may provide evidence later, to the Board, not only to recover the extra rent paid but also compensation; the rent control law of LA provides for penalty for violation of the rent control laws at double the amount of over payment and the beauty of the law is that the landlord is solely responsible for compliance; the tenant is considered a 'victim'. The rent control board officials told the author that 'depending on tenants to bring charges of overcharging works very well', as tenants can sue to recover payments even after leaving the apartments. The law thus ensures compliance through creating distrust among parties. Similar is the case for the minimum wage laws in the US; 75 to 80 per cent of the minimum wage violations are reported by the workers themselves. Most of the regulations of India, however, treat both parties as culprits; hence the code of silence and the problem of lack of information. A simple provision that the victim, sex worker, labourer, or an emigrant who is duped by an agent, even if a willing party to the transaction, is empowered to provide information and evidence and is entitled to get relief, will itself bring about the desired results. The victims will be potential 'spies'—an application of the 'Invisible Foot' mentioned later (Chapter 23). If the rules under the PNDT or Emigration Act were to provide that the citizen even though a willing party to be transaction, can claim and get compensation for any violation of law by the clinic or the agent, it will create a positive feedback loop of distrust among the actors involved and the collusive but illegal transactions are likely to be, if not eliminated, at least much better controlled.

PART IV

Delta and Gamma Regulations: Positive and Negative Public Goods

The Corporate and group entities, apart from the state agencies, play a major role in providing public goods. Incentives of these organisations are primarily commercial and may not therefore be, subject to the cognitive and behavioural constraints and limitations displayed by individuals as discussed earlier in the case of Alpha and Beta services. Considering the nature of public goods, we need also to attend to the governing mechanisms and the design of the game apart from the rules thereof. The context of a particular service is however relevant and what may be appropriate for school education may not work for higher education. Further, whatever the governing mechanism, the major instrument available to the state for making a difference, even without assuming direct responsibility for delivery, appears to be information about the 'score', outputs and outcomes. Regulations concerning public goods therefore need to focus on the obligations of the public as well as the private agencies supplying the public goods to provide relevant, timely and accurate information. Appropriate rules for disclosure of information are therefore needed to equip citizens on the demand side to make informed choices, as may be difficult for governments to directly control or shape the market outcomes through sanctions and other restraints on the behaviour of the private providers of public goods.

The public 'bads' selected for analysis are crime, pollution, and corruption. Some suggestions have been made regarding the design of rules to make them compatible with the incentives of the three sets of actors involved in the case of crime – victims, police and criminal. The role of information is vital in the case of pollution control whereas in the case of corruption, some element of a 'shove' or compulsion may also be necessary in addition to mild 'nudges'.

16

Infrastructure and Public Health

Vi Ostrom and Elinor Ostrom refer to public goods—Delta services—as 'not subject to exclusion and subject to jointness in its consumption or use'[1] and quote Aristotle: 'that which is common to the greatest number has the least care bestowed upon it', to indicate the problem with such goods.

Broadly, one can include under delta services:

(a) physical, communication, and other infrastructure;

(b) education and similar social goods;

(c) services designed to address negative spillovers of spontaneous/natural and commercial actions of actors and enterprises—whether of bacteria or of humans—on the public at large These would cover public health issues (mosquito abatement, fire protection) listed by the authors and other areas such as pollution free environment.

The critical feature of group (c) of the public services is that the negative social impact and spillovers may not be due to any design on the part of the agency causing it and consequently such behaviour may not be amenable to incentives relevant to Beta regulations. In the transmission of AIDS or of polio, the culprit is the non-human virus or bacteria and humans are only passive (or not so passive, in case of the AIDS) agents. It is difficult to identify the 'culprit' or the perpetrator and even the potential victim of the act of omission (polio) or commission (carbon gases/global warming).

'Tragedy of the Commons'

Various solutions to bring these 'public goods' within the frame of economic exchange have been suggested. In the case of common lands, for example, one option is distributing the 'commons' among individuals. Elinor Ostrom has identified conditions under which the consumers of the 'common pool' resources are likely to reach cooperative agreements and implement them through quota systems, though even she is hard pressed to find a large number of functional community systems, barring isolated examples like the community irrigation systems in Nepal. As Landsburg,[2] however, shows, a fixed resource is of use only if it is private property; its gains will be competed away quickly as 'commons'. Very few of the 'commons' of this nature are left now at least in India, with government having taken over most of these and in any case, what is left with the community is not due to lack of rules for their appropriation! Belated attempts like the Forest Dwellers Rights Act are, for the present, miserable failures; not a single state in India has determined these rights of forest dwellers as required by the law.

Physical Infrastructure

Generally, even the market enthusiasts accept the role of government, at least in the planning and financing of infrastructure, even though governments are increasingly depending on private markets to do so. Surface roads may be fully or partly funded by the government and constructed by a private party and the fee for users, or tolls, may be imposed or permitted. Even where the tolls are imposed, it is mostly the government's duty to maintain alternative public roads, however difficult to traverse due to the congestion problems, for the people who don't or won't pay. This courtesy to citizens is denied in India. Infrastructure thus can no longer be described as public goods at least in India. In the case of telephone and wireless communications, the infrastructure is mostly in the private hands and even the government agencies levy charges for use thereof. Though it is feasible to 'exclude' potential users by the levy of charges/encryption of signals, et cetera, the facilities are inexhaustible, though subject to overload problems. Similarly, at the local level, street lights, parks, et cetera, are generally free to users, including those who don't pay local taxes. Public parking used to be free but is now priced, as that is the probably the only way orderly consumption can be ensured.

The regulatory burden is, thus, rather light in the case of infrastructure, and the focus is on the promotion of widespread and equitable consumption by providing free street taps for drinking water, for example. In the absence of market clearing prices balancing supply and demand, the taxpayers fund the cost and the consumers rarely pay the full price. Infrastructure is thus especially prone to inefficient resource use. The main problem in physical and civic infrastructure is inefficient and sub-optimal delivery, as the Urban Governance Study[3] shows in the case of the 'minor' issue of chlorination processes adopted by the ULB's (urban local bodies). Casual and ad hoc chlorination defeats the objective of clean water supply and results in the loss of storage capacity. Furthermore, storage tanks and reservoirs are choked with lumps of chlorine powder!

Economists favour private markets for infrastructure, to address the problems of 'free riders' and a lack of responsiveness among the public suppliers of these goods to effective public demand (roads leading nowhere, health institutions located away from user habitations, and so on). The usual solution for the governments is to organize the supply of such goods through a government or public monopoly, with prices being determined politically. Pricing of power is an exception and is now subject to independent regulation. Most of the civic services such as water and sewerage, street lights, other physical infrastructure —roads, bridges, transport, et cetera, and facilities like parks, recreation areas, et cetera—however, are subject to the problems mentioned.

Unlike 'natural resources' or exhaustible 'commons', where unregulated use can lead to resource depletion, infrastructure is relatively easy to manage as in the short term, extensive or over use may not lead to resource exhaustion, but only result in additional costs such as plying of overloaded trucks on roads. In a way, everybody is a free rider. The use and consumption of infrastructure however does not involve any 'governance interaction' in the sense discussed in Introduction and the sector is mostly the domain of economic and social policy. Governance activities comprise mostly of macro level planning, allocation, and use of resources in response to demand, not necessarily of the public, but also of the budget maximizing state agencies like the works departments. One can generally say that this is an area of economic and social policy with little governance potential (except for corruption, of course, as indicated in another chapter).

Curative and Preventive Health Services

Curative health is essentially an individual product, delivered individually and lacking the character of a public good. Treatment of 'A' may mean exclusion of 'B'. Curative services create little problems of interaction, based as these are on the self selection principle, involving little screening and to the extent they do (for example, free treatment for BPL families), it is better addressed as a resource transfer problem. The systems of health care in different countries reflect political and social preferences—targeted insurance in the USA and universal coverage in the UK and Canada, funded by general taxes. India has a mixed system. It tries to provide primary care free of cost, through the primary health care units set up with the objective of providing free medicines and services for common problems like diarrhea, TB, leprosy, and bacterial infections. Treatment of infants and pregnant women, as well as lactating mothers is also free. Lifestyle diseases and vital organ-related problems, however, need to be paid for, though at concessional rates, even in the government hospitals. A new initiative is the insurance scheme for BPL families (Rashtriya Bima Yojana), where the insured families are eligible for treatment in approved government and private institutions. I realized the irony of the much praised insurance scheme for the poor where the cover, even if the poor manage to have a valid policy (it is to be renewed every year), is limited to Rs. 50000; this is equivalent to one-day hospitalization in a private hospital if you need a ventilator, which costs Rs. 40000 per day! Evidently, the poor are expected only to have diseases for which Rs. 50000 insurance cover is enough! The efficacy of the scheme does not appear to have been investigated, but my hunch is that the turnover may be based on a combination of 'adverse selections' by the insurers as well as the insured, as the scheme is heavily subsidized by government.

Public Health—Addressing Externalities

These regulations are meant to address the harm imposed on the third parties due to private transactions, interactions, or omissions. In some cases, the first party (one polio infected child affecting another) cannot be easily defined, and therefore, one cannot easily control 'behaviour', unlike the regulations for labour, which involve directly affected parties. In the case of health hazards caused by industrial gases/effluents, the specific industry is identifiable but not the parties exposed to negative externalities. Here gains to the entrepreneurs may be substantial and the third parties too numerous, vast, and ill informed to act on their own; these spillovers are dealt with in another chapter.

In the case of preventive health, say polio immunization, individuals may not have adequate information or motivation or may have the usual 'procrastination' problems. Even the doctor couples can sometimes forget to get vaccination for their children. An excellent example[4] is provided in an experiment conducted by Leventhal et al on the campus of the Yale University. The experimenters constituted two groups who were 'primed' in different ways; the group which was provided a map of the health centre where it could get a tetanus shot, had a visit rate nine times more than the group who were only given a passionate lecture to do so. 'Channel' factors, which help to form a mental map, can be more helpful than expensive advertisements, celebrity endorsements and verbal exhortations. What is needed is to make the products, programmes and messages 'sticky'; as Gladwell[5] remarks, teenage smoking is rarely affected by the health awareness campaigns, as these campaigns rarely 'stick' in the minds of the clientele and don't therefore influence behaviour and actions. Small pox vaccination could be carried out to quickly achieve the target of universal coverage due to available institutional links—schools. It is, however, not possible to have polio vaccination in schools, as it is to be done within the first year of birth. Mass programmes of home visits appear to have worked to make India a polio free country; these measures make it costless to families. The approaches adopted earlier—verbal messages promoting awareness of benefits, and so on—had been of little avail.

One has to take note of the trait of procrastination and the factor of convenience, especially in case of the poor for whom vaccination is but a small concern among the numerous problems to be taken care of in the present, and of course, the least urgent. Incentivizing steps ('a phone or SMS to a Health Centre and someone will visit you within 24 hours or even within a week') may work better. Basically, what these programmes need is zero or negligible transaction costs on the part of parents, and in addition, availability of service 'anywhere anytime' at the convenience of the public, not that of the nurses/doctors. In the case of tuberculosis, for example, probably an SMS to the patient on the scheduled date (medicines are supplied free) can work wonders in ensuring timely consumtion of drugs, one of the most important aspects of Directly Observed Treatment, Short Course (DOTS) under the TB control programme as indicated later. An Officer, Sheela Rani Chunkath[6] has highlighted the relevance of the compilation of micro level data and its impact on a dramatic reduction of the MMR in Tamil Nadu, apart from 'death audit'—verbal autopsy of maternal deaths. Officials earlier depended on the SRS data, which had relevance only for the state and was generally too outdated and too loosely averaged for timely and effective interventions. A strategy addressed at the 'human' patients as well as 'agents'—channel factors, simple MIS Systems (an example of which have been given earlier regarding the use of data on the causes of death in Chapter 5) and 'sticky' messages—may be more effective, rather than general awareness programmes and bland instructions about drug consumption routines.

17

School Education: 'Predation' of The Right to Educate

Consumption and use of education does not lead to its exhaustion; the same facilities of staff and buildings can take on more students without creating a significant problem in delivery. It is, however, easy to exclude and limit the users of facilities, even without pricing, by providing for rules, for example, regarding neighbourhood schools. Higher education, on the other hand, is generally priced even in the public sector, and policies are more restrictive—merit, qualifying examinations. School education is considered a public good, as more educated citizens, it is hoped, would add social value, even though specific individuals may be the direct beneficiaries, and it does not, therefore, technically qualify. In any case, most of us do not question the role of State in providing education, though some would limit the rationale of government intervention to issues of equal opportunity, without necessarily supporting the outcome of a 'social good'. Whichever side one votes—education as a private good or as a social good—the issue is whether school education is subject to the phenomenon of under supply associated with the public goods that individual entrepreneurs may not find it worthwhile to supply, and whether any regulatory controls (eligibility and the standards the institutions must conform to, and other similar restrictions) are called for.

In India, school education is best examined against the backdrop of the new law, the RTE (Right to Education) Act. The Act promises to be essentially promotional but is likely to operate as a 'regulatory' law, restricting freedom of choice. The

Right to Education Act provides for a 'right' to education for the children of six to 14 years of age and incorporates the western concept of neighbourhood schools. It also mandates that all the schools, including private ones, need to be approved, and provides for standards of approval, penalties for violation and reservation of up to 25 per cent seats in the private schools, to be compulsorily earmarked for the children of the economically and socially challenged families. The schools must also set up the management committees, not as they wish but as prescribed. Children must not be exposed to interviews or other usual criteria of selection, nor detained in any class. There are elaborate conditions for the approval of private schools—adequate/qualified teachers, toilets and other infrastructure. There are however, some 'game changers'—no examinations, admission through a lottery system in case of excess demand, mandatory approval of the private schools by the Education Departments and reimbursement of expenses of the Economically Weaker Sections (EWS) students admitted there. While the RTE has been presented as a 'game changer', we need to see whether it will be effective, leaving aside the debate on whether it was needed or as some feel, it should have been left to the market (if people value education, the market will provide it). The problem, as pointed out[1], is that one may not value education highly enough to divert substantial resources to pay for it. Nilekani[2] is optimistic of the future of school education in India, due to the commitment demonstrated by the new initiatives, and efforts of the NGO's in translating intentions into outcomes. As we shall see, however, most of it is ideological baggage, and not likely to add either to enrolment or quality of education, having been evolved in a frame which neglects the players involved, their incentives, and the likely behaviour.

Under the RTE Act, the fundamental right to education, earlier limited to the primary stage (upto Class V), has been extended to the secondary (middle) stage. The new system is expected by the framers to rectify a number of problems coming in the way of universal education. The RTE Act consists mainly of:

(a) Strengthening pedagogy in the government schools

and physical infrastructure—buildings, additional classrooms and schools, trained teachers.

(b) Involving private schools (called public schools in India) through regulations providing that upto 25 per cent seats may be reserved for the EWS students. This is under the assumption that the quota will lead to 'quality' education for the selected EWS students, make public schools systems more 'inclusive' and help extend equality of opportunity to the poorer or otherwise challenged sections of society.

(c) Mandating selection through draw of lots, thus eliminating discretion and discrimination.

(d) Providing for reimbursement of expenses for the EWS students in private schools.

(e) Putting in place a system of registration and accreditation, without which no school is allowed to function.

Intention of the law makers appears to be to make education costless through the provision of text books, uniforms and the mid day meals, as these costs of education are high. In a Study conducted by the IDC,[3] 60 per cent of respondents indicated lack of finances as the reason for students dropping out of school. The challenges of school education in India are manifold—access to schools (financial, physical), getting children into schools (enrolment), keeping them there (attendance) and educating them (quality). Some solutions have been shown not to work[4]—adequately trained teachers, infrastructure (buildings, toilets). The history of impact of the government policies on school education in the East as well as the West has been somewhat chequered. Whatever little success such policies had is through simple interventions like 'Opportunidades' in *Mexico* (linking cash payment to enrolment and attendance of children). The problem is to provide regulations which address the dispositions and incentives of the parties concerned—children, parents, their teachers, and the school managements, who constitute the four key players in the game. The RTE policy is intended to influence and affect the incentives and behaviour of all the actors concerned to bring about the desired results and one needs to see how these interactions are likely to play out.

Incentives of Parents

The main requirement from the point of view of the family is evidently free education for the student child. In addition if positive benefits like the mid-day meals can be provided, it is a bonus. Leaving aside the huge costs of education in the private schools, even in the government schools, the cost per month, apart from fees, can be substantial. Uniforms are rarely provided in time and one has to remember that dresses and shoes wear out much faster in the case of children. Additional cash payments will help, as the Latin American programs mentioned shows. These are likely to be more effective than indoctrination of parents and campaigns based on the positive impact of education on family income in future, as some studies have shown.[5] Unfortunately, 'human' parents, especially the poor, are too overwhelmed by the present costs and problems, to modify their choices in the expectation of the remote, future and somewhat uncertain, rewards. And that still involves other costs of children education, psychic and physical, on the poor and uneducated parents—burden of homework, keeping abreast of a child's progress. One can ignore for the moment the opportunity costs if children were to be put to work but needs to take note of the elaborate steps a poor family needs to take, to get into a private school under the new dispensation of the RTE—filling up an application (or rather a number of them!), getting an income certificate for eligibility (this problem is dealt with elsewhere; there are no systems to help parents in processing these), keeping track of, and being present, on the date of draw of lots and so on.

We also need to remember what Mullainathan et al[6] say about the 'bandwidth tax' on the poor; the poor have too much on their minds and this affects their 'cognitive capacity' and 'executive control'. Putting a child in a private school, worrying about getting the child to school and back, ensuring that she does the homework – all of these may only result in the limited number of the poor who choose this 'opportunity,' to regret the decision or suffer more of the 'tax'. Contrast this with the earlier system—if a parent had to enroll a child, the child was taken to a government school and he/she got admitted. Extended choice for the poor has meant more of confusion and cognitive load. The new system appears to have stacked a brick wall of rules and procedures, creating psychological and physical disincentives for the poor parents, right at the stage of admission. It is unlikely that the really poor will go anywhere near the private schools, even if fees et cetera, are paid for. Most of the quota is likely to go to the middle class at the (upper) margins of the qualifying threshold, with parents in the latter case more keen on and able to afford private schools. The poor have a chance only where the school goes out of the way to facilitate such admissions (and some of the schools of course do so) which most of the schools—charitable in law, commercial in practice, and only complying with the legal requirements—are unlikely to do.

Incentives of Pupils

According to the NSSO 61st round,[7] the major cause of the dropout rate is the need to supplement family income (60 per cent for males) and domestic chores (40 per cent for females). An IDC Study[8] found that 'lack of interest' was also a major reason for the high dropout rate. The Rural Governance Study of the IDC[9] indicated similar findings; all of these indicate the need to attend to the much-neglected area of pupil incentives. It is a rare student who likes to going to school in the first few days, pre- school or Class 1. Most of the children dislike schools, have to be cajoled and persuaded to attend school (another cost for parents). Shakespearean wisdom holds true even today:

And then the whining schoolboy, with his
satchel
And shining morning face, creeping like
snail
Unwillingly to school.
(As You Like It)

That is one reason for the 'breaking in' of children at the pre-primary stage so that, as they enter Class 1, it becomes a sort of habit. Considering the pressure for the hard aspects of teaching especially in the private schools—checking home work, preparing for class work—teachers rarely have the time to accommodate the needs of students facing the trauma of schooling for the first time. Student incentives are, however, rarely factored in by planners and policymakers. It is difficult for teachers or institutions to control absenteeism, drop out rates and so on, except by making the school attractive through incentives—for example, mid-day meals—which do seem to make a difference. Hopefully, when the RTE scheme gets over its hiccups, this probably will be seen to have been the only worthwhile intervention directed at student incentives. It is also more difficult today to discipline and motivate students. Any teacher can wield a cane—it does not need much of effort or time. Positive motivation, on the other hand, takes time and effort, which the teachers don't have. Parents' disincentives and pupils' dispositions thus combine to contribute to high dropout rates. And whatever the incentives, in terms of financial concessions and meals, face the final blow—such as abolition of examinations—so that neither students nor their parents know about the quality of education imbibed by the student.

Teachers' Incentives

The problem is compounded by the 'moral hazard' of teachers who have just to mark the attendance of children at present and give a pass certificate. The students are not tested for the skills acquired in any class due to 'social promotion (or automatic promotion) policy and the teachers can pass their departmental 'tests' of efficiency easily, even assuming little student absenteeism. It is impossible under the system to judge the efficiency of teachers in the absence of comparative tests of pupil literacy and skills across various schools. There is no way even to monitor student attendance on a running basis; most of the teachers mark all the students as present, assuming they themselves attend the school, and as and when they do so. And add to this amalgam, the perpetual problem of transfers, with 30 to 50 per cent of teachers trying all the time to move to their places of choice! In the absence of terminal examinations or even a system similar to that of some states in the US (of an independent authority such as Pratham, which evaluates comparative performance of students in different schools and ranks teachers and managements on this basis), the present set of practices is likely to lead to a deterioration in the quality of education, given the structure of incentives of the players concerned. The only indication of the contribution of the teachers is the quality of education but the main objective indicator—examination results—has been done away, with nothing by way of concurrent and comparative evaluation to replace it.

School Managements' Incentives

Before the RTE Act, a system was in place for recognition of schools for the conduct of terminal examinations—for Class VIII and Class X—but the schools were operationally autonomous. The RTE regulation negates this autonomy. Earlier the schools survived on the basis of reputation, relative fee structure, quality of teachers and other factors; now, the single most important factor is recognition by the government department. Recognition/registration of schools is, of course, not a difficult process, but may just add the last straw on the private entrepreneur's 'back'. The problems are likely to be two fold. One is the disincentives of the profit oriented educators who would have otherwise set up schools and devised a fee structure according to their assessment of demand and competition, without having to take note of constraints imposed by the additional process of recognition, bureaucratic interference affecting the school autonomy and the inspector raj of the government 'educators'. This is likely to be a big setback even for the charitable and dedicated NGO's who run schools for slum children or children engaged in domestic work and so on. They will lose their autonomy in choosing the clientele and devising appropriate systems, due to the standard and uniform rules imposed under law for running the schools, admissions, staff salaries and so on.

Oversight and Monitoring

There is another contextual factor relevant for India, apart from the institutional factor of the transfer and posting policy. This is the confusing plethora of the monitoring systems consisting of the VEC's (Village Education Committees), the local officials, the PRI's and so on, with none of them having clear tasks or responsibility regarding what is to be monitored and evaluated, even if they have access, which they don't have at present, to information (for example, school attendance) required for this purpose. Institutions of local supervision, like the VEC, are not likely to work—too many parties, with different motives, get involved (or otherwise) for such unstructured social audit to work. Trials and experiments concerning nurse and teacher attendance listed by the Poverty Action Lab[10] are instructive in this regard. Community monitoring appears to have had no effect in Madagascar; informing villages and raising their awareness about the accountability mechanisms had no impact in India, as also the time clock programme in respect of the attendance of Nurses; impersonal measures were more effective, but were not foolproof and subject to 'gaming'.

'Unwilling Pilgrims' Progress

A simple arithmetic seems to demonstrate some absurd consequences of the RTE Act.

Assumptions

- Total universe of (eligible) students (+5 years) for Class 1 in Punjab: 100.
- Enrolment capacity in schools: 80 government and aided schools; 20 private unaided schools.
- Eligible EWS students: 40 (the income norms are liberal as compared to the BPL criteria).
- EWS quota in the private unaided schools: 25 per cent of 20 i.e. 5.

Outcomes

- Probability of distribution of EWS (all 40 EWS would otherwise have been admitted to government schools) under the RTE: Private Schools 5; Government Schools 35.

- Non-EWS students pushed out of Private Schools: 5 to be adjusted in government schools (assuming no increase in seats).
- Financial impact—expenses/fee of 5 EWS students studying in private schools + expenses of 5 students, who will not mind paying fees in private schools and who now will not pay any fees.
- Enrolment impact – nil.

There is need to recall what has been stated earlier—that in the new system, new schools are unlikely to be set up. The issue is, will it not be more cost effective to let the students who are willing to pay fees of private schools and who are pushed out, continue there, without any additional burden on tax payers and in case of additional demand, add seats in the government schools or set up new schools, thus saving the money spent on the five students *pushed out* of the private schools, who would be happy to pay the fees charged by private schools! The money spent on five free ships in private schools could be used for creating facilities in government schools for accommodating additional children reporting for Class I, and improve the teacher student ratio.

Governing Mechanisms: Public and Private

The McKinsey Report 2007 (*How the World's Best Performing School Systems Come Out on Top*) refers to three crucial ingredients for school education namely: (a) getting the right people as teachers; (b) developing effective instructors; (c) ensuring that each and every student performs well. The report finds no correlation of outlay or teacher student ratio, and similar pet programmes, with performance. A November 2010 report similarly demonstrates the uselessness of structural changes, resources or decentralization; schools improve instead by improving processes such as curriculum.[11] Jean Dreze and Amartya Sen[12] mention the relevance of institutional approaches to economic and social policy but emphasise the difficulty of having an actionable checklist of the needed institutions and rules. They quote Trebilcock and Prado (*What Makes Poor Countries Poor? Institutional Determinants of Development*; Cheltenham: Edward Elgar, 2011) that 'in sum, while much empirical evidence supports the view that institutions matter for development, *we know very little about which institutions matter and what specific institutional characteristics within classes of institutions matter for development*'. Different objectives obviously need different accountability systems and the problem of accountability therefore has to be escalated by the authors (in a section on the 'Centrality of Education') to the 'accountability of the entire schooling system'. The problem is that the accountability mechanisms for quality may be different from those for attendance and different for teachers and students. Macro perspectives therefore, even across a particular sector such as education, do not appear very relevant in defining the measures required to achieve the desired outcomes. In any case, it is clear that, unlike for example the labour laws, the governing mechanisms for school education in the Indian context need to be primarily the public agencies and not the private sector.

Prospects for the Poor

The results of the NSSO survey (NSSO 61st round 2004-05) indicate that about 20 per cent of students (primary) and 15 per cent (upper primary) are enrolled in private unaided schools; the share of the private aided schools is 10 and 15 per cent respectively. In Punjab, there is no enrollment, in the MPCE (Monthly Per Capita Expenditure) size classes of less than Rs.1000 in the private unaided schools. Over 28 per cent of the children enrolled in these unaided schools belong to the MPCE households in size class 1000 to 2000 rupees.

Punjab: Distribution of Children enrolled in Government and Private Schools by MPCE, 2004-05

Size class of MPCE (Rs.)	*Rural*			*Urban*		
	Govern-ment	*Private Aided*	*Private Unaided*	*Govern-ment*	*Private Aided*	*Private Unaided*
< 500	-	-	-	-	-	-
501-1000	-	-	-	-	-	-
1001-2000	94.1	0	5.9	65.6	6.3	28.1
2001-5000	81.1	1.7	16.8	53.3	10.2	35.8
> 5000	39.7	9.1	50.4	18.4	18.0	62.6
All	71.6	3.6	24.4	45.8	11.5	42.2

Source: NSSO 61st round, 2004-05.

The new system evidently will most likely benefit the EWS families in the high MPCE size classes, which already have children in the private unaided schools, as the annual income criterion for the EWS eligibility is rather liberal (Rs. 1.50 lac per annum); this translates to a per capita income of around Rs. 3500 per month for a family of four. The criterion is likely to leave the situation unchanged for the poorest with children either not in school or enrolled in the government schools. The logic of the arithmetic given above needs to be supplemented; not only are the students willing to pay fees pushed out of the private schools, the EWS quota would also mostly result in 'self selection' of the families who would have put their wards in these very schools and paid fees, an instance of 'adverse selection'!

All the drama therefore about equality of opportunity in private schools when it covers only 12.5 per cent (5 out of 40) EWS students, and that too just marginally below the Rich Line, rather than the BPL as indicated above, appears to be a mockery. The RTE Act does not take note of the fact that the poorest may still not opt for private schools; the transport fee itself can be a deterrent. In Chandigarh, private schools are concentrated in two or three sectors on the periphery of Chandigarh. This is apart from many other expenses on the school trips/extra activities, et cetera, which are customary in private schools and which the government has been unable to control even in the case of 'aided schools', governed by the pattern of government schools. Considering the hassles of getting a certificate or rather the ease with which the 'creamy layer' can get a certificate, and the other factors mentioned, most of the seats are likely to be filled by the marginally rich rather than the poor. Further, even in the lottery for admission to private schools, dice is loaded against the poor; the more schools to which a child applies, the more the chance of selection and obviously only the relatively better off can afford to do that.

There is need to take note of another important factor relevant to most of the states in India—the preponderance of the private schools, (called 'aided' schools) operating under the same system as the government schools. A large number of these aided schools are paid grants (and even pensions to teachers) by the government and are subject to the conditions and obligations similar to those of the government schools. The unaided private schools are mostly in the major urban areas/ for pre and primary stages in the rural areas, and given the new systems of recognition, high land prices and the RTE regulations, it may become more and more difficult to open more private schools in future. The window for providing quality education for the EWS through private schools will remain even more limited than the arithmetic above indicates.

It would appear therefore that the genuine EWS are unlikely to be helped through the quota system in the private schools; expansion of the schools in the private sector is likely to get a setback and the quality problem will remain at the present levels, or even worsen due to lack of competitive pressure on government schools. The somewhat irrelevant rules and obligations, such as the teacher student ratio, imposed on the private schools, are likely to lead to the private entrepreneurs withdrawing from this area.

Design of Governing Mechanisms

The real problem is education in the government schools. And some simple solutions may be effective:

(a) Institution of a system of simply comparing and monitoring attendance on day to day basis—of pupils and teachers; the acquisition of data and information can be outsourced and digitized at moderate cost.

(b) Adopting the practice of quality testing through external periodical tests, based on Pratham's model now used only for 'sample' surveys. Individual schools under different jurisdictions subjected to such assessment of performance, may really improve and the authorities could concentrate on the local causes of failure rather than focusing on the 'averages' of a multitude of causes, which only lead to solutions demonstrated to be not very relevant—student teacher ratio, qualified teachers, toilets and buildings.

The positive spillovers of education are generally recognized but as always, there is a debate about the states' role—whether to have more and more government schools and extend free education to cover not only fees, books, stationery, food and uniforms but also transport expenses, or bank upon cash vouchers and similar schemes to give a choice to the parents and create a sense of competition among the schools. The whole edifice of the RTE appears to be built on somewhat shaky foundations, choking the vibrant profit oriented private as well as charitable school institutions, putting a virtual stop to the expansion of private schools. Unlike the Charter Schools in the US, which get funding on the basis of total student enrolment, funding in India is limited to the EWS quota. No school can function without obtaining recognition; so what one may see, is not new experiments and individual initiatives like the Charter Schools in the US but simply 'clones' of the existing schools which strengthen the monopoly character of the education market. It is unlikely that there will be much improvement in providing equality of opportunity, in terms of access to quality education for the poor, as indicated. Instead of mild nudges in a positive direction, the RTI Law provides kicks in the groin, forcing the private suppliers to proceed in directions just the opposite of what is desired. Arvind Panagariya[13] has aptly remarked:

> 'Moreover, just as onerous labour laws have discouraged the expansion of labour-intensive manufacturing in the organized

> sector, the demanding input norms in the RTE Act would discourage the entry of new low - cost private schools—it is a fair bet that an inspector raj would soon emerge whereby bribes will be extracted for delaying de-recognition of recognized schools that do not meet the input norms and for letting unrecognized schools stay open'.

Even if there is no corruption, the impact on the supply side of the education market will definitely be in terms of more scarcity.

The RTE Act provides for child mapping, maintenance of records of children, tracking their progress and so on, but the provisions are only likely to invoke the System I of the government agents and the managements who may evolve convenient rules of the thumb to cope with the situation. For the government agents, these 'heuristic' rules are likely to be to ensure that the private schools file applications for recognition, the departmental responses (scrutinizing, rejection or approval of applications) are given, and that the schools admit 25 per cent EWS students. Major issues—whether the students get all facilities as required, or whether the schools really fulfill the criteria—will tend to be ignored. The government departments will and have already developed amnesia about child mapping and such other sophistications. All the activities are likely to be only on the actionable aspects of rules that suit them. For the private schools, getting recognition and negotiating through the 'hassles' (to them) of admissions of the EWS, are the two verifiable/measurable actions. The government schools have a still happier ending. The pressure of competition is officially off the teachers' backs. Very few private schools may come up in future, and the public dialogue will be cleverly shifted from the quality of education in the government schools to issues of uniforms, fees, toilets and admissions for the EWS.

The RTE is likely to be a big set back to school education, instead of the 'game changer' it is claimed to be. It is likely to strengthen the monopoly of the existing schools, discourage genuine NGO's and create disincentives for new entrepreneurs —charitable or profit oriented—to establish new schools. Most of private schools get registered as charitable (due to incentives available for rebate on income tax to charitable trusts and associations—another instance of perverse incentives generated by tax policy). They had earlier to lobby only for land allotment but could devise their own fee, admission and teaching systems. Now they have to go through the red tape of recognition, which is surprisingly not required for the government schools, even though the latter, admittedly, are poorly resourced in respect of all the parameters—quality, infrastructure, et cetera. There could not be a worse example of the somewhat unconstitutional discrimination against the private schools. The RTE Act appears to be a product of wishful and optimistic thinking, lacking in the inputs of elementary arithmetic and logic, and just provides a soothing 'narrative' for equality in education. It does not provide even equality of opportunity, let alone equality of outcome.

Mancur Olson[14] defines a 'market augmenting' government as one that not only recognizes and protects rights and enforces contracts (and according to him only a 'representative democracy' can do that), but also abstains from 'predatory' activities and regulations. The Indian State appears to be moving in the reverse direction. It needs to provide feasible alternatives and options for the poor in terms of better facilities for education for their wards. The government seeks instead to shift this social responsibility of the State to the private sector, an action that can only be described as 'predation' of the 'property in rights'[15] of the private entrepreneurs, to run the private schools as they wish. 'Nudges' seem to be beyond the Indian government's capacity or understanding or inclination.

18

Higher Education: More Regulation Equals Less Competition

The institutional framework for higher education in India consists of universities established by an Act of Parliament (Central Universities) or of a State Legislature (state universities), Deemed Universities, Institutes of National Importance, Institutions established by State Legislative Acts and colleges affiliated with the universities (government and private). According to the MHRD (Ministry of Human Resources Development) Annual Report 2009–10, as of March 2009, the country had 26455 institutes of higher education—504 universities and university level institutions, and 25951 colleges. Presently about 12.4 per cent of school 'pass outs' opt for higher education. If India were to increase that figure to 30 per cent, it would need another 800 to 1000 universities and over 40,000 colleges in the next 10 years. In India, institutions must undergo a process of State regulated and controlled recognition or affiliation whether as 'deemed university' (the UGC) or the Medical Colleges (Medical Council of India—MCI) or an Engineering College (All India Council of Technical Education—AICTE). Two-third of India's colleges and universities are believed to be lacking in the requisite standards. Based on the recommendations of Yash Pal Committee and the National Knowledge Commission, a proposal for the establishment of an autonomous overarching National Commission for Higher Education and Research (NCHER), for prescribing the standards of academic quality, and for mandatory assessment and accreditation in higher education, is under consideration.[1] As per newspaper reports, the UGC has recently decided that accreditation will be now compulsory for all universities.

As in the case of school education, there was little need for regulating private universities till the State almost threw up its hands in coping with the demand through (supply of) the public institutions of higher education, and what Nilekani[2] calls 'de facto privatization' took place, initially through the spread of professional colleges affiliated to various public universities. The states are now out competing each other in setting up the private universities. There is a demand for effective regulations to ensure quality and standards, and a 'super regulator' across all the professions, even though reasonably well regulated structures of the AICTE, the MCI, the Nursing Council, the UGC, et cetera, are available. The issue is whether we need to regulate —through super or single regulators, and the consequences of the different sets of regulations, given the present structure of demand, supply and the incentives.

The options available are: (i) managing without any regulations and depending on the competition provided by the market, and (ii) design of the specific regulations necessary to improve efficiency and productivity. As mentioned (Chapter 17 - School Education), we know very little about the kind of institutions that will help in bringing about the outcomes desired and governments may do better with some experimentation. Countries like the UK started with public institutions funded by the Church or the State, and the private sector even today is a marginal player. In the US, private nonprofit universities got established first and the state universities—by and large funded by the State—are 'second cousins', even though the quality differentials may not be as high as for the government schools, as compared to the private schools. India initially had adopted the British system and very little resources were devoted to higher education by the private sector and the charitable and religious agencies. Even today, the public sector continues to dominate general education, though the private sector has come up in the professional areas of higher education. There are not many charitable ventures. Reasons for the 'scarcity' of supply of altruism in India are unclear but the facts are not disputed.

Role of Government

There need be little argument on whether the government should provide higher education institutions. Considering the paying capacity of students and the relative uncertainty of benefits to individuals, especially in the general education area, the market is unlikely to meet the demand for higher education at prices acceptable to both parties—the students and the institutions. Public sector needs to help in easing the demand pressure by providing higher education at prices yielding positive utility to the students/parents. Purely private supply channels may not be enough. Countries like the US manage to have quality education, based on a system of voluntary accreditation of the private institutions, except for some professional areas (for example, medicine). The US Council for Higher Education Accreditation (CHEA) is listed[3] as an institutional voice for 'self regulation of academic quality through voluntary accreditation'. It focuses on providing information to the public, without trying to judge the viability of the institutions, and ensures that the private institutions provide complete information and are transparent in their functioning, to enable the students and the parents to make appropriate choices; it has, for example, a checklist to help the users identify the 'diploma and accreditation mills', that is, bogus institutions. India is bringing in more and more regulations even in the face of evidence of the failure of existing regulations and of the regulatory authorities (MCI, Technical Education Boards). One cannot establish and run a private institution, even if no money or other help is required from the government. The result is a proliferation of entrepreneurs, who can negotiate the licence permit raj of the 'approval' processes, and once that is done, extract 'rents' from students whose options are further limited due to the regulatory standards and norms of the fees to be charged; these are in practice supplemented by informal payments especially in the case of the professional colleges. Supply thus gets limited by the mandatory recognition processes and is rarely spurred by demand, as fees are also regulated. The way private initiatives are thus stifled, is aptly demonstrated by the theme of the film

Shivaji The Boss, where an NRI, played by the actor Rajni Kanth, is harassed by the government agencies just because he wants to set up a medical institution free from the curse of capitation fee, whereas the government and its proximate principals are interested only in their 'cuts' in the process of recognition. The Minister tells Rajni Kanth, hero of the film, that unless his demand is met, recognition will not be given, but in case he is 'satisfied', there would be no need to bother about the students —whether in terms of fees or facilities. Higher education appears to be one area where entry of the regulatory authorities may have meant not more, but less quality. The regulations simply translate into an incentive to obtain the initial approvals, and to comply with conditions during the periodic inspections done by ex colleagues and friends; the institution, once it gets initial approval is, however, practically immune from competitive pressures. There is scarcity of supply precisely for the reasons given—the regulations for recognition—and not everybody can be a Rajni Kanth.

It is almost impossible to control the higher education market—may be even more so than the economic markets; it deals exclusively with the 'futures' of dreams and prospects, and the 'herd mentality' makes the game one sided—everybody wants to buy into it, as in medical education. And unlike the share markets, probably the 'bubble' will never burst considering the demand in India, which is mostly a function of numbers.

Regulations, Advocacy, and Incentives

The incentives of the 'punters' who set up the higher education institutions and of those who enroll in them, can only be moderated by competition, regulated primarily through the voluntary accreditation processes by the 'trade'. The State regulations only add to the transaction costs; the competition is limited to somehow managing recognition, and survival is determined by exogenous factors—recognition by the State rather than competition, quality, reputation, or standing. Recognition and approval by the State is the simple route to achieve all of these. What may be more helpful to the students is clear information to be provided by the institutions, the standards to be observed, and a provision for compensation to parties (students in this case), in case supply is deficient.

As indicated in the case of labour regulations for the safety and health of workers, defining a standard of service or compliance may be enough to ensure that malpractices are minimized. Generally, the need for government financing and government regulation is advocated on two grounds—of higher education being a public good and of equity. One may not agree with Milton Friedman[4] all the time, but here the case is made. Evidence for higher education being a public good is unclear; the primary advantage is to the person and often, as many an Indian film shows, the family makes sacrifices for providing education to the 'son', but he (it is mostly a 'he') abandons them to their struggle for existence.

There is another contradiction in the government regulations. Equity is sought to be ensured through reservations and positive discrimination but is decried on grounds of merit,[5] and labelled political interference. Unlike elementary education, where the aim is rightly to have 100 per cent enrolment and retention, the universities can take on at the most 20 to 30 per cent of eligible population, whether from the affluent and/or the poor and the underprivileged. An effective compromise between the paying capacity of students and equal opportunity is an almost impossible task, hence the need for the State to set up institutions to provide easy loans based on the principle that, if you can't pay today, you should be prepared to repay out of the future income stream. Imposing a uniform structure of fees on the private institutions, even if it were practicable, is an invitation to perverse incentives for 'gaming' the rules for recognition.

The case for the need for regulations to improve the quality of education is on a still more shaky ground. If the public universities cannot be depended for providing quality, even in the absence of commercial objectives, how can a regulator ensure it in the case of the private institutions? The fact is that some of the most advanced nations known for the quality of their private universities are managing without any State controls, as in the US, where the only major government contribution is providing educational loans for students.

V. Shantha Kumar[6] has analysed the need for these regulations in India from the point of view of ensuring access to higher education on merit, irrespective of means. The other aspect mentioned by him is the quality of education that the customers (students) may find difficult to assess on their own due to lack of information. The rationale, however, is not supported by facts and the interplay of the owner and regulatory agency incentives as indicated above. A system of voluntary accreditation, as for hospitals, may function much better. We see the evidence everyday of the effectiveness of the voluntary standards like the BIS (Bureau of Indian Standards). Probably the best a government can do is to provide, as it does at present, competitive alternatives to the private sector in higher education. With complex incentives on the demand side—disposition, ambition, talent, paying capacity, expectations—and the commercial objectives of the educational entrepreneurs on the supply side, a free market with clear liabilities for deficiency of service (as under the Consumer Protection Act) may be the best option, apart, of course, from the provision of base level funding by the government through loans for higher education, for those who want them. In fact, 'equity financing' (giving the creditor a share of the future earnings), advocated by Friedman[7], may not be a bad idea.

Regulation of universities and other higher education institutions, mainly through barriers to entry, but also through control over fees and compulsory accreditation, is unlikely to encourage the universities to compete. This is only likely to encourage the 'diploma mills' that somehow manage approvals and make profits under the protective umbrella of uniform fees, whether by compromising on costs or quality, or supplementing income through informal charges levied on students, as some of the private institutions do at present, even though extensively regulated officially in respect of fees by the government and the courts.

Apart from facilitating merit based admissions through the promotion of the public loaning institutions, there is another area where the State may need to intervene—ensuring that the institutions provide full and complete information to students and parents, in a user friendly manner, to enable them to make a proper choice. Regulators need to ensure this, rather than take on the responsibility of approving the institutions under the optimistic but mistaken assumption that the initial and annual inspections, accompanied by reams of written records, will equip them with complete information to take the right decisions and provide appropriate signals to the entrepreneurs and the users. And one needs to add the problem of the agents' incentives (professionals put together for inspections for recognition, officials checking voluminous documentation) to see that the task is impossible. The top levels of the regulatory institutions—not only the agents but even the principals in the institutions like the MCI and the AICTE, have had cases of corruption registered against them. Compulsory affiliation and accreditation would only lead to a situation of oligopoly—consisting of a limited number of suppliers and producers—where the competitive pressure is exhausted right at the stage of getting approval for an institution.

We speak of public goods being undersupplied by the market, but in this case, supply does not appear to be a problem requiring the State to step in. In fact, the position is just the reverse. The scenario is different from that of school education where government schooling may need to continue in the absence of sufficient supply of private schools, available at the price the customers are prepared to pay. Regulation of higher education appears to be a case of 'governance failure,' the government regulations creating barriers for the competitive private markets in education. Government intervention thus causes a more inefficient allocation of resources than would occur without such intervention, resulting in 'double market failure'.[8]

19

Donation of Human Organs: Incentives for Altruism

Governments all over the world have been wrestling with the problem of evolving proper systems, regulations, and processes to ensure orderly removal and transplantation of human organs. The objective of the relevant law in India (*The Transplantation of Human Organs and Tissues Act 1994*) is to 'promote, through appropriate regulations, the removal and transplantation of human organs while preventing commercial dealings. The problem is that neither of the two objectives is being achieved. India has probably the least number of donors per million, barring countries with strong religious taboos. There are two sources of organ donation—from 'living' donors and from 'brain dead' persons and cadavers; the present law appears to have failed miserably in promoting donations and, if one may say, civilized transplantation especially in the case of the latter.

One of the suggested solutions is to allow open trade in human organs as this is likely to bring the buyers and the sellers in direct contact, improve economic efficiency, and reduce the asymmetry of information leading to 'market failure'. This however is generally not acceptable on ethical considerations, whatever the economic feasibility of the arguments. Even short of this politically and socially unacceptable solution, however, governments can probably do a lot if they focus not so much on the macro technical, financial and organizational issues, but on the micro institutions, rules and processes which affect the incentives of different actors—donors, recipients, and the intermediary organizations, the hospitals.

One of these areas is regulations concerning living donors.

The law provides for restrictions on the donation of organs by living persons, who can donate only if they are near relatives or have bonds of 'affection/friendship' with the recipients. These restrictions have been imposed to prevent the possibility of exploitation of the poor who may be tempted to donate their organs for monetary consideration. The result of the restrictions is however the opposite of what is intended. Genuine donors who may wish to donate organs even anonymously during their life time without any expectation—and there may be many—are excluded. Only after death can they hope to satisfy this humanitarian urge! The unfortunate 'friendless' recipients who may not have any relatives or friends willing to make a donation, are forced to 'forge' special bonds of kinship, leading to the emergence of a class of underground experts in 'creative relationships'. The irony is that the underground activities are not carried out in the dingy joints in the back lanes of towns, as used to happen in the case of abortions when the regulations were not as liberal as they are today. The transplantation may be (mostly) carried out in the institutions and by the agencies which are formally authorized. Both the donor and the recipient are getting exploited by the middlemen; the former get a fraction of the market value of the donation, whereas the latter have to pay much more than the market clearing price, mainly due to the heavy transaction costs imposed by middlemen who capture the surplus, which otherwise might have accrued to the donors or the recipients or both. They capitalize on information acquired by them regarding donors and the 'resource persons' who may be willing to trade illegally in the absence of a free and transparent market. The regulations have thus created perverse incentives for all the actors—recipients, donors, hospitals, other intermediaries—to bypass the law. There is a general belief that commercial dealings and illegal trade in human organs has increased over time.

There is also an ethical paradox. On the one hand, the regulations have failed to prevent—and have, in fact, increased—exploitation of the poor, even while these have failed to control illegal trade. On the other hand, these regulations may be responsible for shortening the lifespan of many needy recipients—the wealthy as well as the poor, and in a way, therefore, the cause of avoidable death and suffering, due to delays involved in the tortuous procedures for approval, resulting in some patients becoming unsuitable for transplants especially of kidneys.

The rule design shows lack of realism in another area—harvesting of organs of cadavers, especially unclaimed dead bodies. Despite such cadavers being available in large numbers, there is little harvesting of organs due to somewhat unimaginative rules in regard to the obligations imposed on the medical institutions and/or doctors in charge of the unclaimed bodies and the conditions under which organs can be harvested. The doctor who is in lawful possession of the dead body is required to certify(form 6 of the Rules) that he/she has 'reason to believe that no near relative of the deceased person has objection to the deceased person's organ being used for therapeutic purposes'. It appears unfair to impose this obligation on the Medical Officers (MOs) who have no obvious means of obtaining the appropriate information to be able to conscientiously make the required certification. Why would a doctor go through all the trouble to give this certificate in the absence of information, when a simple complaint against him from any relative or even an outsider may damage his professional career? Denial of permission by the hospital authorities, therefore, becomes the 'default' practice. Moreover, as provided in section 5 of the Act, the mandatory wait for the claim to be made by a relative is forty eight hours from the time of death; most of the transplant options are closed by that time!

The outcomes of these regulations are well known and documented. Solutions suggested, however, are about more of the same useless medicine. A study[1] in Tamil Nadu reports increasing commercializa-tion and exploitation of donors by middlemen with some of the donors getting only 1/3rd of the amount promised. The suggestions made in the study, however, are for further restrictions, a tightening of the definition of persons not related to the recipient, and eliminating discretion of the authorization committees—all meant to control incentives of parties and prevent misuse. Similarly, the Qureishi Report[2] of the Health Ministry recommends additional regulations even while bemoaning the failure of the existing ones; its focus seems to be on more elaborate formalities and placing the onus on the doctors and the authorization committees to take risky and difficult decisions based only on the documentation available. These committees are no doubt responsible for scrutiny, but have no independent sources of information; all they have is the documentation provided by the interested party. In case of any problem, the decision-makers would be in the firing line. Rejection is consequently the normal response, the 'default' practice. The committee may face little problem, or criticism even if genuine cases are rejected, but may face censure if even a single permission or approval goes wrong. The Qureishy Committee recommends by way of encouragement of harvesting of the cadaver organs, somewhat tame social incentives—issuing commendation certificates to the donor's family and tends to ignore the interplay of much stronger incentives in the illegal market. These restrictions and regulations are obviously unable to deliver the outcomes desired. One need say no more about the incentives created by these rules, which encourage officials to respond in a way designed precisely to reduce the number of donors and transplants.

Incentives and 'Nudges'

The question is, can some imaginative 'nudges' help? 'Thaler et al.'[3] devote a chapter to the relevance of 'nudges' for increasing organ donations: moving from 'explicit consent' to 'presumed consent' or if this is socially and politically not feasible, to 'mandated choice', where every person while getting a driving licence is required to tick one of the two boxes 'yes, willing to donate' or 'no, unwilling to donate'. They provide an illustration of a dramatic nudge, the Illinois First Person Consent Registry law, which declares the choice of the First Person (donor) to be absolute; no further consent is required from the donor's family. Given the social and political context and if one may say, the moral hypocrisy in India (widespread commercial trade but zero tolerance rules), similar nudges may be more effective. First, probably there is a case to allow donation of organs by the volunteer donors not necessarily related/friendly to recipients. Surely, the problem of exploitation can be controlled by eliminating direct contact between the donor and the recipient, as any person, if she so wishes, would be allowed to donate her organs during her life time but only to an anonymous recipient. The national/regional registries of donors and potential recipients can be set up for anonymous matching by the authorized institutions and allowing transplantation on first match basis. An appropriate change in the law can thus allow at least the genuine donors to help anonymously. Second, a change in law on the lines of the Illinois one, coupled with 'mandated choice' for all the holders of driving licences, would probably work wonders. No doubt we also need a supportive infrastructure, but that will be provided in due course by the 'invisible hand', once the donors become available.

Third, it may be desirable to revisit the conditions imposed on the medical officers (MOs) in the case of cadavers. The present rules are creating only disincentives for conscientious doctors. The use of cadavers can be promoted, by providing instead, that the medical officer in charge is bound to give a clearance certificate for harvesting the organs of cadavers if no claims have been made within a specified period, say, in cases of death occurring 24 hours after admission; (this can raise a reasonable presumption that the family members may not be making a claim). In order to create confidence among the MOs and the institutions as well as the public, the law could provide for oversight and control by professionals, rather than putting the doctors at the mercy of the network of the police whose incentives have been commented upon elsewhere. This could be done through the empowerment of reputed 'mother' institutions (something akin to what is being done for the Blood Banks); the Directors of these institutions could be authorized to initiate action in case of professional misconduct. To start with, one reputed institution in each state could be vested with the oversight of implementation only for cadaver organ harvesting. Giving ownership to specific institutions may be much more effective than implementing the law through hybrid committees consisting of disparate interests—hospital representatives, civil servants, NGOs et cetera. These entities can, however, continue to operate for screening 'living donors' which is a more sensitive social issue. Quick decisions are required in such life and death issues and some organization needs to be the owner and take responsibility. This mother institution can also be a clearing house for information; it is not possible today to get even elementary information on the hospitals registered under the law. The experience of China which conducts an annual review of the capacity and performance of the approved hospitals and institutions is instructive and could be followed. In any case, once a donor is distanced from the potential beneficiary, there is little likelihood of misuse. Michael Connelly (*Blood Work*) portrays a character who is number three or four on the waiting list for a heart transplant and therefore murders some innocents and makes anonymous calls to the Emergency Services in order to ensure that the recipients above him in the waiting list and he himself get heart transplants in time (in time that is, for him!). Such extremely perverse incentives need not worry us!

Another major problem is that of matching donors and recipients. Despite liberal laws in some of the countries including Iran, where organs can be traded at rates fixed by the state, or Spain with its 'presumed consent' policy, there does not appear to be any fully functional market in this area. The problem is of genetic matching and compatibility between the recipient and the donor. Matching requirements differ depending on the organs and tissues involved. As Davis points out[4], most of the organ transplants need matching between the recipient and the potential donor across a number of compatibility genes; the status of immune reactivity against the donor cells also needs to be checked. The quality of matching is also important; it can affect the life of the graft. Supply of organs suitable for transplants, therefore, even in an unregulated market, is likely to remain limited. A willing relative or friend, even though able to get through rigorous vetting procedures, may not necessarily be suitable as a donor due to these matching requirements. Simplistic solutions which depend on volunteerism and have worked, though in a limited way, in the case of blood donation, may not therefore be adequate for skin grafts, kidney, bone marrow and other organ transplants. Unlike blood transfusion, where a vast supply of potential donors is available locally and the number of blood groups is limited, the level of matching required is much more sophisticated for organs other than the eye. The problem of genetic matching indicates the desirability of encouraging more donors beyond the immediate family. The risk of misuse—sale of organs—may be easier to control, once the data bases of willing donors are developed and anonymity ensured.

Some practical solutions to improve the rate of transplantation of kidneys by matching pairs of incompatible patient-donor units have been suggested[5] by Alvin Roth and others. Such algorithms for patient-donor matching have led to substantial improvement in the rate of transplantation in some of the US states. Such simple measures, supported by appropriate rules, may lead to substantial improvement even without having to compromise on the 'high' ethical principles which form the basis of the present set of macro laws and regulations. This is in addition to permitting barter or exchange between two needy families where the profile of family 'A' donor matches the profile of the recipient in family 'B' and vice versa. The need for attention to micro rules to encourage harvesting of the organs from unclaimed dead bodies has already been mentioned.

In these areas of interaction which may also involve 'meta-economic' motivations, professional, structural and technical solutions may not be enough. We may need to devise pragmatic institutional frameworks and operational rules to create suitable incentives and necessary conditions for achieving objectives of the law, rather than hoping for a change in human nature, with eager donors readily queuing up for donations.

20

Crime and Punishment: 'Nudges' for Police, Victims, and Criminals

Crime is a complex social phenomenon and its control involves prevention of crime as well as dealing with crime *ex post*. This is one area where the academics and practitioners tend to be arrayed on the extremes of the causes and measures favoured—mending 'broken windows', psycho social and managerial (enforcement) interventions and so on, depending on favourite explanations and theories of crime—society, family, a mysterious 'social epidemic.[1] Molecular biology has added its own flavour to the debate on the influence of heredity versus environment. It is now generally agreed that both genetic disposition as well as environmental influence need to combine for a person to take up criminal activities. A study referred by Matt Ridley[2] demonstrated that the low activity monoamine oxidase A (MAOA) genes, generally associated with criminal activity and aggressive behaviour, had much more effect on youngsters who were maltreated as kids. Ridley remarks that 'The low active (MAOA genes) maltreated men did four times their share of rapes, violence and assaults' and that 'criminal parents produce criminal children but not if they adopt them and a bad genotype is not a sentence, it also requires bad environment'.

Eugene McLaughlin and John Muncie[3] trace the history of crime in the UK and provide a glimpse of the almost bewildering variety of measures adopted against crime:

> 'social democratic welfarist cannon of effective crime control (addressing 'social roots' of crime), deterrence and prevention in the 1980s, based upon 'just deserts' to the criminal 'other' (rolling

back the 'moral relativism' of the previous era), comunity and victim obligations ('target hardening'), the Labour Party's 'institutionalization', in the '1990s', of the processes of manageralism established by the Thatcher government in the '1980s' (application of best value and cost effectiveness standards to the police and the courts, privatization of prisons and so on), resulting ultimately in a mix of 'manageralism, community responsibilisation, restorative justice and authoritarian populism.'

Economics of Crime

The 'frames' of various disciplines also provide different perspectives. Psychologists talk in terms of deviant behaviour, sociologists in terms of the social and community environment, and political scientists in terms of laws and institutions.[4] The clearest, though not necessarily the most helpful, perspective on crime appears to have been provided by economists—a criminal is a rational agent and crime is a function of costs and benefits imposed on parties, victims, and perpetrators. The Gary Becker perspective[5] would require trading the costs of crime against benefits. Zero tolerance of crime implies very high social costs and therefore may not be acceptable within the economic framework. As David Friedman remarks,[6] 'eliminating all murders, even all muggings, would no doubt be a fine thing but whether we ought to try to do it depends on how much it costs. If reducing the anual murder rate from ten to zero requires us to turn half the population into police, judges and prison guards, it is probably not worth pursuing'. Despite attempts by economists, therefore, to bring crime wihin the frame of supply, demand, costs and benefits, the laws are mostly framed on the basis of the 'conventional wisdom' and broad value judgments sometimes, may be, not even of the majority. Even in the case of economic crimes (for example, property crimes), a cost benefit analysis is rarely undertaken, or if undertaken, rarely noticed by those who call the shots, the lawmakers. There has been little practical application of economic analysis in the area of crime except in the broad areas of 'target hardening' (for example, antitheft devices for cars, burglar alarms) and in deciding on the severity of punishment —both designed to add to the costs of crime for the criminal.

Moreover, there is little agreement among economists, even in an area that has been the subject of extensive research - drop in crime rates in the US in 1990s. Explanations vary from 'broken windows' and 'staffing' to 'community policing', legalization of abortion,[7] liberal practices allowing citizens to carrying handguns[8] or a mix of all the above. The explanations, all of them, are supported by elaborate statistical tools and analysis. An excellent analysis[9] of research in this area by John Lott, Jr., however, points out some actions and rules that can help. Some of the factors listed as helpful in controlling and preventing crime (in the US context) are: death penalty (for murders and other serious crimes); arrest and conviction rates; and the 'right to carry' (guns) laws. Factors which may not be relevant are: gun control and 'affirmative action' in hiring the police force. The verdict is still out, according to him, on the 'broken windows'[10] theory and 'community policing'. The arrest and conviction rates are especially relevant; as Lotte Jr remarks, 'changes in the arrest rates account for around 16 to 18 percent of the drop in the murder rate. Conviction rates explain another 12 percent. Arrest and conviction rates have an even larger effect on other types of violent crime. And their effect on property crimes is still greater, often two or three times larger than for violent crime overall'. The State of California was the first in the USA to introduce the Three Strikes law which provided for increased quantum of imprisonment/punishment for the second and third time offenders. Gladwell has pointed out[11] that while the law had immediate success in reducing crime, the law of diminishing returns came into play in due course. The criminals probably adjusted their incentives and strategies accordingly. He also refers to studies of criminal behaviour which demonstrate that the quantum of penalty has a negligible impact on the criminal psyche. The issue therefore of penalties and their effect on crime prevention is somewhat complex.

Harnessing Incentives for Control of Crime

Crime thus appears a difficult area to influence through incentives and nudges. Costs of punishment (increasing quantum thereof or the rate of conviction and similar disincentives) may not work for many criminals. In any case, what is probably is not factored in, is the disposition of the criminal. In case of a criminal overrating his or her skills at evading detection, costs may not get the same weight as for other 'econs'. 'Humans' generally overrate their abilities,[12] a sort of 'endowment effect' and probably criminals are as likely, if not more, to do so. The expected cost, therefore, of death penalty for an 'econ' criminal may be very different from that of a 'human' criminal. In certain areas of governance interactions, however, among the concerned parties—victims, perpetrators and the police—it may be possible to design appropriate rules to influence incentives. In the Indian context, two areas which need mention are: (a) in the case of the victims/families and the police, recording and cognizance of crime, and (b) in case of criminals, recidivist crime.

Reporting and Cognizance of Crime

Behaviour of both the victim and the police can be greatly affected by the formal institutions of accepting and registering the FIR's (First Information Report). Recording of crime is itself a process that may respond to some tweaking, as incentives at that stage (on the part of both the police and the complainant) are not strong enough. The FIR is the first point of contact between the police and the informant, victim or otherwise. Generally, irrespective of information given, the contents of the FIR as registered are decided by the police (which sections to apply, who to name as suspect and so on). Mostly an informant has to sign the FIR register even though not required under law, or rewrite the complaint to conform to the *letter* of the FIR. So in the case of a minor girl who may be reported missing, a family may want to lodge a report of suspected abduction, but it may not be so recorded—to allow for the matter to be compromised later, with the third party (the police) being the only gainer in the process. The *thana* (police station) decides whether an FIR is to be registered (abduction) or only a missing person report in the Daily Diary Register (DDR) and sometimes who, if any, is to be named as the accused. The slightest possibility of extraction of a bribe from the complainant and the accused is likely to be exploited, especially if the matter, as is common in such cases, is likely to be compromised. The police will, in some cases, advise the family to be cautious on the ground of family honour, and without recording an FIR, ask the family for resources to apprehend the suspect, recover the girl, and then extract money from the other party also for not recording an FIR! In a case where a complaint for dowry harassment against the boy's family was filed (but not registered!), the police station informally summoned the accused, who was told that he must carry at least one lakh rupees to preempt his arrest at the police station. And this was when a number of influential people accompanied him to the police station! It is no surprise that over 47 per cent of cases of police corruption are at the stage of the FIR registration.[13]

Victims and their families may be reluctant to register complaints and if at all, go to the police station 'well equipped' —accompanied by persons in the good books of the police or believed to be influential. And underreporting of crime is a worldwide phenomenon. Lott Jr.[14] cites an FBI report about the victims reporting only 20 per cent of larcenies, 63 per cent of rapes and 68 per cent of aggravated assault. Many of the victims do not approach the police due to the 'inconvenience of dealing with police and the slim chance of recovery of items'.[15] In India, the quantum of under reporting is much more partly due to the very rules of the FIR registration. There is always the possibility of a cross complaint being made against the complainant (in case of serious injury for example) and complainants are not sure they would not lose more than they would gain, if they go to police. There is not much faith in the police objectivity and neutrality, whether in respect of money or influence. In the general climate of distrust, a small number of 'white sheep' in the police do not matter even if they exist.

Once the FIR is registered, the game shifts to a different level, mostly related to interaction of the accused with the police. It is well known that a person accused of a cognizable offence has, till his conviction or acquittal, to pay substantially to the police and after conviction to the jail staff (the latter for some small privileges and turning a blind eye to the rules of the Jails

Manual). Major incentives are involved here and the redesign of rules to make them 'tougher' is unlikely to work for the police or the criminals. Some attention to incentives at the first stage of interaction—the FIR—may, however, pay dividends but the more the need to change, the more things remain the same. In the 1970s, the police in Punjab were claiming, as an explanation for increase in crime, that they had started registering the FIR's liberally without questioning the *bonafide* of the complainants. The same selectivity in registration continues along with similar explanations for increase in crime even now. Ever since e-governance became the common currency of government departments, police all over India have been claiming that on-line complaints are likely to, or have become a reality. But a perusal of the police websites of different states does not indicate a single state, which has actually done so. The system was initiated by an officer in a district of Kerala;[16] the officer claims dramatic effects of the system of an open line for complaint registration (instead of institutionalizing complaints at police stations) on crime reduction, and increase in reporting, especially of crimes against women, due mainly to an open help line. The 'best practice' however appears to have withered away with the departure of its champion. An examination of the websites both of the State police and the Tiruchy district shows that the present practice is confined only to 'promises' to record online complaints only about misconduct by police. The Delhi state has recently initiated a system of online registration as have some districts in Punjab but the practice remains at an experimental and preliminary stage.

The survey referred[17] gives the example of an e-governance initiative, the e-Cops website in Andhra Pradesh, which claims to provide for automatic and disintermediated recording. It does not however appear to be so, even though listed as a best practice in the India Corruption Report; it just advises you to phone the police at the given telephone numbers, or present yourself at the police station, with no promise of the report being registered. The spread of best practices seems to require a unique amalgam, as indicated by Aiyyer.[18] The best practice of dis-intermediated registration of the FIR's remains a vision statement at present.

The problem of the institution of the FIR in fact highlights one of the few exceptions to our basic premise—that rules are central to public governance. The law requires immediate registration of an FIR, without 'ifs' and 'buts', but the practice is different. Even the PCR (Police Control Room) Vans, even while immediately taking the required action, insist on a complainant visiting the *thana* for completing the formalities. On the one hand, there is much focus on online service delivery in many Alpha services to eliminate the distortions that arise simply because an interaction may be personal and direct. The Electronic Service Delivery Bill circulated by the Government of India seeks to mandate online delivery of public services, even though some of us may prefer personal interaction to avoid the bother or due to the personal preferences; it does not seem fair to deny such people what they want. The FIR on the other hand is one area where only a rare brave soul will prefer personal contact but that is what he/she is forced to do, despite the law.

The only feasible and neutral (neutral that is to the 'game' strategies of police and other parties) solution is making information available to those entitled for it, by making the FIR registration a public act—easily accessible to the interested parties. A simple incentive thus for the victims and families to report crimes could be to depersonalize reporting, delink the FIR from the institution of the police station, enforce the mandate of immediate registration and provide real time display of the FIR registers, indicating the time and date of the complaint or report and of registration. Once the two activities —complaint (receipt) and registration are independently recorded and displayed in real time, some major problems related to incentives of the police and the victims are likely to be substantially resolved. This system will place responsibility for the registration of the FIR where it belongs—to the officer competent to do so. So far as the apprehension of proliferation of bogus FIRs is concerned, the fear of the police, if not the threat of punishment for perjury, would be deterrent enough for the overwhelming majority of resource less victims, who dread going to the *thana*, let alone dare make false complaints. In India in any case, the proportion of charge sheets to the FIR's registered is rather low[19] and registering of false FIRs appears to be a luxury only for people who are influential or have the police backing or complicity.

There is a need to put some distance between the point of registration/information and the point of investigation. It should be possible to make a complaint at a designated office—say a *Saanjh Kendra* in Punjab and/or online, and leave it to the authorized officer to register the FIR, if necessary, after a preliminary and quick check whether the complaint indicates a cognizable offence. Whether the investigation is done through centralization at the district level, say in case of homicides and other serious offences, or by the local *thana*, by and large the complainant would be outside the web of the informal police system while lodging the FIR; registration of the FIR will become an internal process delinked from the reporting agent, thus restricting the space for easy exploitation (or 'gaming' of rules) by the police.

Under-trials and Recidivism

The second area which has some relevance to the control of crime is the police/Jail staff/accused interaction during the criminal proceedings. The problem of the under-trial prisoners continues, even though known to involve wasteful, painful and unwanted interactions due to their avoidable incarceration. About 65 per cent of prison population in India is reported to be under trials.[20] At least 30 per cent of these under-trials are accused of only petty crimes under the SLL (Special Local Laws) and the IPC (Indian Penal Code), who are mostly illiterate or under Matric and are in jail simply because they are unable to furnish security. An NGO in India—the Human Rights Law National—has been able to handle only under 1000 cases of under-trials over a number of years.[21] The problem is obviously beyond the capacity of the society and the government needs to step in. A Report of International Bridges and Justice (LBJ),[22] lists some suggestions regarding release, on personal bond, of those under trials who have served more than half the sentence; the suggestion was reportedly made by the then Chief Justice of India. The social waste implied in the extended incarceration of under-trials even for petty offences is huge and it is a pity that India has been unable to find a solution to this problem by developing systems of bail which are within the capabilities of the 'epsilons' of the world of crime. And addressing this problem is necessary not only from the point of reducing overcrowding in jails, the common argument, but also its impact on recidivism. A study[23] indicates the rate of recidivism, typically found after a four to five-year follow up study in a community in respect of sexual offences, to be 10 to 15 per cent. Predictive factors, stable and dynamic, involved in such crimes by the repeat offenders, are complex and one wonders what impact the psycho social interventions, as argued in another study,[24] can have in this area. In any case, it may be difficult to expect professional administrators, accustomed to going by the operational rules, to devote attention to such sophisticated and individual oriented interventions. The reported recidivism rate in India in 2011 is under seven per cent, with most of the crimes being committed by those convicted only once in the past.[25] Probably if one could have the data on recidivism with respect not only to previous convictions but also arrests, one may get a more realistic picture as the conviction rate is low; crime reports[26] indicate this to be only 41 per cent for the IPC cases.

Incentivizing Under-trial Prisoners

It is likely that the quick release of under-trials may result in reduced recidivism and induce positive behaviour among the repeat offenders—arrested or convicted. There are two complementary aspects of 'nudges' proposed in the case of the under-trials. It is difficult to be sure but possibly the ratio of persons arrested per unit of crime in India may be one of the highest in the world, whereas the rate of conviction is probably one of the lowest. Evidently therefore the expected cost of committing a crime in India may not be much of a deterrent, even ignoring the problem of the optimistic and confident criminals mentioned above. The shadow world of the under-trials, on the other hand, is subject to very different incentives. They are mostly first offenders, and may not have, in case of petty offences, much of an incentive to disappear, committing in the process another offence, in case they are arrested again in another criminal case. One can probably try a different approach: bail to be given on the personal bond of the under-trial in petty offences such as crimes against property, provided the under-trial agrees to be UID'd through routine fingerprinting and genetic fingerprinting and thus leaves the jail with a UID which is retained on the national data base. The law at present does not require the under-trials to be subjected to fingerprinting, et cetera, and hence the reciprocal and 'nudging' nature of the suggestion (bail on personal bond if willing to undergo finger/DNA fingerprinting). The arrested persons get permanent identity in the police records, a disincentive to commit a crime again and be arrested; the jail population becomes manageable, and recidivism is reduced. The prospects of future good conduct can thus be strengthened through this voluntary identification system for the first offenders. James Watson[27] has put the case well for the DNA fingerprinting of the convicted as well as the under trials; criminological data indicate that 12 per cent of sexual assaults in Florida and 28 per cent of homicides are recidivist crimes. The British government has proposed DNA samples for the defendants arrested but never charged or acquitted; nineteen US states now collect DNA samples from all felons, not just those involved in violent crime.

Releasing the under-trial prisonors held on petty offences, on personal bond, provided they are fingerprinted/given a UID, may be a small 'nudge' in modifying the behaviour at least of the first time offenders, if not of repeat offenders. Recidivism actually may be much higher than indicated in the Crime Reports, which deal only with the repeat offences by the convicted. And finger/DNA printing may be a simple deterrent whether compulsory, or if the law and beliefs of the proponents of privacy and choice of the arrested 'innocent' come in the way, voluntary.

Quick release of the under-trials is especially relevant for addressing recidivism as the alternative economic options of economic rehabilitation and livelihood diminish with the time spent in jail and the earlier an arrestee is released, the more his/her chances of reintegration in society. I am not sure whether the proposal will be considered 'asymmetrical' or fully 'patrimonial' (Thaler and Sunstein refer to the debate[28]) but it is likely to be an effective 'nudge.

Police and Criminals' Incentives and Technology

The other area of crime where technology and incentives can be matched is at the stage of investigation where adoption of modern forensic technologies can be of great help. One of the most important is the DNA fingerprinting, as indicated, which is almost infallible, can rarely be misused and abused (unlike the fingerprints) and can be a first rate tool for apprehending recidivist criminals. One needs to remember that genetic fingerprinting is an important instrument of 'justice', which can provide evidence simultaneously against the criminals and in favour of the innocent. The very first use of genetic fingerprinting in the UK was to prove that a person already convicted of rape and murder was actually innocent.[29] A quote from a book (*Actual Innocence*) by James Watson[30] appears appropriate—'DNA testing is to justice what the telescope is for the stars'.

All law enforcement officers can be also required to be DNA fingerprinted to prevent the risk of contamination, if not authoritative exclusion, of the law enforcers from the list of suspects, which, in the Indian conditions, is more than a remote possibility. In the US, all military personnel are fingerprinted, as also police in some of the states. The DNA printing can be linked with the UID data and thus provide a basic, comprehensive and secure national level finger and DNA fingerprint data base, of course only to be used under conditions of strict privacy, in criminal investigations. These technological inputs may help transform, to some extent, the crime detection scene in India, which is dismal today.

The incentives of the police can also be affected by the ICT (Information and Communication Technology). The CCTV cameras can do wonders in respect of empowering citizens—accused, victims or the general public—in their interaction with the police and this technology may need to be mandated for all interactions/exchanges within the institutions of the police *thanas*/interrogation centres/jails as a routine. Facilities for the CCTV are now available in some of the police institutions, but these are utilized only for the convenience of the police (whenever they expect complaints, in the case of the influential and the powerful). There may be a dramatic change in the police incentives, if all the proceedings/activities within the *thanas* and jails are mandated to be video graphed and are 'visible'. The doubting Thomas may feel that these rules can be easily sidestepped in practice, as so often happens. This may be so for the tough ones in the force but may be enough for the majority of 'normal' policemen. Above all, there is need to have simple algorithms or SOP's for police; complex guidelines tend to get simplified/interpreted as per the dominant culture. One illustration of the complex guidelines for desirable police behaviour is the 380 page *Compendium of United Nations Standards and Norms in Crime Prevention and Criminal Justice*[31] which deals with norms for persons in custody, legal and institutional arrangements, good governance, et cetera, Ludwig Von Mises[32] points to the essence of bureaucracy, which stifles initiative and innovation by imposing restrictions on discretion through detailed rules and codes, thus creating incentives primarily for following the 'code of instructions'. The frame and the context of the governance situations is different from that of the economic markets and 'It is vain to advocate a bureaucratic reform through the appointment of businessmen as heads of various departments'. It is futile therefore to look for 'champions' who would emerge from the cocoon of the bureaucratic frame or to expect that the bureaucrats will generally display incentives, divorced from a utility maximizing mode in which they function.

Compounding Crimes: Providing Choice to Victims

The fourth area is incentivizing victims who may have at present no motive, other than revenge, or a desire to teach a lesson to the accused, to pester the police. The Code of Criminal Procedure in India (Section 320) does provide for compounding, but the offences covered are a very small fraction of criminal cases, and the cases settled another small percentage thereof; the provision thus is not visible, readily 'available' or easily recalled. Few defence lawyers would explore this option. Substantially extending the scope and coverage of this provision, to property and other crimes involving financial incentives, may be helpful. Compounding in some cases (theft, motor accidents involving 'rash and negligent' driving, involuntary man slaughter or 'culpable homicide not amounting to murder', et cetera) and a provision for compensation to the victims, may provide much more effective disincentives to criminals and also reduce the policing and criminal justice costs. The choice of compounding and compromise has of course to be left to the victim/family. Compounding can be mandated through the courts, to avoid misuse.

We sometimes use the concept of an 'optimum' level of crime, given the state of law and rules, and the police, courts and other resources. Compounding is a simple strategy to 'reach' the incentives of the victims; the likely scenario, absent victim incentives, of a win-win bargain between the other two rational agents (the policeman and the criminal) is, as economic analysis has shown, likely to leave the victims and the society in the lurch; to keep the criminal law functional, it may be necessary to bring into the 'game', the rational interests of victims. Compounding of crimes is likely, apart from incentivising victims and minimising the socially harmful collusion between the policeman and the criminal, to free a lot of resources for addressing serious crime even at the current level of enforcement, rules and level of crime. This can be a sort of extension of 'plea bargaining' which is now permitted under the Indian laws, though rarely used at present and unlikely to be popular, given the state of incentives of the prosecutors; they think, and rightly, that the public will never believe that the application of this provision in a particular case is judicious and for example not used to help the accused even in an open and shut case. Compounding, providing the victims choose to accept it, is a Coaseian bargain which would transfer (at least some of) the gains of crime, from the criminals and the police to the victims.

We are still far from having the technology to be able to predict crime and apprehend criminals before they commit crime, as shown in the film *'The Minority Report'* and would need to make use of resources and technologies in an incremental but imaginative fashion to influence the choices of all parties concerned with crime, especially the police. These small changes and 'rule based nudges' in the form of (a) depersonalizing the process of reporting of crime and an open FIR registration e-portal (affecting police and complainants' motives); (b) release on personal bond of the under-trials, subject to DNA fingerprinting (incentives for at least the first-time offenders); (c) DNA/fingerprinting of all arrestees/jail inmates as a routine (affecting incentives of potential criminals); (d) use of the CCTV in the police and jail institutions; (e) allowing compounding in most of the offences (incentives of the accused and the victims), may, without too many resources normally advocated – staff, equipment, make a difference.

21

Managing Environment: Information, the Key Incentive

'Tragedy of the commons' is a well-known phrase; 'free riders', indulging in competitive consumption, lead to the destruction of the commons resource. The exploiters and the victims however, constitute a single category; the perpetrator can be a victim himself and in fact may have no intention to harm others. The general public affected by the spillovers is too dispersed to function as an antagonist. The spillovers, however, don't spare the perpetrators of pollution and poisonous gases. The advantage gained by the perpetrator is temporary; the person who cut the last standing tree on the Easter Island would surely have perished, though may be the last in line.[1]

Pollution is a typical negative public good as the perpetrators have incentives for production at minimum cost, and installing and maintaining decontamination equipment costs money. The affected public has—as individuals—no incentive to protest or initiate action as the advantage thereof will be enjoyed by everybody 'free riding' on the hapless 'enthusiast's actions, as Mancur Olson has demonstrated. Governments have therefore stepped in as champions of the public and have prescribed regulations imposing limits on pollution, installation of de-contamination plants and imposing penalties for violation of these regulations.

Environment management and pollution control in India is governed under the Central laws—for water, air, environment protection, hazardous substances, et cetera. The Departments of Environment and the Pollution Control Boards (PCBs) are the main agencies for implementation as well as promotion in the states and are expected to coordinate various programmes and implementation of these laws, in close consultation with the Central Pollution Control Board (CPCB). The basic regulations require industrial and commercial units, designated or defined under law, to obtain 'consent to establish' and 'consent to operate'. There are generally three categories of industries under these regulations: Red (highly polluting), Orange and Green. The PCB duties include monitoring and surprise visits, taking samples and adopting other promotional steps such as the development of common facilities for discharge of effluents.

Some of the well-known problems of direct intervention by the government are:

(a) Agency and Information problems—The staff had no incentive to do the bidding of the Principals; there is little information available to the Principals on their actions and in fact little information even to the agents about the state of compliance or violations by the industry.

(b) Business has high incentives for generation of the by-product even though there may be no intention to do so; incentives are in terms of profits, some of which may be 'passed on' to agency staff, to the avoid penal action.

(c) The affected public has little motivation; individual activism does not result in individual gain and 'rational disinterest' is naturally the common response.

These issues of incentives and information pose difficult challenges in the regulation of public 'bads' like pollution.

Asymmetry of Actors' Incentives

Regulatory agencies also face peculiar governance issues as various stakeholders have different and sometimes conflicting interests and incentives.

Owners are interested in profits and may not be bothered about spillovers and externalities imposed on the society or may not find it profitable to comply with regulations. These problems of cost would especially bother highly competitive industries. An entrepreneur complying with regulations faces a typical dilemma—others will merrily make profits while he or she suffers the consequences in terms of reduced profits. It is true that there is an element of personal and social risk but as noted elsewhere, individuals mostly over rate their skills, competencies and abilities—in this case the ability to able to avoid punishment. The tendency is aggravated as gains are certain while the probability of a loss is small; the laws are so stringent that few can afford to comply.

The employees and staff of the establishments may themselves be affected by the spillovers of production and this issue has been covered in an earlier chapter concerning labour regulations. Employees can negotiate mutually beneficial arrangements provided the rights and obligations are clear and they may not have in that case, any reason to approach the government or the courts.

The public and the society in general is affected by the spillovers collectively but the process is gradual and not easily perceived (the well known analogy of the 'frog and the boiling water'), thus resulting in the citizens being mostly disinterested spectators. It is not worthwhile for any individual to take up the matter when he/she may not gain any advantage more than that of others.

The NGOs play an important role in this area. One need not go into the complexity of their motivations – whether out of altruism ('other regarding') or 'self regarding' notion of doing something worthwhile. The main problem, even if they are committed, is availability of timely and accurate information, especially as the affected public is disinterested and the polluters trying their best to obfuscate facts.

Regulatory departments have 'agency' problems which are further compounded by problems of information. An official may not be aware of the violations or if personally aware, may not, in the normal course, have any incentive to open Pandora's Box.

'Slow Poison'

Another problem in addressing pollution is the global dimensions of concentration of the CO_2 and other toxic gases that have effects beyond the local or even national frontiers. Generally humans rarely modify their behavior in response to problems unless they get clear and immediate signals. The impact of pollutants is in most cases gradual and unobtrusive, the problem we face with the green houses gases. People may find it difficult to attach any emotion to a cognitive appreciation of such problems and even respond by 'if it is slow poison, it must be very slow indeed' sort of skepticism.

Problems of Pollution Control

The approach appropriate for some other services discussed already may not therefore be applicable in the context of pollution control. For entrepreneurs, the costs of compliance with the regulations are substantial in terms of investment and running expenses. Unlike the area of crime against person and property, polluters may not leave a 'smoking gun' or *corpus delicti* in the course of violating the law. In any case the effects of pollution can, given some effort and expense, mostly be masked as the processes of production, contamination and treatment are carried out within the private domain — of manufacturers and entrepreneurs. And even in case a violation is brought to the notice of a regulatory agency by a whistle-blower, consequences can still be avoided due to agency problems, even if the Principals are committed, itself a rather shaky assumption. Enforcement agents and the public don't have information about the effectiveness of the decontamination equipment and even when information is provided by a whistleblower, it may not be possible to gather adequate evidence to prosecute the violators.

Options for bringing about desirable outcomes appear therefore to be limited. One is to provide on-site systems for gathering information regarding the pollutants generated/ treated and monitoring the information gathered, to the extent technology permits, instead of banking on ad hoc inspections and raids. In Punjab, the CCTV cameras, recently installed at the de-contamination plants of major units, are expected to provide information on a continuous basis; these are monitored on-line at the office of the enforcement agency. We found, however, that the monitoring systems are not operational 24x7 and therefore may not serve the purpose; considering the incentives working against such a system, it is unlikely that it will go beyond the pilot stage.

Devising Cooperative 'Frames'

Another possibility is to make it less costly and more convenient for the polluters to comply with the regulations instead of banking upon the deterrent of prosecution and punishment. This can be done for example by facilitating, through active coordination, setting up of de-contamination plants for a group of companies and possibly a little bit easing of the standards keeping in view the economics of such plants. As remarked by Benkler:[2] 'Convenience is a more important factor in determining compliance than material (dis)incentives. Fines may result in illegal dumping rather than compliance in case of home or roadside pick up of recyclables versus a central deposit point'. Social norms do work, but the main driver of motivation is generally convenience and expense/cost of the effort involved. In order to encourage compliance and cooperation, we need to take note of factors such as how burdensome or easy it is for individuals to act on their better instincts of compliance/cooperation. The present rules, tough and unforgiving as they are, seem designed instead to encourage socially harmful behaviour.

Information and Incentives

We don't mean to suggest that stringent laws and punishments do not work or that we should hope for a dramatic calamity to impress upon the public the urgency of the problem of pollution. It is just that when the line between right and wrong is thin, the regulations complex, and the measurements relative, there is enough scope for rationalization of the spillovers caused by productive activities undertaken by the industrial units. Probably the main instrument for bringing about better compliance is information. It need not be 'radical transparency' as suggested by Daniel Goleman,[3] that is, transparency right from resource to production to consumption to disposal. Information may all that is necessary to jog the conscience of all concerned in the hope that a spark of action may be ignited.

There are two sets of information that need to be in the public domain and can incentivize the players involved—enforcers, polluters, the public. One of these is information about the nature and quantum of pollution emitted by different industries, manufacturing units, towns and city inhabitants and so on. The second is information on outcomes. Much needs to be done in respect of these information sets. In India, the industrial units are required to send a report to the PCBs annually regarding details of production processes as well as the quantities of pollutants discharged by the industrial units. Only a negligible percentage of the establishments covered, however, send these reports at present and these are, in any case, rarely assessed and analysed. Similarly, the Urban Local Bodies (ULBs) are also required under law to send reports on the status of solid waste handling and similar issues but they also mostly default. Restructuring the disclosure and display of critical information would help in reducing information asymmetry among the stakeholders, provide information to all the stakeholders including the public, the NGOs, clients and the officials themselves, and incentivize the stakeholders, by bringing into the public domain, relevant information regarding the activities and contribution of the PCBs and the clients.

There is one more advantage of such information. It is not that every case of spillover or externality concerns undefined parties, the public. Innovations in legal practice have brought together the undefined mass of the affected through what are known as class action suits, as, for example, filed against the cigarette manufacturers in the USA. Similar actions are possible regarding pollution caused by mining and other extraction industries. More important, citizens need to know what impact the regulators are making, armed as they are with the panoply of stringent laws. They also need to give an account of their accomplishments, given the regulatory resources and the costs they impose on business and industry. Information is a critical weapon for the accountability of the regulatory agencies which are unlikely to have sufficient motivation on their own. It is difficult for the government departments to administer competing objectives, act on the basis of an optimum mix of development, growth, ecological and political objectives, and to balance the punitive and promotional roles. They tend to develop simple rules of the thumb and the simplest is to perform the routines, visit, inspect, and prosecute a limited number of polluters to demonstrate that they are active. That is why people in India have welcomed independent Green Tribunals.

Another option that operates on the principle of information and does not involve any compromise on the standards is to use the instrument of social motivation through 'naming and shaming' systems. This has been done successfully in the US, by displaying the pollutants emitted/discharged by the industry on the website of the concerned agency—known as the 'Toxic Release Inventory'. A simple display of this information and making it open to the public has resulted in substantial improvement even in the absence of any penal provisions. Such practices can have substantial impact, as also demonstrated by Diamond[4] in the case of illegal logging and destruction of forests.

Needless to say, the available economic and technological options also need to be tried (for example, carbon tax). Statutory and absolute prescriptions and prohibitions have made dramatic impacts—economic incentives in the case of sulphuric and nitric gases and penal restrictions in the case of fluorocarbons, leading to restoration of the hole in the ozone layer. Further, as remarked by Harford,[5] alternative technologies, say for power generation, also offer tremendous potential (a number of promising technologies are indicated by him). These economic and technological options have to be used where applicable, but we no longer appear to have such simple solutions available for our problems.

One also needs to consider carefully the impact of various 'nudges' enthusiastically provided by the regulators. A number of examples of regulatory 'nudges', which lead to perverse and counterproductive outcomes, have been given by Tim Harford[6] in *Adapt*. The Merton Rule devised in South West London mandated that new construction projects must generate 10 per cent of their energy needs, but was inappropriate for the congested areas in London. The European Union's Renewable Energy Directive mandates the member states to ensure that 10 per cent of the energy for transportation comes from renewable energy sources; this led to diversion of available lands from growing food to producing ethanol. Appropriate use of information would appear to be the main, and possibly the only weapon, left in the armoury of governance interventions, in addition, of course, to technology and economic incentives and signals. Aggressive interventions, mandates, and somewhat casually designed 'nudges' may only enrich the enforcers, add to the transaction costs of the owners and sometimes even generate perverse outcomes without making any impact on the social costs imposed by private businesses.

22

Corruption: The Moral of Incentives

Academic perspectives on corruption have shifted from efficiency theories in the 1970s and 80s to the view, popular now, about its toxic effects on the gross domestic product (GDP)[1] and other economic parameters of development. Refinements have been added by some academics by distinguishing between the impact of organized and centralized corruption on the one hand, and disorganized and polymorphic corruption on the other.[2] Alan Beattie[3] has assessed this comparative dimension in the trajectories of organized corruption in Indonesia under President Suharto, and of polymorphic corruption in Tanzania under President Nyerere. On the other hand, we have the simplistic but popular algorithms such as that of Robert Klitgaard:[4]

Corruption = monopoly + discretion – accountability.

The problem is that the ideal mix of zero monopoly + zero discretion—100% accountability or any other permutation, is never available in real life situations. One is not sure, for example, whether 100 per cent of accountability is enough to offset 50 per cent each of monopoly and discretion. It is also easy to trivialize such algorithms as Vikram Karve[5] has done by adding transparency on the credit side.

A separate chapter is being devoted to the specific attribute of corruption and it is the only exception to the framework adopted here of examining specific governance exchanges on the 'playgrounds' and 'battlefields' involving different players and public and private entities. The issue of corruption tends to dominate the discussions and discourse on good governance and the two terms are sometimes used interchangeably; there are few voices now advocating the efficiency aspects of corruption, a popular hypothesis till the 1980s. The second reason is that corruption is mostly not an act of omission but of commission and tends to structure and affect the 'play of the game' and its outcomes, unlike sports where (mostly) such acts take place off the field. That leads to the third reason. We believe that corruption is best understood in the context of specific interactions and their unique context, rather than in terms of simplistic models like the one provided by Klitgaard.

Speed Money/Assembly Line Corruption

Generally corruption is distinguished in terms of speed money (bribery in the nature of tipping) and big-ticket corruption. The former mostly relates to alpha services. I prefer to call it 'assembly line' corruption—it is 'orderly', 'organized', 'predictable', and mostly a function of the transaction costs involved in exchanges among citizens and the 'cutting edge' officials. A study[6] estimates the annual volume of such corruption in eleven basic services such as land administration, police, civic services, judiciary and school education, to be over rupees 2000 crore in India. The number of households involved in giving bribes is estimated in the same study at over 145 million. Debroy and Bhandari provide estimates of corruption in the case of different alpha services, based on reports in a newspaper.[7] My assessment is that alpha services in India involve approximately one transaction per household per year, the transaction costs are more material than formal fees and the average incidence of bribery is Rs. 500 (excluding property sales). The total transaction costs based on the national estimates extrapolated from the Punjab data would be approximately Rs. 12000 crores. Bribes in these cases mostly originate from the potential created by transaction costs, which are themselves a function of rules and processes. It appears that a transaction-based perspective for governance interactions may be appropriate for most of the areas which involve petty corruption or speed money or *tukkap* (money for rice cakes in the Korean language). Imagine a simple application for a copy of the revenue record—*jamabandi*— being handed over at the Tehsil, being sent to the Patwari (who happens not to have any fixed office), the matter then personally pursued by the citizen and the papers got sent back to Tehsil for issue (and this was happening in a state with digitized land records—the ostensible reason being that only a Patwari is authorized under rules made by the State to attest the copy); or a birth certificate being sent by the single window Suvidha Centre to the Chief Medical Officer, who is the District Registrar, the only officer authorized to issue the certificate, even though the Suvidha Centre has direct access to the digital records and can easily authenticate and issue the certificate through a single window process. The parties would naturally minimize their costs on repeated visits and waiting by facilitation payments. Transaction costs can go up to 50 to 100 times the fee in the case of these basic services. Surely corruption appears to be a more efficient and economic solution under the present 'rules of the game', as it is mostly a function of and is limited by transaction costs as will be apparent from the preceding sections.

Structure of Corruption in Public Services

This area was covered in the two IDC studies referred earlier. In urban areas in Punjab, bribery is quite common for the resolution of complaints (64 per cent of the respondents) and over 60 per cent report that bribery is in the nature of extortion. Over 50 per cent of the respondents perceive corruption to be disorganized and unstructured. Bribery as well as patronage/ *sifarish* is believed to be necessary for getting any work done or service delivered. About 54 per cent of respondents felt that there had been increase in bribery over time. In rural areas of the three states also, bribery was believed to have increased over time. The Panchayati Raj Institutions (PRIs) fared better with 68 per cent of respondents believing that there is no corruption in the Panchayat institutions vis-a-vis only 22 per cent in case of government. What seemed to bother most of the respondents is not so much the speed money or 'assembly line' corruption, as the harassment, especially in the case of complicated regulations like those for approval of constructions and award of contracts by the public agencies.

Demise of Assembly Line Corruption

In the case of Alpha services where the incentives or disincentives are moderate, with little competition or exclusion, corruption is mostly small ticket, and mainly a function of transaction costs as anticipated, apprehended, and (possibly) avoided through this route. Even in case of Beta and (most of) Gamma services, the distinguishing feature of interactions and exchanges is a lack of *mens rea* on part of citizens/corporates and to a large extent even of officials, who get what we may call *dasturi*—something which is customary and not very burdensome, assuming that it saves more than proportionate transaction costs (there is otherwise little motivation to pay). For example, if somebody wants a licence, without having to learn driving (as indicated earlier however this is unlikely, as the person's own safety is also at stake), the maximum he/she may be prepared to pay would not exceed transaction costs, added to the cost and expense of taking driving lessons. Traffic violations provide an ideal illustration. When offences were not compoundable, costs of having to appear in court, et cetera, mattered to the public. After the authority for compounding was given to the police, limits on bribery have been set by the amount of the prescribed compounding fee. The potential for extortion, therefore, in such cases, is limited by the transaction cost curve. In case of the Beta services, transaction costs are limited by the cost of technical violations—maintenance of registers and returns or non provision of facilities for labour, at a level probably stopping short of legal penalties and of course by the fact that enforcing agents rarely have enough information or evidence or commitment to proceed to the logical outcomes of honest enforcement. Lack of information similarly limits the options for Gamma services—for example, the environment laws—apart from the problem of 'rational disinterest' in cases concerning the public at large.

These transaction costs have almost disappeared in many states in India or are getting minimized. This is because of the adoption of the rules and processes appropriate to the digital resources and technologies now available. Once the transaction costs disappear, so would the speed money exchanges in respect of the Alpha services. With accelerating digitization, doorstep delivery windows, Common Service Centres (CSCs) and on-line delivery, transaction costs and consequently the costs to avoid or minimize them are likely to get substantially reduced. More and more citizens are acquiring personal identity documents which constitute at present the bulk of the demand for alpha services—birth, domicile and income certificates, ration cards and so on. We found to our surprise that even an innocuous service—the UID—may not be free from corruption. The poor especially may be paying bribes to get some identity document that is a must for the issue of the UID. Hopefully the process will be completed in a couple of years. Process compression is also likely to take place in areas like approval of buildings and driving licences, with the adoption of alternative models of delivery, third party enforcement and outsourcing, as indicated earlier. Unnecessary procedures like affidavits are being done away with. More and more of the states in India are mandating service delivery standards (under the *Right to Service Laws*) and even in the absence of re-engineering of processes, the 'street level' bureaucrats liable for timely delivery are, one can be sure, likely to be inventive, innovative and adaptable enough, to extend the argument of Lipsky,[8] to short circuit processes, given the mandated thresholds in terms of time limits and the (dis)incentive of fines, provided, of course, the governments don't persist with the 'jumping genes' interventions as indicated earlier.

Social Learning and Corruption

The only puzzling phenomenon appears to be the speed money corruption (generally ½% of sale value) in the case of registration of purchase and sale of property, an alpha service. A small percentage of the purchase price is paid informally on the registration of sale deeds almost all over India, despite excellent initiatives taken in simplifying rules, elimination of discretion of officials in challenging the purchase price and mandatory registration on the day of presentation, and even though the purchase may be clean and above board. Originally, the discretion was vast as the collectors' rate for property and lands was not fixed by government. This discretion of the officials has been eliminated. Structures on land to be sold do leave some scope for discretion in valuation—one can question the quality and the year of construction et cetera. Innovative solutions, like acceptance of valuers' reports, have been adopted in many states. Punjab has simplified matters by treating the value of construction as a specified percentage of the collector's rate for the area covered. One major reason for corruption in these services appears to be the ubiquitous presence of property agents in these transactions; they have regular dealings with the officers and may sometimes be involved in fishy deals and do need official goodwill. In any case, they have no problem with incentives; it is the purchaser who pays. One hopes that such informal customs—a sort of 'herd mentality', or perhaps peer pressure—will also disappear in due course.

Assembly Line Corruption: Purchases and Contracts

Petty corruption in the case of the alpha services is likely to disappear with time, digitization of services, online delivery and so on. Contracts and purchase of goods and services by the government agencies however also involve transaction costs and petty corruption. These transaction costs relate to information and enforcement of goods contracts (for example, timely payment by government) whereas 'hard corruption' is more in the nature of a *quid pro quo* rather than a facilitative payment; incentives of the suppliers don't substantially change, though risks do. Incentives of the public agents, however, depend on different factors in the two situations. In case of assembly line corruption, they tend to strike compromises below the optimum—depending on their personality, moral commitment and prevalent social norms. A small minority, blessed with confidence about their cleverness (mostly people over estimate their abilities!), may exploit the potential to the hilt. Others are happy with 'normal' behaviour and while ensuring compliance with contract obligations by the supplier, quietly pocket the customary commissions – 5 to 10% of cost in major projects, which are considered by contractors as transaction costs. The amount is of course shared among a number of official functionaries. This is probably common even in the corporate sector. Purchase departments are notorious all over—from army at the top to the purchase clerk buying office equipment for the company, to the librarian getting a fixed commission on purchase of books. These customary commissions are a benchmark the suppliers in any trade have to accept as a condition for operating in the market and can differ depending on specific markets—power plants, paper, army rations and so on. A supplier takes it to be a transaction cost (though recovered later) for entering and operating in the market. Post contract transaction costs incurred by the suppliers of goods and services can be viewed as a substitute for the costs avoided—waiting for bills to be passed, payments to be received et cetera. These facilitation costs are incurred to avoid uncertain costs/losses due to delay in payments and of course, vindictive monitoring; it is impossible for a student to be so perfect as to avoid caning from a determined teacher—at least till it was banned.

Transaction costs involved in contracts and purchase of goods and services, unlike noneconomic exchanges in the Alpha services, are therefore likely to continue; these are moderate and above all, pass through. It is the buyer who ultimately bears the cost; they are already loaded in the contract offered. The route to minimizing such transaction costs lies within the (government) organization; it can provide disincentives, say by providing for interest on delayed payments. On the other hand it is pointless for the government to intervene through rules for suppliers by, for example, prohibiting employment of middlemen, as in the infamous Bofors deal or in a Power utility.

'Gaming' the Rules

A Power Utility in Punjab took inspiration from the Government of India rules for prohibiting employment of middlemen by the suppliers, and banned the practice of appointment of local Agents—mostly called 'Advisors'—by the suppliers of equipment; the Advisors were considered a conduit for speed money and facilitation payments and (it was thought) also affected smooth procurement due to constant lobbying. The firms found an ingenious solution; most of the Agents were designated as Directors; a company employee is not a middleman!

Purchase of goods and services by the government is thus also an area for small ticket corruption. Private sector addresses this problem through long term bilateral contracts and supply agreements with selected suppliers/buyers, in place of the practice common earlier, of producing in-house everything a firm needs for the final product. Transaction costs are eliminated by integrating the supplier's incentives within the buyer organization, which is the rationale for integration of economic transactions within the 'firm'[9]. Government agencies are not permitted to do so and whenever they do venture (as the recent Tatra trucks and similar cases show), the organization and its officials come to grief sooner or later. The safest strategy for officials is to invite competitive offers. The cycle of transaction costs and speed money corruption therefore is likely to continue in government contracts and purchases. In the case of alpha services which are by nature 'transactional', however, the focus on speed money corruption is 'putting the cart before the horse'; this type of corruption is simply a function of transaction costs.

Big-ticket/Custom made Corruption

That leaves the other area prone to corruption, relating not to transaction costs but the economic value of the what is to be exchanged—contracts and purchase and sale of goods and services. 'Big-ticket' corruption or custom made corruption[10] (I prefer the latter term), can be distinguished from speed money or facilitation payments described above as 'assembly line' to indicate the context dependence of the latter. *The India Corruption Report* (cited above) expresses the hope that the elimination of speed money and petty corruption will also lead to reduction in big-ticket corruption. This is unlikely as the two operate in different dimensions. Unlike other governance interactions, goods and services contracts are typical economic transactions as in the market; rules are set by the government, whether as buyer or seller (through auctions/two stage bids/open book bids, sealed bids et cetera). Generally, in the private bilateral exchanges, both of the parties gain; the exchange will not take place otherwise. This may, however, not be the case where the government is one of the parties, for various reasons (agency problem, lack of incentives, monitoring). This area of corruption provides different sets of problems specific to the public agencies.

Cronyism, Monopolies, and Procurement

The basic processes of procurement have to exclude the obvious route of monopoly suppliers, as happened in Indonesia (under Suharto's Presidency) in the case of toll roads and leases for forests. The allotment of coalmines on the basis of the memorandum of understanding (MoU) route in India is already under scrutiny. We have seen the fate of the MoU route adopted for attracting the Foreign Direct Investment (FDI) for power generation in the 1990s; the experiment failed miserably and has been formally buried. With urgent economic pressures for developing and exploiting all possible natural resources, the potential for 'rents' is likely to disappear, as has happened in the West and even in countries like South Africa and Botswana. That leaves the field generally open for adoption of standards for transparent bidding and auction systems, governed by elaborate rules providing for a level playing field for parties, open house briefings/tenders/bids, properly conducted negotiations, and so forth. Residual problems of opacity due to manual handling will be addressed through e-procurement systems. India already has a draft of the elaborate law on Public Procurement based on international practices. The 2G spectrum, coal and gas blocks in India and sand mines in the northern states may have been practically the *Last of the Mohicans* in the noncompetitive allotment of privilege and 'rents' in India.

One should then expect such transactions to be above board in due course, but it may not be so simple. It is widely believed that the federal government in the USA pays much more than market prices, despite very open and transparent procurement practices. Only the outcome is believed to be an amazing failure! James Q Wilson has tried to put the record straight in respect of two frequently quoted instances of such imprudent purchases

—of hammers at US$ 465 a piece and a coffee maker at US$ 3000;[11] the belief, however, is widespread. Any observer of, or participant in, the process of award of contracts and purchases by government agencies in India, all of whom follow elaborate and transparent procedures of bidding and allotment, is aware of the under ground machinations going on. It will be a rare deal where corruption is limited to negotiating the transaction costs. The problem of big-ticket corruption is on a different plane. The rules can rarely be made corruption proof in the face of the potential of huge profit and costs, objectives of the suppliers and motives of the 'rationally self interested' public agents.

Auctions are no solution either. Auctions can be subject to gaming and of course collusion, depending upon information and incentive intensity of suppliers. The example of easy gaming is provided by the New Zealand government's auction of the radio spectrum. It adopted the sophisticated Vickrey auction rule (the highest bidder pays the second highest price); in one case this led to a successful bidder (bid of NZ$ 7 million) getting the deal at NZ$ 5000 only, the second bid price![12] The difficulty of getting over such problems is illustrated by the (successful) experience of auction of airwaves in the UK, as indicated by the author. Further, as Landsburg remarks, there is always the possibility of a wrong choice being made in the rules, even without any *mala fide,* while adopting the auction system.[13]

Incentives of Suppliers

A number of factors regarding the incentives of private suppliers, especially in major contracts need to be kept in view. First, there is rarely 'perfect competition'. The number of suppliers, as in the case of defence equipment, is limited; some times these are mostly branded products or company specific technologies for similar functions (for example, turbine for a power plant). Evaluation is a complex process and the lowest cost is rarely the cost effective option. One can imagine the difficulty of buying a car on the basis of the lowest tender—an almost impossible task. Each car has pluses and minuses, even given fixed specifications. You can imagine the difficulty of having to decide on a boiler or a turbine or a coal handling package for a power plant, among a limited number of reputed suppliers (these are expensive units to set up), promising the same outputs and functions, with somewhat differing technologies and product features. All the shortlisted suppliers have got experience and appropriate certificates, prices are closely matched, except when a vague supplier indulges in a 'dumping' practice—offering a price others cannot match, and which the buyer knows is not a serious offer. Shortlisting of parties has also to be somewhat broad based to ensure competition. The purchaser is thus caught in a difficult situation —compromising the project if the lowest offer is accepted, or putting his or her neck on the block for vigilance and similar agencies to chop at! For hindsight auditors and evaluators, there is no difference between 'slips', 'mistakes', and violations;[14] it is difficult to prove intention. In any case, Section 13 (d) of the Prevention of Corruption (PCA) Act in India dispenses with the issue of intention. Add to this the disposition of the professionals responsible for deciding: they have their favourites, which may be mostly based on contacts and incentives, but sometimes also due to a sincere conviction about the relative quality of one or the other product or supplier.

It is tempting for suppliers to informally divide territories and contracts for similar reasons. In the lottery trade in India for example, the limited number of bidders used to informally divide territories (at least 20 years ago when I had occasion to observe it closely) and decide who would get the bid in a particular case; the state lottery contracts are dominated by a limited number of parties making bids in different names. The only thing they would lose by walking out on their offers was the earnest money; there was no alternative but to accept the lowest *available* offer, the top lowest having collusively withdrawn. It is mostly impossible to prove collusion. Informal price agreements are common for items involving a limited number of suppliers. Adam Smith's observation, about the traders 'conspiring', continues to be relevant today. In case of major contracts, a company's survival may be at stake forcing even 'good' entrepreneurs to engage in corruption as the 1960s

Lockheed example shows; the CEO of Lockheed admitted to paying a bribe of US$ 12 million as his 'moral and ethical considerations gave way to commercial gains for the company'[15] which badly needed the contract to survive.

Incentives of Government Agents

So far as the government agents are concerned, there is little incentive for them to go out of their way to ensure competition. Even given that they have no vested interests and financial incentives, there is little to be gained by an official by raising problems occasioned by genuine efforts to promote competition. Rigid hierarchies ensure that a wooden compliance with the rules is the only feasible way out, given the preferences (even assuming there is no *malafide*) of the different agents involved in processing a contract. Top decision makers are rarely qualified professionals; in case of major purchases, a Minister—especially a very honest one—will go by the book. The main attempt at the top levels is to avoid direct responsibility by not questioning the processing of tenders and refraining from imposing own judgment; the top bosses in any case don't have enough information and expertise to be able to upset the apple cart. Needless to say, sometimes this apple cart is, in many cases, loaded by the very same top levels and in these situations processing is leveraged by informal signals, all off the record.

Further, not only is a contract never 'complete', there is the problem of valuation of complex offers and 'loading' for differential features of a product offered. Some of these may not be even amenable to empirical verification. A power utility used to buy transformers after 'loading' for transformation losses; the losses however were accepted as claimed by suppliers; there was no facility to check!

Complexity of contracts, difficulty of incomplete contracts, the inevitability of transaction costs involved in delayed clearances, inspections and payments, high incentives for collusion, the overriding profit motives of private parties coupled with interest on the part of at least some officials in the hierarchy to make money (or at least to get their personal preferences for pet brands accepted), lack of commitment in the part of officials to apply the rules in the light of expected results, the difficulty of designing rules to address the strong material incentives of principals of one party (supplier) and agents of another (government)—all these make it almost impossible to take the correct decision in the interest of government. Even in cases where a decision later proves to have been right, it may be difficult to avoid criticism in the immediate present.

In major purchases, there is also the problem of proximate principals—Executive Director of a company, Secretary/ Minister in a department, who have, as citizens, a very small share in the national or corporate gain; the gains are disproportionate and there is little incentive individually to economize on contracts—the general public is after all, the Principal. Big-ticket corruption can thus occur irrespective of whether rules are followed. Prima facie this area seems to defy any solution, given these constraints and the structure of incentives of the parties to procurement/sale.

It appears that the government agencies can either comply with the rules or get 'value for money' but rarely both. Rules are easily subject to 'gaming' as indicated above. It is our economist brothers who have popularized 'game theory' among rational economic actors, and the suppliers can easily shift from a competitive to a cooperative or collusive frame. The question is, who are the officials who in this situation have an interest in winning the game for the government *vis-a-vis* the private party. Official hierarchy is an amorphous matrix consisting of politicians, nonprofessional executives, layers of technical professionals, finance people, audit, and so on. The answer is obvious; the outcomes are likely to be in favour of the private parties with strong interests, as Mancur Olson[16] has demonstrated.

Controlling Corruption: The Market Solution

An interesting perspective is provided by Johan Lambsdorff.[17] He brings out the problems of 'zero tolerance' and difficulty of preventing corruption through ethical training and similar activities which are costly and time consuming and subject to gaming even in respect of transparency, which can sometimes facilitate corruption ('bid rigging can be facilitated by introducing transparency at the wrong stage of procurement and tendering'). He refers approvingly to a 'tangible construction market' for public procurement organized in China, where a '*mixture of transparency and obfuscation is fruitfully employed to minimize corruption*' (for example, experts don't know which project they have to evaluate and are selected randomly). He advocates a micro analysis of criminal activities and a focus on the where and how of specific corrupt transactions, and addressing corruption through a strategy of the 'invisible foot (cf. 'invisible hand' of Adam Smith) by making use of the corrupt actors' self interest and their capacity to betray each other, and bringing about honest and efficient outcomes in the process. The problem is how to do so? And who is to do so? The answer is difficult due to the agency problems mentioned and the 'invisible foot' is unlikely to be a successful strategy. While some interesting applications are possible as indicated in case of the Beta regulations, harnessing the competing objectives of different actors to bring about socially productive outcomes may need a visible 'kick' instead.

'Nudges' and Corrupt Behaviour

New methods are being tried to tackle the problem of customized or 'big-ticket' corruption. Stiglitz[18] is optimistic and appreciative of developments such as providing information to the public on the school funds in Uganda and oil revenues in Nigeria. These instances however do not seem to have resulted in any substantial change in the ranking of these countries in the Governance Index of the World Bank or the Corruption Perception Index (CPI) of The Transparency International. Isolated successful interventions (for example, the possibility or threat of external audit in the case of road construction in Indonesia[19]) appear to have limited application. External agencies are either integrated into the game or suitable gaming strategies devised to neutralize them.

In any case, most of these best practices tend to undergo *apoptosis* with the departure of their champions. On the other hand, incentives for reversion to old practices are rather strong – a natural 'regression' to the bad old mean! One of the insights which behavioural economics has given us is that cost benefit analysis and the probability of getting caught in particular, does not seem to have much influence on dishonesty in small matters: 'Our internal honesty monitor is active only when we contemplate big transgressions'.[20] This indicates the futility of the policy of zero tolerance of speed money and similar aberrations. And of course the frame of the situation makes a difference. A group asked to write down as many of the Ten Commandments as they could recall, cheated much less in an experiment[21] even through there was no chance of getting caught! A 'moral frame' made a difference. In practical life, however, it is difficult to devise such frames. The scene of action is far away from the ethical 'nudges' in the classrooms and 'integrity pledges', signed by staff, lie forgotten in the executive suites.

Some experts dispute the relevance of regulations even for narcotics and would like the trade to be legalized and have the problem resolved through the market solutions. Not going that far, and in view of the difficulty indicated above, the issue is whether 'nudges' may be effective for corrupt behavior, as even economists agree that it may be difficult to develop an appropriate market for the problem of corruption. Some 'nudges' can be useful. Imagine *Nineteen Eighty Four* of George Orwell; everybody is being watched; no crime can be committed without being recorded. Rules are needed for relevant information to be provided and made available in the public domain, as for example is done in the case of information provided to customers on the price of goods and the manufacturing date. Enforcing the ban on the sale of a drug after the expiry date is not a big problem; information is available, right on the package. In the case of contracts and big-ticket corruption, simple information on the assets of the government officials, if made available to the public/ whistleblowers, might work in India, a country which, most of us feel, seems to be characterized by a lack of 'social capital'! One can 'trust' the third parties—whistleblowers, compulsive complainants, affected parties (parties denied contracts) and their incentives—to do the rest, 'the invisible foot' working!

Apprehend or Prevent: Asset Investigation

An appropriate course may be to delink the issue of rule compliance from outcomes and treat the two differently—the former for administrative monitoring and the latter for criminal action. As indicated, a violation of the rules may sometime be necessary to bring about a good outcome and rule compliance will, as likely as not, bring about an inferior outcome when, say, an orchestrated lowest price offer is accepted. Sophistication of processes or procedures will not ensure that corruption will not occur. Solution lies not in establishing more and more of rules and institutions, oversight/monitoring/audit, but *ex post* investigation and the evidence of 'money bags'. It is no doubt difficult to gather such evidence in the Indian context; the economy is flush with black money but the task is not impossible. It may be easier to address corruption, once this unnecessary complication of dealing simultaneously with violation of rules and corruption is taken care of. Obviously, massive payments cannot be detected 'red handed'. The law, however, provides a solution—asset investigation of the suspected officials and proving that the assets are disproportionate to the income earned.

It is puzzling why this provision is not used more often; at present, this is invoked mostly in cases where specific charges of corruption are made. This may not happen in most of the situations where the rules are complied with, both sides—officials and the suppliers—are happy, and the government loss does not pinch a citizens' pocket/or taxpayer directly. One has only to thank the whistleblowers in such cases. From our personal experience, more than 75 per cent of the 'wet' departments' officials—sales tax and excise, police (SHOs and above), Revenue (top to bottom), Transport, Works Departments (Junior Engineers (JEs) and above), if investigated, won't be able to explain their assets. Open and shut case! But who is to do it? On the other hand, the conduct rules for officials create perverse incentives by making it easy to explain away disproportionate assets. An innocuous looking amendment was made long back that officers don't even need to report assets to government in case these are acquired by spouses having independent sources of income! The beauty of assets in the modern economy is that the evidence does not decay (and even if it does, leaves traces like the radio-active isotopes) but rather accumulates. And the evidence does not need to be collected from the scene of crime —the crime is noted much after the crime or offence is committed. The evidence of assets is somewhat like the immortal DNA fingerprints. The only complication is created by transactions that culminate in the stashing of assets abroad, but most of the John Does of corruption keep them right in India. In a way you may consider it unfair to target such middle level 'fish' of the corrupt world, the middle level government officials, but each line of attack is independent and one does not preclude the other. The Law provides a simple method for 'big-ticket' corruption: investigate assets and income and the disparity therein. It is unlikely that a 'decoy customer' method, useful for vigilance raids on the lowly functionaries will work for the proximate principals; the latter have a number of agents to take care of the logistics of handling, disposal and parking of such funds.

Disclosure of Public Officials' Assets

One pre-requisite in this strategy is to empower the whistleblowers, complainants and the NGOs through public information on the assets of officials as reported to government. Internationally, disclosure of assets of the public officials to the public is a well-accepted mechanism (the USA for example has the *Ethics in Government Act* 1978) but surprisingly even the IInd ARC in India has maintained silence on this. We need, in addition, a law on freezing and confiscation of illegally acquired assets; this is reported to be on the anvil. And of course, given all the problems and massive incentives, an independent authority is needed to investigate and prosecute. An independent authority with powers of investigation appears necessary as the vigilance wings (mostly) get monthly payments from the 'wet' departments' officials and mostly the traps are motivated and in inverse proportion to the opportunities available for corruption. In the case of 'big-ticket' or 'custom made' corruption, interventions need to be made through *ex post* measures—'shoves' as well as 'nudges' as in case of crimes, rather then invoking moral values.

Institution of Transfers and Corruption

In the countries of South Asia, the institution of transfer of government officials adds another dimension to the problem of 'big-ticket' or custom made or the RNA[22] corruption. Wade[23] had 30 years back formulated the hypothesis that the 'transfer industry' is the lynch pin of corruption. Any observer or insider knows this to be true but while there has not been much follow up research on this aspect, one can venture to state that the links are fortuitous: not everybody participates in the game. If that were to happen, political gains of the 'transfer industry' would soon be competed away.

Impact on GDP and GHP

Economists describe transaction costs and corruption as transfer payments which don't therefore affect national income. Psychologists,[24] however, have shown that the disutility of loss may be two to three times that of gain; losing rupees 100 may be equivalent to the utility from a gain of rupees 300. The parties incurring such costs thus detract from the total sum of happiness or utility even within a macro economic frame. This negative utility gets added on top of the negative experiences mentioned earlier. The gross happiness product (GHP) of the nation is definitely shifted downwards due to costs of corruption, whatever its impact on the gross national product (GNP).

Rules, 'Shoves' and 'Nudges'

Sophisticated rules for the award of the government contracts are not likely to have any impact on the big-ticket corruption. Incentives of various actors and parties are too strong and their gaming strategies always one step ahead of rules. It is better, as in crime, to go by the fingerprints left on the scene of crime leading to the assets and life style of specific officials. The auction of airwaves in the UK, mentioned above, is an excellent example of a successful bidding process but it was conducted by reputed economists who took it as a challenge; the government agencies are rarely equipped, or have the knowledge and incentives for that to happen frequently and generally.

The components of an effective frame for addressing corruption in case of the assembly line/speed money would thus be elimination/reduction of transaction costs. In the case of 'custom made'/'big-ticket' corruption, preventive measures are mostly irrelevant for 'humans'. The focus needs to be on 'shoves'—sanctions and other *ex post* measures. Supportive 'nudges' would be mostly negative - independent investigation, public disclosure of the assets of politicians and officials and incentivizing whistleblowers and interested parties.

PART V

Alpha and Omega of Public Services

We cover in this part, an Omega service—food for the poor—as also a miscellany of rules and institutions across a wide range of governance interactions, and conclude with some suggestions about the redesign of the micro rules and institutions relevant to the governance interactions in the course of exchange and delivery of public services.

23

Poverty Alleviation: Harnessing 'Wisdom of the (Poor) Crowds'

Poverty alleviation is a major component of the Millennium Development Goals (MDGs) and this area continues to get both resources and attention, even while there is pressure for the abandonment of welfare policies (social security, 'health for all') for the populations at large. It is also no longer enough to provide for Work Houses as in the nineteenth-century Britain with their strict regime of diet ('six ounces of bread and a pint of gruel for supper'[1]) and the prison-like regime, which the poor sometimes had to choose, instead of staying out and starving. By the end of the nineteenth century, however, 'a feeling began to grow that life's losers deserved better'.[2] Some welfare schemes such as disability allowance, child allowance, orphanage homes address specific handicaps of the vulnerable sections and seek to protect them and prevent exploitation as they may not, for some reason of incapacity, be able to take care of their interests; they may not be considered rational agents fully responsible for their choices, admittedly an exception even accepted by the Chicago School; this is listed as the fourth duty of government by Friedman:[3] 'duty to protect members of the community who cannot be regarded as responsible individuals.' These challenged groups, whether involved in voluntary or involuntary social and economic exchanges, present problems different from those of the 'rational agents' voluntarily participating in exchanges (consumers) or production (labour in the case of industry regulations). Governance in the case of Beta regulations, as we have seen, seems to support Friedman's[4] remark that 'every government measure bears, as it were, a smoke stack on its back', causing governance failure though unintended consequences of such interventional regulations. On the other hand, the Omega services are concerned with classes and groups who admittedly need state assistance and intervention. There are a number of programmes In India—Mahatma Gandhi National Rural Employment Guarantee Act —(MNREGA), targeted public distribution system (TPDS), housing (Indira Awaas Yojna), sanitation, health insurance, and micro credit tied to the status of the families as Below Poverty Line (BPL) families. This chapter deals with one of the most important measures—food for the poor.

There have been intense debates over what constitutes the poverty line; various formulations have been proposed and adopted from time to time. There is no problem in adopting any formulation for estimation of the poor—whether based on the NSS Surveys of household expenditure or even a simple criterion of income per day—now about $1.25 in the purchasing power parity (PPP) terms. The Oxford Poverty and Human Development Initiative at the University of Oxford has come up with a Multidimensional Poverty Index[5] (MPI) based on selected indicators of deprivation in basic amenities, living conditions, sanitation, education, health, et cetera. The poor constitute 41 per cent of the population in India on the basis of $ 1.25 income (PPP) criterion and 57 per cent on the basis of the MPI.[6] The problem, however, is identification and selection and, for example, properly identifying all of the 57 per cent of population in a vast country. Moreover as remarked, 'measuring poverty is not the same as alleviating it'.[7] Identification and selection of the poor, irrespective of the criteria adopted—income or the MPI—is not an easy task and a major 'governance' problem in the case of the poverty alleviation programmes continues to be the mechanisms and institutions for identification and selection of the poor.

'Poor' Selection: Rules and Processes

Governance interaction with the poor is at two stages—the process of selection/inclusion within the target group—the BPL, and the transfer of material benefits—supply of foodgrains or whatever.

There has been little focus on the issue of who and how to select, as compared to the issues of what the poverty line should be, its measurement, benefits and similar issues of policy. The selection process, however, is a key governance issue. How do you select? What information is available? How inclusive, participatory, objective and fair the processes are, and whether effective grievance redress systems are available. The systems for inclusion/selection of the target groups have changed over time—from the simple criterion of per capita income/consumption to the complex 13-point criteria in the year 2002; probably another one is under way, based on a multi-dimensional poverty index. The procedures and processes have changed over time with increasing voice in selection given to the Gram Sabhas; the BPL lists are required to be approved in these meetings. In the 2002 survey in Punjab, the officials conducted the survey and devised a cut off (eligibility on a 52 point scale) at thirteen points, so as not to exceed the ceiling, that is, the poverty estimates for the state indicated by the Planning Commission! The Gram Sabha voice consisted of 'ayes' to the numbers qualifying this cut off, whatever its own appreciation and information about the poor in the village. Officials involved in the exercise practically decided all the vital issues—the number of poor in a village, who is to be given the BPL card and approval of the gram sabha was mostly therefore a formality.

While the GoI is still deliberating on the identification systems for the Food Security Act, now proposed in place of the TPDS, many states have taken up surveys for updating the BPL lists, based on income or other criteria. Generally the system of selection of the BPL families consists of forms being filled in by the applicants, endorsed/verified either by independent NGOs, or by the government officials, and the lists are placed for decision in the Gram Sabha meetings. There is a provision of grievance redress by an authorized officer for the Antodaya scheme—selecting the poorest of the poor—and a merit list is also to be prepared[8]. This is however not done in the case of the BPL families. At some point of time, the Block Samities in Punjab were authorized to entertain complaints from the excluded poor but now that authority is vested with an officer at the district level. Grievance redress has mostly been a ritual, however, in view of the limit on the total number of BPL families for the state and consequently for the districts and so on.

The present system of selection/identification appears to be riddled with misdirection and inefficiency. The complex thirteen point criterion of the year 2002 stresses the capacity even of the well meaning survey agencies. The family circumstances as reflected in the criteria can vary from day to day. An out of school child may get admitted in school. There are problems also with multipoint criteria, such as the MPI. Poor families, which may be better informed or motivated, and choose to make some sacrifice to build a toilet or enroll a child in school, would tend to get excluded in the 2002 type survey.[9] One problem is that nobody knows whether there is any correspondence between the poor identified on basis of the multiple criteria and the simpler ones based on income and household expenditure.

Affluent nations generally use a relative poverty measure; this is typically set at 50/60 per cent of the median income.[10] Even though there are problems with the year-to-year variation in this indicator, caused by illness, unemployment, et cetera, for the moment 'income remains the most useful measure for assessing progress.'[11] Even this simple criterion poses problems in the Indian context. A study[12] indicates that the proportion of wrongly excluded (from BPL list) households is 44 per cent whereas that of the households wrongly included is 33 per cent. The Rural Governance Study,[13] which surveyed over 500 respondents from three adjoining villages, one village in each state, highlights perceptions of the poor regarding the selection processes. About 57.8 per cent of even the BPL cardholders view the process as unfair; the non-BPL respondents have a much higher percentage; 37.8 per cent of the BPL families believe that 25 per cent of the Non BPL families are wrongfully included; over 40 per cent of respondents believe that 40 per cent of the BPL families are wrongly excluded. Studies even by the Planning Commission indicate similar problems. Evaluation of performance of the TPDS in March 2005 by the Planning

Commission indicates the quantum of wrong selection (inclusion and exclusion) to be 57 per cent. A November 2009 Planning Commission report shows that 40 per cent of households (APL + BPL combined) had been issued wrong ration cards.[14] Jean Dreze and Amartya Sen[15] refer to three independent national surveys—the National Family Health Survey, the National Sample Survey and the India Human Development Report—all of which indicate that about half of all poor households in India did not have a BPL card in 2005. The need of improving procedures of selection has also been pointed out in various forums.[16]

The State of Haryana conducted a fresh survey of the BPL families in 2009–10; this was based on the income criterion and conducted by independent NGOs. A review ordered by the Courts, however, as per newspapers reports, has found the quantum of wrong selection to be 25 to 50 per cent in some districts. The fact that governments have not been able to make proper identification and selection is one of the main reasons for the argument that in the Indian conditions, food subsidy should be universal; in fact over 70 per cent coverage is envisaged under the Food Security Bill now passed by the Parliament. This extension of the rather tight 'starvation line' is expected to lead to improvement in proper identification of the poor and would, it is hoped, minimize political pressure for extending the lists and the numbers. Even though, however, huge resources may need to be provided (over Rs. 1.25 lakh crores) under the Food Security Act, substantial population (approximately 50 per cent in urban and 30 per cent in rural areas) will still be excluded and the issues of targeting and selection are not likely to go away.

Selection Process, Actors and Incentives

One can look perhaps at the processes of identification and selection in the context of incentives and behaviour of various parties engaged in the transaction—the Gram Panchayat and the Gram Sabha members, persons who want to be included (whether eligible or not) and the non-poor who form (at least in the case of Punjab) the majority who would have a decisive voice in the Gram Sabha, if properly convened and organized. This majority of Gram Sabha members would have no personal interest in the outcome except, may be, for transient clannish or clientelistic preferences. They are not in the hunt and therefore 'rationally disinterested' as Mancur Olson[17] would put it. Opinion leaders including Panchayat members are likely to function in a 'public choice' mode, supporting persons who may be politically or personally helpful. Thus the village assembly, even if capable of making an objective selection, assuming it has the information, may have little incentive to do so. A poor family patronized for some personal, social, or political reasons, may have more likelihood of inclusion in the list than a still poorer one lacking such support. Needless to say, officials would have little interest except in ensuring that there is some definite end product; they have forms to fill, boxes to check, and time lines to complete the process.

That leaves the families who wish to be included as the main interested parties. Unlike alpha services, where the clientele don't have conflicting interests and there is little competition, the situation here is different. The stakes in terms of financial benefits can be quite high. It is estimated that on average the subsidy on foodgrains alone for a family would be approximately Rs. 500 to Rs. 700 per month, enough for a family of two to survive at the current poverty line. The benefit is substantial if one adds monetary benefits of other schemes linked to the BPL status. Contrast this with the rate of pensions for the old and the destitute which is only Rs. 250 per month in Punjab. The poverty line is so low (at present approximately Rs. 30 per head per day) that many consider it no more than a 'starvation line' and one can expect many more families, than the estimates of such families would suggest, who would consider themselves eligible by social standards. Some families —labour, informal trade—may have more income but the flow is uncertain and subject to seasonal variations.

Competition among the BPL

These factors should normally translate into an intense competitive pressure for inclusion in the list (as in the jobs market or admissions to professional colleges), forcing the adoption of transparent and objective systems of selection and grievance redressal for the excluded. Surprisingly, despite these factors, the fact that even the poor are generally perceived to be vocal especially in northwestern states, and the economic and social motivation which the direct stakeholders, the potential beneficiaries have, this pressure is missing. In some states like Rajasthan, with the somewhat accidental best practices (presence of the Mazdoor Kisan Sangharsh Samiti (MKSS) and the NGOs), things may be different, but dedicated NGOs are generally missing in the states of Punjab and Haryana. It has not been possible to ascertain the quantum of complaints filed in the course of earlier selections. No records are maintained. The problem is generally sought to be resolved through a wholesale review, a sort of 'management by revolution' as was done in the case of Haryana.

Incentives of the Poor

A number of factors mostly related to the rules and processes of selection appear to be relevant for this lack of assertiveness by the excluded poor. One of these is the silent, anonymous and, in a way, secretive process of filling in forms, applications and completing the documentation. As seen in case of the basic services, public officials are likely to endorse eligibility of the applicants including stipulations of income or whatever other criteria are adopted. Applications for the issue of a BPL card are filed practically by all the persons who consider themselves poor—this number being much more than the limit on numbers imposed centrally; all of them fulfill on paper the criterion say of income. These applications are then supposed to be presented to the Gram Sabha. Eligibility is listed in identical terms; every applicant family may show the income as less than say, Rs. 1000 per month or whatever the threshold, as we observed in a village in the Haryana state. So the Gram Sabha has say twenty applications, all certified to be eligible as per criteria, but has to select only ten, with little available by way of a gradation of income or deprivation or a 'merit list of the poor'. The outcome of selection is bound to be erratic and whimsical. A lottery draw may be more effective! In any case, the Gram Sabha rarely makes the actual choice. As we found in the Rural Governance Study referred earlier, meetings are rarely held or if held, not conducted properly, and the paper work get completed quietly by officials ('in the meeting held on——the following were identified/selected').

The issue is why the interested parties, the poor who are excluded, don't protest, given the substantial gains accruing to the BPL cardholders. And these are advantages available immediately and not in the remote future, which as noted elsewhere, people may not value due to 'temporal inconsistency'. One reason could be lack of information—that they don't even know who applied or who were selected. The first process is private and the second only an exercise on paper. They only come to know after the BPL cards are issued. These problems could also be attended to by ensuring the presence of official observers in the Gram Sabha meetings. Not many complaints however are filed even after the 'excluded' come to know of what has happened. Authorities report very few complaints being received. Many of us have personal experience of being approached by the aggrieved parties and finding that (a) nobody is aware clearly of who is to accept a complaint and document it; (b)who is to decide the case; (c) how it is to be decided. If, for example, X represents that he should be included in a list of 10, do we start examining X's eligibility (which is meaningless as all the slots are filled) or reopen the whole list? Obviously the easy way out is to sit on it, as 'X's inclusion is subject to 'Y's exclusion which is a very different ball game. Everybody, the public officials, panchayat and the families, knows that the list cannot be modified as the number is artificially determined and allocated by the central government for the state, by the state for the district, and by the district for block, the village and so on. The grievance redress process is a charade without meaning, as redress, even in genuine cases of exclusion, is by definition not possible, given the ceiling on numbers.

'Rule of Seven' and 'Poor' Selection

Howsoever the preliminary list is prepared and irrespective of the veracity and reliability of an independent survey (or rather census), and the check points and systems of verification/ preparation, the institution of approval/choice by the Gram Sabha introduces the problems indicated above—personal preferences, possibility of whimsical choice or a simple endorsement, without any independent judgment being exercised by the participants. A list of 20-30-40, or whatever persons verified to be the eligible BPL families, is presented, without any ranking order that may help the Gram Sabha members make a selection based on their impressions of relative deprivation. In the absence of rules providing for such structured information to the Gram Sabha, a relative assessment/ranking of so many persons is almost impossible. Malcolm Gladwell[18] refers to 'channel capacity', the amount of space in our brain for certain kinds of information, well expressed by the magical number Seven provided by George A. Miller, which is the basis for organization of telephone numbers (generally seven digits). We find it difficult to distinguish between more than six variations in tastes or flavours. Humans find it difficult to remember or relate to more than a limited number of entities—whether beauty or flavour or the pitch of a sound. These cognitive limitations are rarely taken into account while designing systems in which the Gram Sabhas or even individuals have to make a selection among a large number of individuals, most of them in similar circumstances. A different system for selection may be required.

Using 'Wisdom' of the BPL 'Crowd'

The problem highlights the need for devising appropriate rules for incentivizing and empowering the Gram Sabha and the poor to exercise their 'choice' rather than having to acquiesce in their incapacity. In fact, these forums appear ideally equipped to exercise 'wisdom of the crowds'.[19] They are not subject to problems of 'Groupthink'; the numbers are rather large. Surowiecki[20] lists the basic conditions for a crowd to be wise—cognitive diversity, independence and decentralization.

Unfortunately the way the system is organized, decentralization does not allow for the first two. The Gram Sabha 'crowd' does not get advantage of the diverse information available with the individuals constituting it; the meeting is a formality. In the example given, of a cut off point in the 2002 selection of BPL in Punjab, there is nothing for the Gram Sabha to do but to endorse the list prepared by surveyors or officials.

Probably one of the most problematic issues in the game is the definition of 'eligibility'—of who can enter the *akhada* or the playing field meant for the poor, whether it is the 13 point criteria adopted in 2002 or a slightly less complex one (each lobby for the poor adds its own priority—education, health, nutrition, diet, social, and economic disabilities!). Only 'econs' could have devised such involved parameters, parameters, which even the better informed among laypersons find difficult to follow and the poor don't understand the logic of. A family may make sacrifices to buy transport for selling milk—if a 'Grameen Bank' comes to her aid and provides a loan for transport—or be unfortunate to have an ungrateful son who has a job but who refuses to support it. Such a family may be disqualified; clever lawmakers have, after all, provided the costly and somewhat useless remedy of filing a case against the son for the maintenance of the old parents! We need to carefully and clearly define the line separating the 'poor' from others. As Yunus remarks, 'Where non-poor are co-passengers in a programme, the poor are elbowed out by the better off.'[21]

Kahneman and other experimental psychologists have demonstrated the need to keep things simple so that they 'stick'. Atul Gawande[22] puts it well: 'We have accumulated stupendous know how... [but] avoidable failures are common and persistent; the volume and complexity of what we know has exceeded our individual ability to deliver its benefits...' It may be prudent to keep to a simple criterion—say of income—which everybody, especially the poor understand, and can relate to. The MPI or 13-point type multiple criteria are only likely to lead to situations like the one described by Kahneman[23]: patients were dying not because experts were not available but were taking too much time and adopting too many criteria to decide who among the patients needs emergency care! The problem was resolved through a simple protocol; the example given is Dr. Apgar's algorithm for identifying neonatal babies in distress who are not breathing normally; this was based on five simple variables that even a nurse could assess; this ensured medical attention to serious cases, which tended to get delayed due to personal preferences of experts for different cues of distress among patients and their relative weight. The standard and simple protocol helped identify the danger signs in time and saved lives. There is a need for a simple set of rules and systems for selection, systems which individuals with incentives and stakes can understand and in which they are provided a distinct role in decision-making, rather than simply being a part of the entity of the 'disinterested' Gram Sabha crowd in which the role of the latter is structured to encourage 'whatever you say' mentality.

Reframing Selection Architecture

Gram Sabhas have local information ('tacit knowledge' of Friedrich Hayek) and can be useful for proper identification of the BPL families, but they don't have the motivation to assert; this only the affected individuals can have. There is need to structure proper processes for the expression of incentives and choice by the poor, by properly 'framing' the process of selection. This could consist of: a) accepting applications on a specific date in a village/locality and displaying/announcing the list before/in the Gram Sabha meetings held for this purpose; (b) a sort of merit or deprivation list of the selected families, in order of deprivation—a 'poor' merit list; (c) some agency for receiving complaints and responsible for deciding quickly. This could be on the basis of First In, Last Out (FILO)—the first complaint to be accepted means the last on the selected list goes out. Aggrieved parties now don't file representations because even if accepted, there is no way for authorities to issue an additional card, the numbers having been decided already at state level! Aggrieved parties will then have an incentive to agitate as they would have a definite stake by being included if somebody is taken out of the list on their complaint.

Governments need thus to: (a) disclose information whether given by applicants or collected by independent surveyors/ officials on all the applicants openly, to trigger individual incentives to assert rights/protest; (b) provide a ranking order; (c) incentivize parties to complain/agitate through the FILO or some other similar principle.

'Group Selection' by the Poor

Persons excluded may have enough motivation but one cannot ignore the stakes of those included. The merit list itself may be a repeat of a similar paper exercise as the current one. The problem is ensuring that the list includes the poor and not many others who may also need such assistance and are in the running. One expects that the poor in a village will have more information about each other than say the richest man in the village. Possibly a model of 'peer group selection' (on the lines of micro lending to self help groups) may be appropriate. Once the Gram Sabha has finalized the list, the selected BPL group can collectively provide the ranking and endorse it. They know of the relative deprivation, have stakes in making the list conform to reality and are unlikely to be able to exert disproportionate influence individually. This may be the route for the government to internalize the 'wisdom' of the BPL 'crowd'.[24] Charles Mackay[25] has documented madness of the crowds—whether regarding tulips or the South Sea Bubble. The context of the BPL 'selection' however appears ideal for harnessing the wisdom of the local crowd of the poor, charting the middle path between 'groupthink'[26] and 'herd mentality'. The present process seems to be a mix of the 'group think' of motivated officials, opinion leaders and an acquiescing 'herd' of the Gram Sabha generally noticed during (most of) the 'Public Hearings' mandated for environmental clearance.

The architecture for the BPL Selection Process would consist of:

(a) Self-selection (filling a form).
(b) Selection of the group by the Gram Sabha (specified limit on numbers)—a participative process involving all the stakeholders, including the self-selected poor

in the list.

(c) A 'poor merit list' of the selected families, endorsed/ selected by poor—a peer 'group selection' process.

(d) A system for addressing complaints, on the basis of FILO principle—a 'bureaucratic process'.

BPL Benefits and Perverse Incentives

There is another dimension to the problem. At least so far, the BPL card has been the gateway for all deprivation based entitlements—housing, MNREGA, concessional loan for trade and business—a sort of 'open sesame'. Making the BPL card the pillar for all entitlements is likely to create further perverse incentives for inclusion in the BPL list, especially as it cannot be revised frequently. In India, where the difference in the economic conditions of the bottom 40 per cent and the next 10 per cent, or even 20 per cent, is marginal, and the families, especially those with uncertain income sources, are constantly sliding across the line, this can create serious problems. A process of identification more aligned to incentives of the target groups as suggested, may help address such problems more effectively.

Delivery of Subsidy: Cash Vouchers and Foodgrains

The second set of interactions comes into play at the time of transfer of the material or financial benefits. Policymakers have been worried about the failure in delivering these benefits, even discounting the fact of misdirection in the primary process of selection – 30 to 50 per cent of the beneficiaries are, as generally agreed, the gainers/losers due to mis-targetting. The two failures however are closely related. A person who, for example, is in the APL category, but is issued a card, may not value the material benefit, as the relative utility may be much less than for a destitute. An ineligible farmer, who holds a BPL card but produces his own wheat and rice, may not value foodgrains and may not even want them due to quality and other issues. He would be quite willing to trade off the entitlement with say 50 per cent of cash. Interventions such as the smart card would not help in such cases, as a person would and can take delivery on paper, or even physically, and have appropriate entries made. The sophistication of the process of entries in the smart card and electronic registers may only result in increasing the premium of the supplier, the depot holder—due to the higher risk now built into the system, and the transaction costs of 'sale,' thus reducing the total utility of the beneficiary. Some of these arguments apply also in the case of genuine BPL cardholders. An agricultural worker, who needs and has a card, may not need foodgrains—part of the wages of labour are generally paid in kind in many states, and would be subject to a similar set of incentives. Further, as Duflo and Banerjee have shown, families generally don't consume optimum qualities of coarse foodgrains and may prefer other foodstuffs if provided subsidy; 'getting more calories was not a priority; getting better tasting ones was';[27] and sometimes the problem may be 'less the quantity of food than its quality'.[28] There may be acute financial needs of the family, such as illness or social obligations, which may force them to sell the only 'family silver' they have available—the foodgrains entitlement.

Advocates of cash coupons argue that these enable a family to make appropriate economic choices, and would not cause huge disruption in the existing market for food, as a compulsory food rations program is likely to. If we factor in the element of motivations and incentives of the recipients of this subsidy, the appropriate option is to provide cash coupons. One problem with cash coupons, however, can be that the system may destroy the present elaborate system of food procurement and jeopardize food security, a major macro objective; we would look ridiculous if we find the expected off take does not take place as estimated and the stocks pile up. This can be a major problem with extended coverage (70 per cent of India's population) as proposed under the Food Security Bill, in case open ended cash coupons are provided. That also shows that while micro interactions are important, we also need to keep major policies, objectives and context in view. Possibly food coupons, made tradable only at ration/notified shops will be a viable alternative; this will align the choice of the poor to the broad government objectives, address the BPL family incentives and give them some options. The objective of maintaining the present food procurement system will also be achieved. Economic rent or arbitrage would then be available to the entitled BPL party, rather than the middleman or the depot holder.

I have referred earlier to Mullainathan et al. who highlight the problem of economic 'scarcity' imposing 'cognitive load' on the poor. The authors have a pertinent suggestion[29] about helping the poor, not only in respect of big shocks such as medical emergencies but also small shocks and fluctuations in income. In this case, one of the ways could be to permit the poor (in case token money is to be charged), to lift the permitted monthly quota in more than one installment and at their convenience, rather than their having to arrange and shell out a fixed sum for one time monthly supplies; the rules are not clear on this but, knowing the bureaucracy, the procedure is likely to be for food-grains to be supplied only once in a month!

Magic of 'Free'

There is one other area where a behavioural focus may be helpful. Quite a few of the poorest might find it the most difficult to shell out even the token money (Rs. 2 to Rs. 3 per kg. of cereals). 'Free' food for the poor may work better than a scheme which requires even a token contribution. One needs to remember that the oft quoted failed experiment of free distribution of contraceptives is not appropriate in the present context; that was an imposed demand unlike food, which has a direct and experiential utility. Experiments by behavioural economists have conclusively established magic of the 'free'. Dan Ariely[30] devotes a whole Chapter 'The Cost of Zero Cost,' explaining the magic: 'zero is an emotional hot button—a source of irrational excitement'. As he remarks, 'if you want people to drive electric cars, don't just lower the motor vehicle taxes but eliminate them'! If necessary, the quantity can be reduced *pro rata; it* may be better for a family to consume 60 per cent calories rather than forego all, just because it cannot raise cash for the token contribution. At least in this area of social policy where the government is providing food that is practically free, making it fully 'free' for the poor should not be difficult.

In view of the needs and incentives of the poor and other stakeholders, it would be appropriate to devote more attention to the processes of selection and identification, instead of hoping, against all historical and empirical evidence, that the current or proposed processes will magically throw up a proper list of eligible families. Selection processes may need to be structured as indicated, incorporating some features of self selection by the poor but also involving a political and broadly participative process by allowing people to make use of information only they possess. Considering the attention we give to systems for selecting candidates for jobs/admissions/ getting best price auctions, it is a pity that, for a scheme which costs the exchequer over Rs. 1.25 lakh crore, professional inputs and professional advice in the design of selection criteria and processes is missing. In any case, there is little harm in conducting randomized controlled trials to assess the effectiveness of the proposed (or any other) methodology and rules considered appropriate in the context of expectations and incentives, and provide some element of choice, so that the outcome is socially productive. Stakes are high enough and the problem is long term.

24

Micro Rules and Institutions: Problems, Possibilities and Prospects

This chapter adopts an eclectic approach across a range of services and regulations. Some of these may not fit the taxonomy of public services indicated in Chapter 4, but illustrate the variety of governance markets, exchanges and interactions, where some attention to the incentives of the parties involved may pay dividends in terms of improved public satisfaction and social efficiency, without necessarily affecting the core of a particular policy, service, or its objectives. Some of the services are amenable to simple solutions in terms of the rule design required for achieving the desired policy objectives; income certificate is one example of such alpha services. Some areas of public governance such as acquisition of lands and resettlement and rehabilitation (R&R), highlight the perverse incentives likely to be generated by the apparently pro-poor provisions and indicate the relevance of micro rules of interaction for policy outcomes. Some examples are also provided of the somewhat quaint and/or inefficient rules and point to the need for care in the design of micro rules, keeping in view not only the policy but also the context and incentives of parties.

Third Party Injury Caused by Accidents: A Market Solution

Accidents are 'normal' and will happen despite various checks and safety measures. Tim Harford[1] provides some instances of the 'contribution', of these very safety measures, to accidents whether in nuclear reactors or oil drilling rigs. The US death rate from fires is reported to have come down by 2/3rd over the last 20 years but serious accidents happen even now. The regulatory regime for safety in India, however, is based on the premise that accidents can be avoided simply by adopting adequate safety measures. The tendency of the post-mortem analysts is mostly to find scapegoats—that is how their jobs get defined through the heuristic processes common to bureaucratic organizations as, for instance, in the case of police and other agencies. The National Disaster Relief Agency in India, in its bulky manual on fire accidents, does not have a word about post facto measures; it is all about training firefighters, having adequate infrastructure, official inspections and so on; the assumption is that somebody or the other has to be liable for an accident and only such an entity should pay. The specifics of the liability however are nowhere defined and people have per force to approach the civil courts in the case of third party damage (except in the case of motor vehicles, where insurance for third party liability is mandatory).

In the case of Dabwali fire in 1995, where over 400 persons including schoolchildren died, the High Court judgment settled compensation after over 15 years of the accident and allocated liability, amongst government, the marriage palace owner where the function was held, and the school management, presumably in the ratio of their liability.[2] It is not clear as to how the apportionments would have been determined on the basis of the available evidence, in case it was not possible to allocate responsibility for criminal negligence; victims' families would still be entitled to compensation. The series on investigation of air disasters on the National Geographic channel indicates the difficulty of pinpointing causes of accidents—whether caused by man, machine, or an act of God.

One of the 'nudges' for the owners and managers of units liable to fire and other accidents can be to provide that any damage attributable to private parties and their property will be the owners' liability, even in the case of third parties. At present, the owner is liable to compensate for third party damage as in the case of motor vehicle accidents, but clear rules for liability of the property owners are missing—something similar to the problem mentioned earlier in case of China where liability for fire accidents and damage caused is limited to meagre compensation for labour and presumably none for the affected third parties. Civil claims take a long time for settlement and there is need for providing speedy settlement mechanisms on the lines of Motor Accident Claims Tribunals. There is a need, not for more and more regulations and clearances for safety of buildings and factories, but for allowing a market to emerge through mandatory insurance of the property for third party damage and provisions for speedy settlement of claims. Once that is done, the aggrieved parties are likely to settle their claims bilaterally through insurance companies rather than approaching courts; at present this is the only option.

Commercial and industrial enterprises which are prone to hazards and accidents, could be legally required to go in for insurance cover even for third party damage as against the present practice of getting insured only for 'own' damage and that too if they choose to do so. Damage to third parties through fire accidents needs to be brought into the ambit of the liability of the owners of a particular property, even as the governments continue with the regulations regarding the safety equipment to be installed. Once third party liability and insurance cover is made mandatory for the owners, insurance companies will see to it that due precautions are taken by the owners. This is one area in the insurance markets that creates little problem of 'moral hazard' and 'adverse selection'. And of course, premiums are fixed on actuarial basis. Mandatory insurance in such cases is likely to be a win-win situation—for the owners, the victims, the government, and the society at large. Incentives and behavior of the owners would change dramatically if rules were to provide for mandatory third party insurance in the case of fire (as in the case of motor vehicles).

Such specific provisions for third party liability in respect of fire accidents will make a difference to the incentives of builders and the industry in regard to adopting fire safety and similar other precautions. There will be a 'market' for compensation—premium paid by owners, insurance companies paying compensation and victims/families getting timely and adequate payment, instead of waiting for years for settlement of their claims, as in case of the Bhopal Gas Tragedy or the

Dabwali fire. The debate at present is fruitlessly centred on liability and culpability. One can imagine the disastrous consequences, if similar practices (absence of mandatory third party insurance) were to be followed in the case of motor accident claims. At present most of such properties are no doubt insured but, not surprisingly, only for 'own damage'—that is what the owner is bothered about! The State needs to intervene through appropriate regulations to help establish a market for third party claims that, in the context indicated, can be characterized as restrictive but 'mild' nudges, not involving a major sacrifice— financial or otherwise—on the part of owners. There may be some resistance but the government could make a start with companies whose turnover exceeds a prescribed threshold.

Land Acquisition: Compensation, Rehabilitation and Resettlement (R&R)

A Policy Generating Perverse Incentives

The compensation, rehabilitation and resettlement policy, for the families whose lands are acquired, provides for processes and norms for compensation to persons whose property may be needed for public projects of physical infrastructure or other equally important investments. The law provides for certain processes and systems of compensation under the Land Acquisition Act, and these have been supplemented substantially by the policy which seeks to go beyond the legal parameters of compensation for acquisition and addresses issues of rehabilitation and resettlement even of the landless. The R&R packages are being made more and more attractive with some states like Haryana even assuring long term annuity for the affected parties. Even the National Rehabilitation and Resettlement policy of 2007 provided for mandatory assistance even to the landless/BPL families.

The detailed processes and rules for relief and resettlement have been designed to address the 'moral hazard' problems of the project authority (government or private) which, if left to itself, is likely to soft pedal these problems, as the costs thereof are ultimately borne by the project management. This is especially relevant as the cost of land acquisition and resettlement, as a component of the total project cost, has increased substantially over time and project managements may address these problems only to the extent they consider necessary for 'selling' the project. Despite all these measures, there is little indication of any substantial change in terms of improved outcomes for the affected parties. I had an opportunity to study this aspect in the case of the hydropower projects in Himachal Pradesh and Uttarakhand. There is still an almost absolute dependence on 'court ordering'—'award', contest in the District Courts followed by appeals to the High Court and the Supreme Court. There are no alternative dispute resolution (ADR) mechanisms and there is rarely a project where 'closure' is achieved. Most of the packages for relief and resettlement are rather complicated. It is difficult even for experienced bureaucrats to make a mental map of these. There is little structure and transparency in the systems of communicating such information. The complicated rules are just posted on the websites, or printed and distributed, without any effort at effectively communicating as to what they mean to the families affected. The resources for the affected families receiving legitimate compensation and benefits flow from status, property, and education, which the socioeconomically challenged lack, in addition to the problem of lack of negotiation skills. The problems of accountability of officials in the case of acquisition for private projects, coupled with the overriding profit considerations of the project management, and absence of advocacy of the affected parties in case of 'invisible' and small projects, leads to sub optimal decisions—affected parties not getting full deserts, officials getting richer in the process, and projects exploiting the ambiguous processes of 'participation' in decision making in collusion with the influential.

The ambitious Land Acquisition and Resettlement Bill passed by Parliament cuts the 'Gordian knot' of these problems by providing for liberal compensation at *two to four times the 'market rate'*. It is expected that the new law will tilt the outcomes of acquisition effectively in favour of mostly small landholders. This appears unlikely. Powerful people have generally managed to avoid acquisition of their lands when compensation is considered inadequate. A report on water logging in the Malwa region of Punjab attributes the problem to defective alignment of drains, mainly due to influence of the big landowners whose lands were left out thus leading to improper alignment of drains. The same landowners would however readily preempt the poor, by purchasing lands under the new law, if the compensation is expected to be lucrative. If the powerful are tempted by the 'surplus' in compensation, they would buy off the small owners at say twice the amount, and increase the base market price in the process!

There can be a way out. While determining entitlement, the law can provide for disregarding sales made by small owners before acquisition for any project—say within two years of the notice for acquisition. Neither the possibility of such misuse, however, nor the remedy, appears to have occurred to the policy makers.

The major reason for a lack of 'closure' in these cases is litigation regarding the 'market value' and this problem has not been addressed even under the new law; rather, there are now stronger incentives for litigation. 'Market value' has still to be determined through the same ambiguous and subjective processes. One wonders whether a more pragmatic provision, that *the compensation will be market value or four times the collectors' rates, whichever is higher,* will not be more appropriate; it will eliminate the whole process of disputes and corruption in manipulating market rates while also achieving the objective of fair compensation. Collector's rates are fixed with a view to optimize stamp duty, are reviewed for the whole state systematically and periodically, and are not, therefore, likely to be affected by perverse incentives on the part of local officials to fix lower rates in individual cases; compensation is payable, not by the government, but, by now, mostly the private agencies handling the projects.

The rules are also more than likely to neglect details about how the consent of 70 to 80 per cent of owners (as the law requires) is to be obtained and this may introduce more distortions in the policy's outcomes. If, for example, a 50-acre plot to be acquired has 40 *khewats* (landowner holdings) and the number of the total shareholders is 200, would the rules require consent of 80 per cent of 200 stakeholders, or 'one holding one vote' of those present, or what? Is the government prepared for a secret ballot or will it be enough to have a 'consensus' of the 'herd'? Banerjee and Duflo highlight[3] the need to look into these micro issues of organization of village meetings that are relevant to the outcomes; governments need to attend to them, to avoid escalation of litigation and to preempt redistribution of resources to the rich through this well-intentioned law. The regulation in its present form will otherwise be just a signal for easy 'gaming' by the powerful.

Sex Determination Tests and Selective Abortions

Incentivizing 'Victims'

The PNDT Act (The Pre-Conception and Pre-Natal Diagnostic Techniques, Prohibition of Sex Selection Act 1994) prohibits screening tests of embryos for sex determination. The authorized officer, however, can choose to ignore some and prosecute others. Observations and discussions also indicate a large number of unregistered units which are operating in the rural areas and have portable equipment. As in the case of labour laws, enforcement is mostly about proper maintenance of registers and forms, whose formal compliance suits both parties, even though irrelevant for the outcomes. Surely clinics are not going to record the details of illegal tests! The system of automated alerts through remote controlled systems taken up in some districts does not appear to have prospered and spread as a bes practice. This does not suit the enforcers who are, after all, rational agents. A regression analysis would probably show little correlation of the outcomes with the PNDT Act. This is apart from the fact that the very denial of choice to the mother is abhorrent—if, for example, she believes this to be better than having to sell off the baby after it is born. There is also the problem of 'free rider' temptation in the case of a public good—in this case a balanced sex ratio. A family enjoys the benefits while it can itself afford to indulge in foeticide.

The annual number of sex selective abortions is estimated,[4] even after 20 years of the law, at three to six million (two to four per cent of all pregnancies). Dreze and Sen, while dealing with the problem, are however reduced to making a somewhat optimistic appeal, as in case of organ donations mentioned earlier, to 'enlightened public reasoning' to solve this social problem. We seem to have run out of solutions, even while sharpening the legal instruments.

One could possibly consider a 'nudge' for the women who may be parties to the collusive transaction of sex determination tests at the clinics. Can the Law provide immunity to them, treating them as 'victims', and thus provide an incentive to these victim whistle blowers, in case they file a complaint later against the clinic/doctor? And, of course, provide them compensation from the fines imposed in the event the clinic or the doctor is convicted—an example of the 'invisible foot' working, as suggested for Beta services (Chapter 15). Once the clinic knows that the complicity of the woman in the illegal activity of diagnostic tests will be no bar to her being a witness or a complainant, it may hastily review its incentives!

Drug Resistant Microbes

Structuring Disclosure of Information

One of the major public health problems today is the increasing bacterial resistance to more and more sophisticated antibiotics; the primary reason seems to be unnecessary or irregular intake of antibiotics. Pharmaceutical companies have to come out with more and more sophisticated antibiotics to address the problem. Penicillin, a wonder drug during the Second World War, is no longer heard of. The problem is especially acute in India with a number of systems of medicine with over lapping drug use. A large number of patients take antibiotics not prescribed by the qualified doctors, but instead administered by quacks. Patients, even if they have the prescription, may not buy the complete drug dose due to financial reasons, especially in the case of expensive drugs. The doctors, for various reasons, prescribe more and more expensive drugs even for ailments where cheaper but equally effective substitutes may be available in the market. One hears of the promotion of generic drugs by the government but the combination of the big pharmaceutical and medical interests is rather strong and there is not much impact in practice.

Physicians may have reasons of their own to prescribe branded drugs but the problem is also compounded by the human tendency among patients to relate the effectiveness of a drug to its price. This has been well explained by Ariely[5]—the higher the price, the more the believed quality. Preferences of doctors and biases of patients result in expensive drugs being prescribed and consumed, but not in the required dosages. Most of the patients may stop taking drugs before the full course is over, once they start feeling better. One of the reasons may be that of cost; the more the expense, the harder it is to sustain the full dose especially in conditions prevailing in India, where most of the households cannot afford them.

The law requires most of the antibiotics to be dispensed under a doctor's prescription, but 'over the counter' sales are a reality in India. The conflation therefore of the patient and the physician preferences for expensive drugs, in consumption as well as prescription, and inadequate financial resources of patients to sustain the full course of expensive drugs preferred by the physicians as well as the patients, could be the main reasons leading to discontinuation of antibiotics mid way, and the resulting problem of drug resistant microbes.

So is there a way out? The problem of promoting socially productive consumption of antibiotics is commonly resolved in other countries by requiring mandatory prescriptions for sale but this is unlikely to work in the Indian context. One possible 'nudge' could be for the pharmacies to be asked to display advisory notices and posters to promote proper drug usage and to be instructed to ensure that the customers buy the minimum dosage prescribed. This requirement would fit in nicely with the incentives of the pharmacists—more sales to the same customer—while sending appropriate signals and 'sticky messages' to customers and sensitising them to the importance of following the prescription and taking the full course.

Prescription Narcotics

Addressing Addicts' Incentives

One problem in India is consumption of and addiction to narcotics, most of which have been declared illegal. Legal substitutes however also available and in India and especially in Punjab, excessive consumption of pharmaceutical narcotics such as cough syrups is becoming a big problem. A study in Punjab[6] estimated that 30 per cent of addicts consume pharmaceutical narcotics. No worthwhile interventions, however, seem to be available, even though, unlike opium and other banned substances, this is an area where details on manufacture, trading, and sales are available for the asking. Control over opium and other narcotic derivatives and their use in pharmaceutical drugs, however, remains confined to the ritualistic processes of issues of licences and permits.

The data on the consumption of these pharmaceutical narcotics can be obtained easily by requiring the manufacturers, wholesalers, and retail pharmacists to inform the department, say by uploading the traded and sold quantities of such designated drugs, on a website of the department. Technology can be used to make the process autonomous and to provide access to this information real time. Once the data on the structure and flow of trade and consumption of pharmaceutical narcotics is available, appropriate control strategies can be devised based on real time information about the changing patterns of consumption, specific drug usage, and so on. This may be more effective than imposing more and more restrictions by say, limiting the number of pharmacists licenced to dispense pharma narcotics liable to misuse. Such measures will only add to the costs of transaction, and create 'rent' opportunities for the limited number of licenced dealers; somebody will always be available to arrange supply if there is demand. The simple act of asking for real time information may itself be a deterrent for some of the traders. This example also illustrates the pitfalls of 'double jeopardy' under the Indian federal structure and its fragmented governing mechanisms of accountability, involving the federal (central) government and the state governments.

There is another option suggested by people in the trade, a ban, not a 'nudge'. Government can ban the use of codeine, for example, in cough syrups; it helps most users no more than warm salt water and its only utility seems to be for addicts, and of course, the industry! I am not qualified to list other examples where a 'ban' on the use of addictive narcotics in pharmaceutical drugs may be feasible, but this is an area worth exploring. After all, governments do declare these products illegal just to make it difficult to procure them in the market and the same holds true in case of pharmaceutical narcotics.

Control of Tuberculosis: DOTS Programme

Lest patients forget

The WHO (World Health Organization) website provides an elaborate strategy for implementation of the tuberculosis control programme—political commitment, capacity building, staff skills, gender sensitivity and a whole host of requirements, for the base level DOTS (Directly Observed Treatment, Short Course) workers to be in touch with the patients. The DOTS is mostly considered the best feasible strategy in the Indian situation;[7] an Internet search, however, indicates disagreements on its effectiveness and also the need for more attention to multi drug resistant (MDR) patients. The issue is whether the basic weakness of the programme—discontinuity in the drug consumption regime as prescribed—can be addressed through invoking incentives of the human agents, the patients, assuming that the problem of logistics and availability on the supply side have been resolved (as claimed, by securing dosage for the full course, right at the start of the DOTS administration for a particular patient).

Some issues relating to behaviour may not be amenable to interventions, for example if a patient discontinues the drugs due to actual or perceived adverse side effects. What can possibly be done however is to create incentives to counter the human tendency in case of patients who just forget to consume. This may especially hold for patients who do not find the drugs pleasant to consume. The workers assigned for patients are expected to help in these situations. The programme however depends on a horizontally organized workforce who has multi tasking duties and therefore it may not be advisable to exclusively depend on them to check with the patients; and we need to remember that they can also forget. This is apart from the well known 'agency' problems. Technology is now available for a more effective route to jog the patients' memory; an automated alarm SMS sent to each patient having a mobile in the family would probably do the trick. Workers won't be required to physically monitor and in fact the community worker or volunteer assigned for the patient could herself get an SMS from the program control center. This simple system of reminding the patients of the drug consumption schedule, on the relevant days, at the cost of a simple SMS may work wonders for patients who tend to forget—and that applies to most of us. And the Telecom companies may well agree to provide free SMS service as part of their corporate social responsibility!

Acid Attacks

Fighting a Losing Battle

The problem of rejected suitors turning vengeful and resorting to throwing acid on members of the fair sex has been highlighted by the media. Statistical data is not available to indicate whether this is becoming a more serious problem over time, or it is just a case of 'visibility' and media focus. In any case, whatever the statistics, the crime is abhorrent and heinous. The question is whether the solutions worked out will help. One of these is mandating that all acids should be sold only on the production of an identity card. It appears that this by itself may be rather irrelevant to prevent or deter such crimes. In the first place, the culprit is mostly recognised by the victim and the by standers. Even otherwise, the victim would find it easy to identify the culprit in view of whatever social interaction or tension the two had, which would have provided the motive. Third, it is not possible to link the specific use of a common product like acid to a specific purchase.

Rules appear to be made just to demonstrate that some action being taken. It has been mentioned earlier that some policies and rules continue due to 'status quo bias'; this is however an example of new institutions and rules being generated which have little relevance to the objectives sought to be achieved.

LPG Subsidy: Direct Cash Transfer to Consumers

'Sound and Fury Signifying Nothing'

There is a move to link subsidy on the LPG (liquid petroleum gas) to the bank accounts of customers, with a view to prevent misuse but causing in the process tremendous transaction costs and strain for the consumers. They have to make the *Aadhar* UID Cards. This requires some other document of identification and address. The difficulty in the processing of these documents and the costs involved especially in terms of time, have been indicated earlier. Probably most of consumers would have some ID as the gas connection is itself sanctioned only on that basis. One in any case needs a bank account and many of the consumers may need to open an account. And of course the dealer has to be informed and the two accounts linked. Newspapers are full of reports about most of the consumers not having an Aadhar Card in districts where the experiment is being introduced. People in hilly areas also complain about the inaccessibility of banks.

The effort may be worth it if it ensures proper use and consumption of the LPG only by the genuine consumers and in genuine quantities. But would it? A similar issue has been dealt with earlier—supply of food to the poor—where the fallacy of such assumptions has been indicated. So long as an LPG consumer is in a position, for some reason or the other, to consume less than the prescribed number of cylinders (the limit is nine per year), there is nothing under the new system to prevent him/her selling it to a neighbour or even indirectly through the dealer, who pockets some of the surplus through arbitrage. There is no doubt, however, that the measure will prevent misuse by dealers who can under the current system book cylinders to consumers not lifting their quota, without their knowledge and thus pocket the subsidy; that route of leakage will be closed. But surely that result could be brought about with less effort and expense by a random check of entries made in passbooks issued to consumers or even by random phone calls to consumers. In fact, limiting the quota for subsidy has itself ensured, in most cases where a household has a single connection, that there would be little surplus left for consumers to generate a black market premium. The consumers with multiple connections are the ones who may not utilize their sanctioned quota fully but for whom the procedure of random checking may be enough, as they are unlikely to develop a collusive understanding with dealers, considering the small sums involved. And of course, the program has not taken account of the cost of money invested in advance by customers who recoup it later, and the load on the Banking system having to make millions of unnecessary transactions every month. And a consumer who finds the subsidy missing in his account might as well console herself with a reading of Kafka's *Castle!*

[The system has since been discontinued]

Income Certificates

A Matter of Missing Details

An income certificate may be required for different purposes —admissions of EWS children in private schools, the SC/ST/ minorities below defined income limits, for admissions in professional institutions/scholarships. The procedure in most of the states is to have verification of family income done by public officials—elected as well as the revenue staff—Municipal Commissioner, Sarpanch, Patwari/Tehsildar, on the basis of particulars/affidavit given by the applicant.

There are two areas where attention to rules of 'process' and 'detail' may be required. One is the issue of verification entrusted to ignorant and disinterested public officials, which has been referred earlier (Issue of Caste Certificates). Generally, the present income certificate formats do not always require details of information such as (a) occupation of the applicant/ guardian—agriculture, petty business/trade, employment (Government/Private) and income from each; (b) details of family members (husband/wife/all children), their age/marital status, occupation and income; (c) in case of the head of family, information about land holding, shop/house and income, if any, from these. The present format of income details and design encourages falsehood rather than truth. The prescribed application form leaves a lot of gaps in respect of details of income and, consequently, puts the onus of correctness mainly on the revenue functionaries whose reports are called for in each case before the certificate is issued by the competent authority. These authorities in turn bank upon the reports of Lambardar/Sarpanch in the rural areas and the MC (Municipal Commissioner) in the urban areas. Verifications are based on actual ignorance but professed knowledge—a sort of 'information cascade'.

The second aspect is the critical and almost criminal neglect of an important detail in the rules which vitiates the reliability of these certificates whether issued after third party verification or self certification. The omission is regarding the parameters for assessing agricultural income which is crucial for a large number of rural area residents—the farmers. Some research studies in Punjab, taken up by the public universities *indicate net loss from agriculture in Punjab* and *a farmer may well be entitled to deduct agriculture losses from other income while listing total income!* In one case brought to our notice during visit to one of the Suvidha Centres in Punjab, the revenue authorities had asked for a report from the agriculture department to have the income from agricultural land verified! It would appear that the present structure of rules, formats and procedures encourages false declarations generally and 'gaming' of the system by exploiting this ambiguity. This makes the objective of proper targetting very difficult and results in the wastage of resources expended for example on the ineligible poor.

Changes in format alone would not solve all problems and strategies have been indicated earlier for proper targeting; small changes in the design of applications, providing incentives and 'channels' for truthful declarations may prevent false declarations by people generally. This may be the more feasible route rather than verification by officials who have no information and little incentive to acquire that information. A newspaper report (*The Tribune*, 25 September 2013) mentions that 50 per cent of approved cases of pensions were found to be ineligible in some districts in Punjab. We found a huge disparity between the numbers of those eligible as per the state demographic and income data and the sanctioned cases for old age pensions and marriage grants for the poor; and all of them were verified and vetted by the officials!

It may be a little more challenging for the applicant to state the truth (or tell a lie) consistently on all the relevant details of income, an aspect missing at present. Anybody who has tried to fudge the income tax self assessment would know the difficulty of being consistent in falsehood and such details, if required to be provided, may function as 'nudges' for truthful statements.

Civil Justice: Delayed But Not Denied

The narrative below of a civil case in my personal knowledge is self-explanatory. Surely the delay is not all due to structural and staff problems! There is need to look into the micro institutions and the system of adjournments, rotation of cases, norms of daily case load for hearing and so on, which tend to get neglected while making macro and grand plans for systems of selection, infrastructure, accountability and so on.

Journey of a Civil Dispute Through Courts

'A' and 'B' are two real brothers. 'A' lives in a house that was once owned by their father. 'B' claims his right on half portion of the house allegedly on the grounds that he has equal/half share in his father's property. 'B' files a suit in April 1975. His claim is dismissed on 8.3.82 after 7 years.

'B' files an appeal (1st appeal) against the decision of Trial Court. His claim is again rejected on 23.11.85 after 3 years.

'B' then files a second appeal in the High Court in 1986.

From 1986 to 2004, the RSA (regular second appeal) passes though 14 Judges and the RSA under the Rotation System is shifted to different Benches/Judges.

2005: 13 adjournments, 3-PH

16 March (PH), 22 March, 30 March, 6 April, 11 May, 18 May (PH), 6 July, 13 July, 27 July, 10 August, 24 August, 14 September, 22 September, 28 September (PH), 5 October, 14 December.

2006: 8 adjournments: *9 January, 2 August, 2 September, 11 October, 1 November, 15 November, 29 November, 13 December.*

2007: 7 adjournments, 1 (PH): *8 January, 10 January, 31 January (PH), 7 February (additional record sought), 7 March, 14 March, 2 May, 17 December.*

2008: 10 adjournments: *1 January, 20 February, 19 March, 2 April, 6 May, 12 May, 21 May, 2 July, 16 October, 12 November.*

2009: 10 adjournments, 6 (PH): *13 January, 2 February, 3 February, 4 March (PH), 2 April (PH), 21 April (PH), 13 July, 11 August, 2 September (PH), 7 September, 7 October, 26 October (PH), 9 October, 4 November 5 November (Hearing over).*

2010: 6 adjournments: *9 April, 2010 (rehearing announced after 5 months): 28 June, 8 July, 17 October, 29 October, 19 November, 10 December.*

2011: 11 adjournments: *21 January, 4 February, 14 February, 11 March, 29 April, 27 May, 3 October, 9 November, 12 October, 30 November, 7 December, 9 December (RSA dismissed).*

Total number of adjournments: about 100

Period of pendency in High Court: 25 years

Total Effective time for hearings: 3 hours.

I was a little unsure of including this 'case study' as it appeared to be the 'odd man out'. A retired Justice of the High court, however, assured me that this, in fact, may be very 'representative' of the fate of numerous cases in higher courts!

And adding new judges may not resolve such problems. As Lipsky remarks[8], with reference to the paradox of more and more resources and staff turning out to be an inadequate, whether schools, or mental health institutions or emergency care or judicial courts: "Additional judges do not necessarily decrease court delays because with more judges courts may be more tolerant of lawyers' delaying tactics thus restoring the lengthy time it takes to bring cases to trial". Or, for example, additional resources may exhausted by the increased workload of new cases, without any impact on the disposal of pending cases.

Airport Security Procedures: Rules in Aid of Social Losses?

This is an example of what Taleb[9] calls an 'opaque heuristic': 'routine performed by society that does not seem to make sense yet has been done for a long time and sticks for unknown reasons'. All countries today provide for elaborate security checks; passengers as well as their hand baggage are thoroughly screened. India is probably the only country, however, where you are required to affix a baggage tag, which along with the boarding card, is stamped by staff as proof of security clearance. The purpose of the stamping of boarding cards and hand baggage of thousands of passengers is not clear. In case of violation of security, say if a passenger is noticed later or during flight to be carrying a prohibited article, it is impossible to determine who of the large number of security officials was responsible for the lapse.

It is difficult to estimate the cost of time of staff as well as passengers lost in this process but surely, it is also one of the reasons for the long queues in India at the security check points. And a passenger has to go back all the way from the boarding gate to the security check point and re-enter at the end of the queue, in case he or she loses the stamped tag or forgets to get it stamped! A newspaper report[10] shows a typical bureaucratic response to the problem mentioned. In major airports, the security has graciously agreed to do the frisking at the Boarding Gate to avoid inconvenience to passengers who lose the stamped tags!

High Security Plates for Motor Vehicles

Private Costs, Little Social Gain

These are being made compulsory in India with the objective of making them tamper proof. Only a few countries, so far as I could ascertain, have the system and while it adds substantially to expense (one has to remember the need to change plates frequently in the 'bumper' to bumper', but rather impatient traffic, in the urban areas, which leads to a frequent damage to plates), it is not clear how it will help the society. The transaction costs of changing the plates—one has to visit the authorized centre, which is not as accessible as a wayside shop—can be high. On the other hand, the system of assigning registration numbers clearly violates the 'rule of seven'; there can be as many as 10 or 11 digits (numerals and letters) to remember. No attention appears to have been given to this problem by the rule makers who have designed the system for India. One simple suggestion is to use a different colour code for the two letters used to denote the state name and display the state code vertically along the borders of the plate. This will provide additional space for the registration number; a 'human' can then just have a mental 'imprint' of the State, without having to remember the letters, and the basic registration number of seven digits would be more easily remembered, a 'nudge' for the memory of people in the 'hit and run' cases.

I reserve my views on the reliability of the plates and their being tamper-proof when computers, ATM cards and electronic meters are 'hacked' in routine. Only time will tell! Tyler Cowen[11] remarks that many markets are designed to help people avoid or circumvent regulations. He gives the example of a British entrepreneur selling 'squirt bottles of spray-on mud for licence plates' so that the police cameras cannot record the number on the plates of speeding vehicles! Some similar '*jugaad*' may be in the offing for high security plates in India.

25

Conclusion
Designing Institutional 'Nudges' for Public Services

Tyler Cowen points out that markets are universal: 'sometimes, it seems like there are markets in everything'.[1] While applying economic logic, however, to social interactions (the subtitle of Cowen's book is '*Use Incentives to Fall in Love, Survive Your Next Meeting and Motivate Your Dentist*'), he goes beyond Gary Becker's approach and highlights the need to appreciate 'the power (and limits) of incentives and a recognition of the complexity and diversity of human beings'. Governance markets (and it is Cowen's remarks which inspired this term), while similar in many ways to the economic and social markets, present some distinct features; these always involve some government agency as one of the parties to the interaction and exchange, which is mostly imposed by the government rules and regulations. The micro institutions and rules of exchange are ostensibly designed for the benefit of customers and the public, who constitute the stakeholder universe. They do not, therefore, usually provide scope for the kind of 'one-upmanship' advised by Cowen in social interactions, or even for game theory, which is usually applied (though rarely with success) to economic exchanges. Moreover, the motives and incentives of actors in the governance markets, while not as utilitarian as in the economic markets, are also not as complex and diverse as in social exchanges. One can therefore afford to be more optimistic about the impact of the redesign of rules, as suggested in the preceding chapters, on the outcomes of government policies and programs, than about Cowen's advice, for example, on what to order in a restaurant or how to become a connoisseur of Art.

Examples have been provided earlier of rules that make little sense even from the perspective of objectives. The absurdity of some of the 'victimless' social and economic regulations, and the perverse responses these invoke, is well illustrated by Beattie in *False Economy*. The British farmers and wool manufacturers were adversely affected by the imports of Indian silks and cotton and this led to the English parliament decreeing in the year 1678, that the English people should wear only woollen apparel during winter. All corpses had to be wrapped only in the woollen cloth! In the year 1700, import of silks was similarly banned. Despite these measures, many consumers still preferred to wear cottons. This led to the incidents of 'calico chasing'—'gangs of weavers roaming the streets of London, tearing cotton cloths off the backs of hapless female passersby and triumphantly parading their captured trophies, around the streets on top of poles.'[2] Such absurd laws had at least some logic; they had strong lobbies of weavers and wool producers. In the case of some of the government regulations, even this justification may be missing. The main problem is that of 'framing' appropriate institutions and rules which address these asymmetries in the incentives of the government agents and the citizens.

Default Rules and Discretion

It is, however, difficult to devise rules that can anticipate all situations, options and choices by the parties involved in governance interactions. In sports, apart from formal and elaborate 'rules of the game', informal rules and norms have evolved to address unanticipated situations. One example is the benefit of doubt to the batsman in a 'stumping' appeal in the game of cricket. In a football game, if a player is injured, one of the opposing team members kicks the ball out of play and the gesture is reciprocated; the 'throw' is made in favour of the opponents. While such informal institutions are, probably for good reasons, missing in the governance markets, governments need to realize the impossibility of defining all situations permitted or prohibited by rules, and instead need to have a master 'default' rule; any action or behavior, not specifically prohibited or prescribed, could be presumed to be permissible. An entrepreneur from the drug industry provided a good example. He had installed an item of equipment, a dry powder filling machine, purchased from a reputed supplier; the equipment had a laminar flow technology with a 'closed sterile system' that was technically more efficient and an improvement over the traditional 'open sterile systems'. The drug department officials, however, objected to this, refused to grant a licence and insisted that the owner should have only the traditional 'open sterile systems'; they had to be 'persuaded' to waive the objection—that the manufacturer was guilty of violating the Good Manufacturing Practices (GMP) prescribed for the drug industry! A 'default rule' would have resolved the departmental doubts on the efficacy of new equipment, assuming the same were based on a sincere but uninformed belief, rather than an excuse to extract a bribe. The 'default rule' is an extension of the 'natural justice' principle—what God or law have not forbidden, is socially appropriate. A complaint made to the Administrator of Chandigarh during an open meeting illustrates its relevance.

'Only 4 attended Patil's hearing'

Ajay Kumar, proprietor of Millennium Outdoor Advertisers, urged the administrator to allow the display of an illuminated LED screen panel at Neelam Theatre. *The UT officials said there was no policy on LED screens.*

Source: *Chandigarh Tribune*, 16 April, 2013

The Chandigarh Administration, in this case, need not have a policy for the approval of 'neon signs'. Such signs are not prohibited under the present regulations and therefore could have been approved straightaway. In another case of approval of a commercial building in Chandigarh, the government agency objected to a particular aspect of the proposed building design which was neither specifically prohibited nor permitted by rules. The architect and the owners tried to persuade the government agency through a number of meetings that the plan had to be approved as it did not violate any rule; it needed however, more than interpersonal and reasoning skills! The problem was the absence of any 'default rule'.

Discretion of 'Street Level Bureaucracy'

Related to this 'default' principle is the issue of discretion and its misuse. The current focus among the academics and even the intelligentsia, on limiting the discretion of officials, appears somewhat misplaced. The rules cannot provide for all contingencies and the 'local circumstances of time and place' (and person), and that is where the public agencies need some discretion. If, for example, I need a birth certificate but cannot produce the midwife's or the doctor's certificate (see Chapter 5), even the Chief Minister may not be able to approve the issue thereof; it will be considered a violation of the rules! Discretion is an essential input into human interaction, whether social or governmental, and the only question is, who is to be authorized to exercise it. By denying discretion to 'street level bureaucracy', we simply add to transaction costs and the consequent 'shadow' costs of corruption. There is little point in creating situations where the Head of the State is required to intervene through the *janta* or open *darbar*s in such petty matters, and still unable to help in any case, as indicated in the Chandigarh example above. The rules not only need a 'default' setting but also transparent systems for the use of discretion, for the officials to be able to respond to unique situations and problems.

In the final chapter, *Managing Street-Level Bureaucracy*, written for the 2010 edition, Lipsky[3] lists a number of case studies, where the discretion of these workers was sought to be curbed, which showed mixed results. While the studies do indicate that managers can influence the behaviour of street-level bureaucrats, efforts to turn them into case processing machines—a 'Screen Level Bureaucracy'—are, in any case, unlikely to work. Most of the operational and international rules and institutions in India seek to 'de-invent' the problem by denying discretion to the 'cutting edge' or front desk officials, leaving them with the only feasible option of informal and sometimes socially damaging compromises. A power utility lineman, for example, may help a consumer design the re-routing of electricity wiring to bypass the metering equipment. Many others, as Lipsky remarks, may "go out of their way to respond generously to people in need, despite rules to the contrary" and join what psychologist Lisa Dodson (in the 2009 book, *The Moral Underground*) smartly calls the "moral underground"[4] where helpful officials have perforce to violate the rules. The discourse and practice on discretion of 'street-level bureaucracy' needs a serious review; it turns most of these workers into confederates of the (limited number of) violators of rules who, as we have seen, are forced to take these shortcuts, to avoid the tyranny and rigidity of these very rules.

Institutional structures, in many cases, result in situations of universal non compliance, and only encourage exercise of a personalized, rather than organizational and functional discretion, as has been noted in the case of the health and welfare regulations for labour where pragmatic statutory provisions have been supplanted by rigid operational rules, making it difficult for the 'street level' staff to exercise 'positive' discretion to promote the policy objectives. Discretion needs to be agent-centric, rather than hierarchy and committee centric as at present.

'Framing' Incentive Compatible Micro Institutions

In India, governance failure in most of the areas of public policy appears to be a bureaucratic rather than political or social failure, whether caused by micro rules, or the structure of tasks, as Lipsky believes, or the incorrigible 'street level' bureaucrats as seems to be the common belief in India. I had earlier (Chapter 23) referred to 'normal accidents' which is the title of a book by Charles Perrow. Accidents demonstrate the extreme failure of maintenance, planning or operations but as Gladwell[5] explains, accidents like 'plane crashes are much more likely to be the result of an accumulation of minor difficulties and seemingly trivial malfunctions'. He refers to Perrow's analysis which shows that the (near) disaster at the Three Mile Island nuclear Station in Pennsylvania was due, not to a major human or technical error, but to five completely unrelated events "each of which, had it happened in isolation, would have caused no more than a hiccup in the plant's ordinary operation". Governance failure, we hope to have demonstrated, is mostly occasioned by the relatively minor 'hiccups' in the 'capillaries' rather than the 'jugular' of policy (see Introduction) and that is the reason for a focus on specific governance interactions and micro institutions of interaction or exchange.

It is somewhat difficult to devise appropriate models for public governance, macro or micro, even if one makes a number of somewhat unrealistic assumptions, as in the case of most of the economic models. Even a basic model, such as the Monetary National Income Analogue Computer (MONIAC) or the 'Phillips machine', set up by Bill Phillips in the 1950s, which used hydraulics to model the national economy of the UK, and its financial flows, may present innumerable problems in the case of public governance, despite extensive digital support available today. The area of public governance has rather complicated models, as for example the 'logic of governance' model provided by Ingraham and Lynn.[6] No doubt the factors mentioned by the authors, as indicated in the notes, are relevant; the problem is in applying them in appropriate quantities and proportions, to make a 'recipe' for the governance markets, covering diverse areas of the public and private interactions, which, unlike economic markets, neither have a common currency—money, for utility, measurement and exchange - nor any quantitative relationships. It is rarely possible for the government to take note of the complexities of human behavior while devising macro policy. It is however very much feasible to factor in some of these aspects, especially the incentives of the clients ('C') and managers ('M')—two of the 'nodes' in the 'logic of governance' model referred above— while designing the micro 'rules of the game' under a particular policy, whether for school education, or crime, or the donation of human organs.

Framing Rules: Convenience and Cost

'Framing' of choices is important for shaping individual behaviour and there is need to suitably design the rules of interaction to take note of the context, the situation, the incentives of parties, their expectations and so on. A 'cooperative' frame for interaction may not work with a professional killer, but may be effective for a purse-snatcher. Most of the rules encourage precisely the opposite behaviour—of 'gaming' the rules. Further, as Benkler[7] elaborates, social norms can be put to work, but the material factors relevant for compliance are the convenience and expense/cost of the effort involved. In order to encourage compliance and cooperation, we need to take note of factors such as how burdensome, or easy, it is for the individuals to act on their better instincts of cooperation. It is difficult for citizens to act cooperatively and to voluntarily comply with regulations when the frame of the regulations itself encourages adversarial responses. The problem with the governance institutions and rules appears to be that they adopt the rules of the market and assume self serving behaviour (hence the rules obsessed with the prevention of misuse of the Alpha services and stiff penalties for industrial pollution), while expecting outcomes which can only flow from cooperative behaviour on the part of citizens and clients. As the Toxic Release Registry example (Chapter 21) shows, naming and shaming, rather than the (threat of) punishment may be a more effective strategy in the case of pollution. Most of the regulations, on the other hand, shift the focus of private parties from compliance to avoidance of detection and punishment, through whatever means—a model of selfish behaviour. This is not to say that there should be no punitive provisions, but only how the rules need to be structured to encourage compliance by making it as convenient as feasible.

Rules in Small Print

Most of the rules and regulations referred in the previous chapters cover a wide range—verification before the issue of documents such as the birth certificates, ensuring the safety and health of workers, restrictions on the freedom of 'rational' choice in the case of social and economic governance, monitoring the pollutants discharged and so on. These rules relate to 'acts of commission', tend to encourage perverse incentives and defeat the objectives of a particular programme or policy. Some instances of the areas of 'omission' that need more, rather than less, of formal rules, for orderly and productive governance interactions, have also been provided in the last chapter. Some interesting examples of the perverse incentives generated by rules are provided by Harford.[8] The 'camelback' houses in New Orleans in the USA were due to the local tax system—of taxing houses according to the number of storeys at the front, and owners therefore built one at the front and the rest at the back! The policy in Britain, in force for over 150 years, till 1851, of levying house tax on the basis of the number of windows, caused people to build dingy houses. The examples given indicate the importance of the macro rules which can result in unanticipated and harmful outcomes. The fact that it is difficult to find many contemporary examples of such perverse macro policies and institutions appears to indicate that such instances are now rare. What appears alarming, however, is the proliferation of inappropriate and dysfunctional micro operational rules and institutions in many areas of social and economic policy. The drafting and design of these micro rules does not appear to get adequate attention, as mentioned in the Introduction. The history of enforcement of the Immoral Traffic Act (Chapter 14) may have been very different, if the definition of 'brothel'— a minor detail—had covered up to *four or more* sex workers instead of '*two or more*' as is the case at present.

Legitimacy of 'Nudges'

All of these problems may not necessarily need polite 'nudges' and the government can, and should, impose restrictions, bans, and sanctions if required. Some of these may need more study and experimentation than what has been possible here, but they do illustrate the scope of 'framing' and 'choice architecture' to reduce or eliminate social loss and waste in the governance markets.

The 'nudges' that some governments, whom the critics call the 'nanny states', are designing for the welfare and well being of the citizens, have not been all well received. It is apprehended that these may well be turned by the bureaucracy into 'shoves', 'kicks', and 'shots'. The problem with most of these nudges is that these may be 'sub legal', as for example the prescriptions limiting the size of fuzzy drinks (for citizens' own health, of course!) in the restaurants, in one of the cities in the US, which was later held to be unconstitutional. Governments would do well to provide 'nudges' only where they are competent to prescribe 'shoves', 'kicks' and sanctions, instead of attempting to influence social problems like obesity, which even if they may not cause 'double market failure', gives rise to apprehensions of a 'manipulative' government trying to change the behaviour of individuals—*individuals who may be making a rational (Becker's) choice to be obese*! The areas proposed for incentive-compatible rules, procedures, and systems need to be those where the State has the power and the legitimacy to intervene.

The foregoing analysis of the public services in a way demonstrates the (monetary and fiscal) 'policy ineffectiveness proposition' in the sphere of public governance. The phrase, coined by Thomas Sargent and Neil Wallace, was based on Robert Lucas's 'rational expectations' hypothesis. As Cassidy remarks, in an excellent exposition: 'According to the rational expectations theorists, the government was either powerless or a source of trouble'.[9] In public governance in fact, ineffectiveness of public policy can, many a time, be traced back to the irrational expectations of the policy makers about the incentives and behaviour of the agents—government and private.

Two other issues need to be mentioned. One is the need to constantly assess and evaluate the results of the rule design, governing structures or other measures and interventions taken up to address governance failure (or achieve success) in the delivery of public services. The other issue is how to do so.

Feedback

Harford in *Adapt* refers to Karl Sims who created a virtual environment, with virtual creatures competing for survival according to the rules set by Sims. The blind evolutionary process (of variation and selection) produced a wide range of workable solutions in this 'fitness landscape'—"a vast, flat, landscape divided into a grid of billions of squares[10]", each square representing a different strategy whether in terms of biological evolution, or business, or recipes for dinner. I found it fascinating to watch (in a short video available on the net[11]), the unpredictable patterns of evolution of different 'virtual' creatures in the 'struggle of survival'. Harford refers to this experiment in the context of advocating 'trial and error' as an effective tool for solving problems. What is also of interest is the fact that even Sims, who set the rules, was not able to predict success or failure. A similar fate may await the self-confident policy makers who set the design and rules of economic and social policies. We need, therefore, a constant feedback on unanticipated outcomes—evolutionary or 'emergent'—so as to be able to adapt the institutions in response to perversities like the 'camel back' houses and the Merton Rule—two of the examples given by Harford and referred earlier—as also the instances given in the previous chapters. As has been noted, what works is a particular situation and context, may be ineffective in different 'circumstances of local time and place' and constant feedback may be necessary irrespective of the level of confidence of the rule-makers.

Assessing Outcomes: Regression Analysis and RCT's

The second issue is about assessing and evaluating the suggested framework for the design and structure of (in some cases macro, but mostly) 'operational', micro rules and institutions in different areas of public governance. It may not be possible to wait for the long term; in the long term we are all dead, as Keynes observed. In any case, considering the efficiency of the human brain in selective retention, the 'status quo bias' would have by that time shifted the issues to the back burners of collective memory. Two possible options for immediate evaluation are regression analysis and randomized controlled trials (RCTs). Regression analysis may present some difficulties as most of the experts qualified to do so may not be interested in such noneconomic 'trivial' issues. Moreover, availability of reliable primary level (rather than sample based) data required for this purpose is a major problem in India.

Tim Harford[12] has provided an excellent critique of the second option, the RCTs. Such trials have been invaluable in many cases, as in Kenya for example, on the impact of antihistamines on student attendance and performance (positive) and supply of textbooks and flip charts (no effect). Moreover, as he explains, the context and content of a particular policy or service is a material factor affecting outcomes. Community monitoring was effective in the case of functioning of the health institutions in Uganda but not for controlling corruption in the rural roads programmes in Indonesia (the latter is based on a study which has been mentioned earlier). Lipsky provides an excellent critique of the RCTs relevant to the operational situations and exchanges in public governance, and explains how its application across the board for most of the public services is not practicable. *The Economist* has provided an excellent summary of the contribution made by the RCT's, in the last ten years. (*The Economist*, December 14, 2013: Free Exchange/Random Harvest). The RCT's can be of use in evaluating public services where possible, to see what works in a particular context. As observed earlier, however, the problem is not always that of identifying the appropriate approach or solution to a particular governance problem. It is, for example, agreed that fortifying cereals with iron may be an effective strategy for combatting mal-nutrition, especially of children. As Banerjee and Duflo[13] remark, to fight malnutrition, 'governments can provide fortified foods to pregnant mothers and parents of small children, by treating children for worms in pre-school or at school, by providing them with meals rich in micro nutrients or even by giving parents incentives to consume nutrients supplements'. Surprisingly this solution doesn't appear to be getting serious attention even though the market for foodgrains in India is controlled by the government and this should be much easier to enforce than iodization of salt, a free market commodity. The problem is that of directing the attention of governments to these minor interventions rather than the popular 'grandiose' issues—the percentage of population to be covered, quantity of food to be supplied, the pricing thereof and the resources required. The policymakers, while designing macro and micro rules and institutions of governance exchanges and interactions, would do well, to keep within their sights, not only the political and economic, but also the social and psychological legitimacy of policy and the incentives, motives and behaviour of the interacting agents and actors. In the hierarchy of rules and institutions—social, economic and political, legal (constitution, statutes) and administrative law/delegated legislation—it is the micro institutions and rules of interaction at the 'bottom of the pyramid' which need to be the locus of public governance.

Notes and References

Introduction

1. Daron Acemoglu and James A. Robinson (2012), *Why Nations Fail: The Origins of Power, Prosperity and Poverty*, Crown Business, New York.
2. Mancur Olson (2000), *Power and Prosperity*, Basic Books.
3. John Cassidy (2009), *How Markets Fail*, Allen Lane, Penguin Group.
4. Dan Ariely (2010/2011), *The Upside of Irrationality*, Harper Collins, UK.
5. Richard H. Thaler and Cass H. Sunstein (2008), *Nudge*, Yale University Press, New Haven, London.
6. Cass Sunstein, 'Nudges.gov: Behavioural Economics and Regulation', (eds) Eyal Zamir and Doron Teichman, *Oxford Handbook of Behavioural Economics and the Law*, www.thegovlab.co.
7. Free Exchange/Nudge nudge, think think, *The Economist*, 24 March 2012.
8. www.microgovernanceblogspot.in.
9. Chris Anderson (2006/2009), *The Long Tail*, Random House Business Books, UK.
10. Ludwig Von Mises (1944/2002), *Bureaucracy*, Liberty Institute, New Delhi.
11. James Q Wilson (1989/2000), *Bureaucracy; What Government Agencies Do and Why They Do It*, Basic Books. He is of the view that the 'organization' of bureaus-whether 'coping' or 'production' or 'craft organizations'—is important for the outcomes.
12. Daniel Kahneman (2011), *Thinking Fast & Slow*, Farrar, Straus & Giroux, New York.
13. Milton Friedman and Rose Friedman (1980/1990), *Free to Choose*, Harvest Books/Harcourt.
14. Kahneman (2011), ibid, Introduction.

Chapter 1: Public Governance: The Four Dimensions

1. Hobbes (1651), *Leviathan* (quoted) in Jonathan Wolff, 1996, *Political Philosophy*, Oxford University Press.
2. Adam Smith (1776/1978), *The Wealth of Nations*, pp. 240–5, Penguin Books, UK.
3. Adam Smith (quoted in) John Cassidy (2009), *How Markets Fail: The Logic of Economic Calamities*, Allen Lane, Penguin Books.
4. Niall Ferguson (2008/2009), *The Ascent of Money*, Penguin Books provides brief details of the Bubble.
5. Charles Mackay (1852), *Memoirs of Extraordinary Popular Delusions and Madness of Crowds*, The Project Gutenberg e-Books.
6. Niall Ferguson (2008/2009), ibid.
7. Yochai Benkler (2011), *The Penguin and The Leviathan*, Crown Publishing Group.
8. John Cassidy (2009), ibid, pp. 76–8.
9. Niall Ferguson (2008/9), ibid, p. 203.
10. Janet Newman (2001), *Modernising Governance: New Labour Policy and Society*, Sage Publications, London.
11. Taming Leviathan (2011), 'A Special Report on the Future of the State', *The Economist*, 19 March.
12. Niall Ferguson (2008/2009), ibid, p. 203.
13. Milton Friedman and Rose Friedman (1980/1990), *Free to Choose*, ibid.
14. A. Kaletsky (2010), *Capitalism.4.0: The Birth of a New Economy*, Bloomsbury, London.
15. Daniel Steele Jones (2012), *Masters of the Universe*, Princeton University Press, Princeton and Oxford.
16. David Osborne and Ted Gaebler (1992), *Reinventing Government*, Prentice Hall of India, New Delhi.
17. Newman (2001), ibid.
18. 'History of NHS reform' @nhstimeline.nuffieldtrust.org.uk.
19. Newman (2001), ibid, p. 43, quoting a department of Health document.
20. Impossibility theorem is defined as 'a proof that it is impossible to devise a constitution or voting system that can guarantee to produce a consistent set of preferences for a group from the preferences of the individuals making up the group'. (Graham Bannock, R.E. Baxter, Evan Davis, 1972/Seventh edition 2003, *The Penguin Dictionary of Economics*, Penguin Books).
21. Paradox of voting is defined as 'the paradox that a majority voting system can produce a set of inconsistent social preferences from a set of individually consistent preferences'; *The Penguin Dictionary of Economics*, ibid.

22. R.V. Ayyar Vaidyanathan (2006), *Navigating the Public Policy Terrain: Primer on Policy Process and Politics*, Indian Institute of Management, Bangalore. Ayyar lists three paradigms relevant for modern policy making: neo classical liberalism, human rights and governance.
23. H.B. Milward and K.G. Provan (1999), 'How Networks are Governed'; Unpublished paper quoted in Hill Michael and Peter Hupe, 2002. *Implementing Public Policy: Governance in Theory and in Practice*, pp. 14–15; Sage Publications, London.
24. Jan Kooiman (2003), *Governing as Governance*, Sage Publications, London.
25. Newman (2001), ibid.
26. Michael Hill and Peter Hupe (2009), *Implementing Public Policy*, 2nd ed., Sage Publications, London.
27. P. Selznick (1957), *Leadership in Administration: A Sociological Interpretation*, Row and Peterson, New York.
28. M. Lipsky (1980/2010), *Street Level Bureaucracy: Dilemmas of the Individual in Public Services*, Russell Sage Foundation, New York.
29. Enrique Cabrero (2005) 'Between New Public Management and New Public Governance: The Case of the Mexican MC's', *International Public Management Review*, Vol. 6 Issue 1, at http://www.ipmr.net.
30. Newman (2001), ibid.
31. Subrata K. Mitra (2006), *The Puzzle of India's Governance*, Routledge, Indian Reprint.
32. Joseph Stiglitz, (2006), *Making Globalization Work*, pp. 54–5, Allen Lane, UK.
33. Taleb (2012), *Antifragile*, Allen Lane/Penguin.
34. Dani Rodrix (2011), *The Globalization Paradox*, Oxford University Press.
35. www.sgi-network.org
36. www.bertelsmann_stiftung.de
37. www.moibrahimfoundation.org
38. www.mcc.gov.
39. Kaufmann, Kraay, Daniel Aart and Mastruzzi Massimo (2005), *Governance Matters IV: Governance Indicators for 1996–2002 (update)* www.world/wbi/governance. Indicators are Voice and Accountability, Political Stability, Government effectiveness, Regulatory quality, Rule of law, Control of corruption.
40. UNDP (2004), *Governance Indicators: A User's Guide* (www.undp.org/oslocentre)
41. *Millennium Development Goals*, India Country Report, (www.mospi.nic.in)

42. Stigler George (1982), *Economist as Preacher,* Basil Blackwell, Oxford.
43. R. Coase (1937), 'The Nature of the Firm', *Economica,* New Series, November Vol. 4 to 16, pp. 386–405 (@http://links.jstor.org).
44. *The Blind Men and The Elephant* John Godfrey Saxe (1816–1887) (http://www.constitution.org/col/blind_men.htm).
45. Kaletsky (2010), ibid.
46. Jacob Torfing, B. Guy Peters, Jon Piery and Eva Sorensen (2012), *Interactive Governance: Advancing the Paradigm,* Oxford University Press.
47. Taleb (2012), ibid.
48. Yochai Benkler (2011), ibid.
49. Jacob Torfing, et al (2012), ibid.
50. Dan Ariely (2008), ibid.

Chapter 2: India: 'Planning' for Governance

1. Dewan Jermany Dass (2008), *Maharaja,* Hind Pocket Books.
2. Planning Commission (2008), *Eleventh Five Year Plan 2007–2012,* Vol. I, Oxford University Press, New Delhi.
3. www.india.gov.in/e-governance/national-e-governance-plan.
4. www.prsindia.org.
5. George Stigler, 'The Theory of Economic Regulation', *Bell Journal of Economics and Management Science* 2, no. 1 (Spring 1971: 3).
6. R.N. Gupta and A.D. Sud (2007), *Evaluation Report of Ghaggar River,* IDC, Chandigarh.
7. www.prsindia.org.
8. Ronald H. Coase, 'The Nature of the Firm', *Economica,* New Series, Vol. 4, No.16 (November, 1937) pp. 386-405 (http://links.jstor.org).
9. www.prsindia.org.
10. DPARP GoI (2013), Addressing the Challenges of Public Service Delivery, (unpublished).
11. DPARPG (2008), *Splendour in the Grass: Innovations in Administration,* Penguin Books.
12. GoI and Human Resource Development Centre, UNDP (2002), *Successful Governance Initiatives and Best Practices* published jointly with the Planning Commission.
13. National Social Watch (2011), *Citizens' Report on Governance and Development 2010,* Sage Publications.
14. Sudipto Mundle, Pinaki Chakraborty, Samik Chaudhary and Satadru Sarkar (2012), *The Quality of Governance: How Have Indian States Performed?* Working Paper No. 2012-104 July, National

Institute of Public Finance and Policy, New Delhi. (www.nipfp.org.in).
15. DARPG (2009), *State of Governance: A Framework of Assessment*, Department of Administrative Reforms, Public Grievances, Pensions, Government of India, New Delhi.
16. Bimal Jalan (2005), *The Future of India: Politics, Economics and Governance*, Viking/Penguin.
17. www.oecd.org/derec/worldbank/36489212.pdf.
18. Eshetu Bekele, *Citizen Report Cards in Ethiopia* (www.capability.approach.com/pubs/4_5_Bekele.pdf).
19. R.N. Gupta and Ramanjit Kapoor (2007), *Study on Urban Governance in Punjab*, Institute for Development and Communication, Chandigarh.
20. R.N. Gupta, Ravinder Paul and Vaishali Mishra (2009), *Rural Governance: A Study of Rural Peripheries in North India*, Institute for Development and Communication, Chandigarh.
21. R.N. Gupta, et al (2009).
22. H.S. Shergill and Varinder (2009), *Evaluation Study of Punjab Nirman Programme*, Institute for Development and Communication, Chandigarh.
23. Bimal Jalan (2005), *The Future of India*, Viking/Penguin Group.
24. Abhijit Banerjee and Esther Duflo (2011), *Poor Economics: Rethinking Poverty and the Ways to End It;* Random House India.
25. K. Shreedhar Rao (2013), *Governance, Security and Development*, South Asia Foundation and Concept Publishing Company Pvt. Ltd., New Delhi.
26. William Easterly (2006/2007), *The White Man's Burden*, Paperback, Oxford University Press.
27. Easterly (2006/2007), ibid.

Chapter 3: Incentives, Behaviour and 'Rules of the Game'

1. Oliver E. Williamson, 'The New Institutional Economics: Taking Stock, Looking Ahead' (University of California, Berkeley; owilliam@haas.berkeley.edu) refers to institutional environment in terms of macro 'rules of the game'—property, judiciary—as first order governance and describes second order governance as 'play of the game'.
2. Taleb (2012), ibid, p. 417.
3. Cassidy (2009), ibid, p. 134.
4. P. Mauro (1995), 'Corruption and Growth' *Quarterly Journal of Economics*, Vol. 110, No. 3, p. 681-712.
5. Taleb (2007), *The Black Swan*, Revised Ed. 2010, p. 241, Penguin Books.

6. Ian Bremmer and Preston Keat (2009), *The Fat Tail*, Oxford University Press.
7. Taleb (2012), ibid.
8. Paul McGarr and Steven Rose (ed) (2006/2007), *The Richness of Life*, Vintage Books, London.
9. Matt Ridley (2003/2011), *Nature via Nurture*, Fourth Estate.
10. *The Times of India*, March 21, 2013; "Vitamin A Pills don't cut Child Mortality".
11. Vivek Dehejia and Rupa Subramanya (2012), *Indianomics: Making Sense of Modern India*, Random House India refer to Debraj Ray and Siwan Anderson's *The Age Distribution of Missing Women in India*, New York University Working Paper 2012 and their critique of Amartya Sen's *'Missing Women'* 1992, *British Medical Journal*, Vol. 304-8.
12. Taleb (2012), ibid, p. 417.
13. Kooiman (2003), ibid.
14. Tim Harford (2011), *Adapt*, Little, Brown, Great Britain.
15. Acemoglu, et al. (2012), ibid. In a section "Breaking the Mould", the authors explain that one of the contingent factors in Botswana's success was the visit of three chiefs of the then Bachuanaland, in the year 1895, to England to persuade the British government to exercise greater control, so as to pre-empt the annexation of their lands by Cecil Rhodes' British South Africa Company; the mission was a success and the relative autonomy they kept enjoying, under the British Protectorate, helped build inclusive institutions in Botswana.
16. Dani Rodrix (2011), ibid.
17. Jared Diamond (2005), *Collapse; How Societies Choose to Fail or Survive*, Allen Lane/Penguin Books.
18. Muhammad Yunus (1999/2007), *Banker to the Poor*, Penguin Books, New Delhi.
19. Ridley (2003/2011), ibid.
20. Shankkar Aiyaar (2012), *Accidental India*, Aleph Book Company, India.
21. Cassidy (2009), ibid.
22. Jared Diamond (1999), *Guns, Germs and Steel*, Vintage Random House.
23. Tim Harford (2011), ibid.
24. Richard O Zerbe Jr. and Howard Mc Curdy (1999), 'The Future of Market Failure'; *Journal of Policy Analysis and Management* 18(4), 558.
25. Stephen D Krasner, *Governance Failure and Alternatives to*

Sovereignty, CDDRL Working Paper 2004, FSI Stanford.

26. George Akerlof (1970), The Market for Lemons: Quality Uncertainty and the Market Mechanism *Quarterly Journal of Economics* 84, 489.
27. Cassidy John (2009), ibid.
28. D. North (1990/2007), *Institutions, Institutional Change and Economic Performance*, Cambridge University Press.
29. Avner Greif (in *The Institutions and the Path to the Modern Economy; Lessons from the Medieval Trade)*, indicates the relevance of cultural and religious institutions-individualistic versus communitarian, for development of Western Europe especially trade. However, Gregory Clark (*Journal of Economic Literature*, Vol. XLV, September 2007, p. 727-43; www.econ.ucdavis.edu/faculty/gclarkbooks_reviews) questions the relevance of such institutions for trade, let alone their contribution to economic growth.
30. Acemoglu, ibid.
31. Cassidy, ibid.
32. Milton Friedman and Rose Friedman (1980/1990), ibid.
33. Ferguson (2008/9), ibid
34. Malcolm Gladwell (2000/2010), *The Tipping Point*, Abacus/Little Brown, London.
35. Dehejia and Subramanya (2012), ibid.
36. Thaler, et al (2008), ibid.
37. Richard Hawkins (2009), *The Greatest Show on Earth*, Transworld Publishers, Black Swan.
38. Elinor Ostrom, "An Agenda for the Study of Institutions", *Public Choice*, 48 (1986): 3-25; (in) B Guy Peters and John Pierre (ed) (2007), *Institutionalism*, Sage Publications.
39. D. North (1990/2007), ibid.
40. James Watson (2003), *DNA: The Secret of Life*, p. 32, Arrow Books, UK.
41. Ludwig Von Mises (1944/2002), ibid.
42. Nate Silver (2012), *The Signal and The Noise: The Art and Science of Prediction*, Allen Lane/Penguin Books.
43. Oliver E. Williamson (2000), 'Why Law, Economics and Organisation?' UC Berkeley School of Law, Working Paper Number 37.
44. Ferguson (2008/9), ibid.
45. North (1990/2007), ibid.
46. See reference 1 above.
47. Deepak Chopra and Jim Clifton, Is India Having a Crisis of Soul? *The Times of India*, April 9, 2013.

48. Avinash K. Dixit and Barry J. Nalebuff (2010), *The Art of Strategy,* Viva Books India.
49. Robert Axelrod (1984, Revised Ed 2006), *The Evolution of Cooperation,* Basic Books.
50. Milton Friedman and Rose Friedman (1980/1990), ibid.
51. Kahneman (2011), ibid.
52. Kahneman (2011), ibid.
53. Antonio Damasio (2010), *Self Comes to Mind: Constructing the Conscious Brain,* William Heinemann, London.
54. Thaler and Sunstein (2008), ibid.
55. Amos Tversky and Daniel Kahneman, 'Judgement Under Uncertainty: Heuristics And Biases'; *Science,* Vol. 185, 1974.
56. Kahneman (2011), ibid.
57. Banerjee and Duflo (2001), ibid.
58. Thaler et al (2008), ibid.
59. Thaler et al (2008), ibid.
60. "Disclosure and Simplification as Regulatory Tools", June 18, 2010 issued by OIRA (Office of Information Regulatory Affairs) as a part of 'Open Government Initiative'; www.reginfo.gov.
61. Taleb (2012), ibid.
62. Taleb (2012), ibid.
63. Matteo M. Galizzi, 'Label, Nudge or Tax'? A review of health policies for risky behaviours; *Journal of Public Health Research* Vol. 1, 2012 (http://www.jphres.org/index.php/jphres/article/view/jphr.2012.e5/html).
64. Thaler and Sunstein (2008), ibid.

Chapter 4: Governance Markets: Taxonomy of Public Services

1. Timothy Besley and Maitreesh Ghatak (London School of Economics, London, UK), 'Reforming Public Service Delivery', *Journal of African Economies,* Vol. 16, AERC Supplement 1, pp. 127–56.
2. N.K. Singh and Nicholas Stern (ed.) (2013), *New Bihar,* Harper Collins.
3. M. Lipsky (1980/2010), ibid; Preface to 2010 ed.
4. M. Lipsky, ibid.
5. M. Lipsky, ibid.
6. Lane Kenwothy (2011), *Progress for the Poor,* Oxford University Press.
7. Ridley Matt (1999/2011), *GENOME: The Autobiography of a Species* in 23 Chapters refers (p. 303) to Huxley's *The Brave New World* (1932).

8. Rogers A.J. (1973), *The Economics of Crime*, Dryden Press, Illinois, p. 160.

Chapter 5: Registration of Births and Deaths

1. Banerjee and Duflo (2011), ibid.
2. Frederick Forsyth (1971), *The Day of the Jackal*.

Chapter 6: Verification of Caste Certificates

1. Character in a British TV series of the 1990s, *Mr. Bean*.

Chapter 7: Motor Vehicle Regulations

1. Steven E. Landburg (1993), *The Armchair Economist*, Simon & Schuster UK Ltd., London.
2. Marianne B., Simeon Djankov, Rema Henna, Sendhil Mullainathan (2007), 'Obtaining a Driving Licence in India; An Experimental Approach to Studying Corruption', *Quarterly Journal of Economics*, November, 1639–1676.
3. *The Times of India*, 28 August 2013.

Chapter 8: Civic Regulations for Buildings

1. Loretta Napoleoni (2011), *Maonomics*, Seven Stories, New York.
2. Ronald H. Coase (1960), 'The Problem of Social Cost', *Journal of Law and Economics* (http://links.jstore.org).

Chapter 9: Transparency: The Market For Information

1. George Akerlof (1970), 'The Market for Lemons; Quality Uncertainty and the Market Mechanism', *Quarterly Journal of Economics* 84, p. 489.
2. Universal Declaration of Human Rights, www.un.org/overview/rights.html.
3. John Cassidy (2009), ibid.
4. www.reginfo.gov. Sunstein advocated, during his association with the Federal Government, intelligible and simple formats for regulations and information disclosure.
5. Government of United Kingdom (2003), *Freedom of Information Act 2000: An Introduction*, www.informationcommissioner.gov.uk.
6. Government of Thailand (1997), *Official Information Act*. http://www.oic.go.th.
7. Republic of South Africa (2000), *Promotion of Access to Information Act*. www.polity.org.za/html/govdocs/legislation/2000/act2.pdf.

8. R.N. Gupta (2007), *Towards Transparency in Government*; IDC, Chandigarh.
9. punjabgovt.gov.in/punjabrti.
10. Yochai Benkler (2011), ibid.
11. Thaler & Sunstein (2008), ibid.
12. Thaler & Sunstein (2008), ibid (citing Kurt Lewis).
13. Ridley (1999/2011), ibid, p. 129–30.

Chapter 10: Alpha Services: Aligning Incentives and Institutions

1. Ariely (2010/11), ibid.
2. *India Corruption Study* 2005, Centre for Media Studies/TI India, www.tiindia.in.
3. Bimal Jalan (2011), *Emerging India,* Viking, Penguin Group.
4. Simar Halarnkar, 'The Ides of May', *The Hindustan Times*, 11 April 2013.

Chapter 11: Labour Laws: Regulation 'In Excess of Situation'

1. Rajiv Kumar; Revisiting Manufacturing Policy [Chapter 4] in Bibek Debroy, Ashley J. Tellis, Reece Trevor (eds.), (2014), *Getting India Back on Track: An Action Agenda for Reform,* Random House, India.
2. Milton Friedman and Rose Friedman (1980/90), ibid.
3. Bibek Debroy, www.cato.org/econom86ic-freedom-India/Economic-Freedom-States of India-2012-Chapter-4.pdf.
4. Milton Friedman and Rose Friedman (1980/1990), ibid.
5. R. Coase, 'The Problem of Social Cost', *Journal of Law and Economics*, 3:1-44, October 1960.
6. Taleb (2012), ibid.
7. James Q Wilson (1989/2000), *Bureaucracy: What Government Agencies Do and Why They Do It*, Basic Books, p. 343.

Chapter 12: Fertilizers' Quality: Neglect of Incentives

1. Federation of Indian Micro, Small and Medium Enterprises, www.fisme.org.in.
2. Bibek Debroy and Laveesh Bhandari (2012), *Corruption in India – The DNA and the RNA*, Konark Publishers Pvt. Ltd., New Delhi.
3. Tim Harford (2013), *The Undercover Economist Strikes Back*, Little, Brown, Great Britain.
4. Compilation by The Fertilizer Institute (TFI) Product Quality and Technology Committee, www.fda.govt/ohrms/dockets.
5. Adam Smith (1978), ibid, Introduction by Andrew Skinner, p. 20.

Chapter 13: Emigration Law: The Ban on Rational Behaviour

1. Migrant Workers Act 1995, RA8042 @ www.poea.gov.ph/rules/ra8042.html.
2. Blog, 27 September 2010; Philippine Industrial Relation Society @ pris08.webs.com—/4891375-externalmigration-and-the-overseas-filipin.
3. *Human Rights Watch*, July 2004, Vol. 16, No. 9B (www.hrw.org).
4. *'Smuggling of Migrants'*, 2009, UNODC (www.unodc.org/india).
5. Kashif Aziz, 'Protection of Emigrants or Exploitation of Pakistan's Working Class', 19 December 2008, (Current Affairs) www.chowrangi.pk.
6. Rogers (1973), ibid, p. 98.
7. Praveena Kodoth, V.J. Varghese, 'Protecting Women or Endangering the Emigration Process—Emigrant Women Domestic Workers, Gender and State Policy', *EPW*, 27 October 2012, Vol. XLVIII No. 43, www.epw.in
8. 'International Migration Policy', Binod Khadria, Perveen Kumar, S. Sarkar and Rashmi Sharma (www.jnu.ac.in/library/IMDS_Working_Papers).
9. V. Santhakumar (2011), *Economic Analysis of Institutions*, Sage Publications.
10. N. Vittal (2010), 'Designing Value Based Systems for Dispensing Justice', in *Restoring National Values,* (ed.) E Sreedharan, Bharat Wakhle and Pratyush Sinha, Sage Publications, New Delhi.

Chapter 14: Immoral Traffic (Prevention) Act

1. Stephen D. Levitt and Stephen J. Dubner (2009), *Superfreakonomics*, p. 55, William Marrow, imprint of Harper Collins, New York.
2. Sudhir Venkatesh (2013), *Floating City: Hustlers, Strivers, Dealers, Call Girls and Other Lives in Illicit New York*, Allen Lane/Penguin Books.
3. Definition of brothel: "brothel" includes any house, room, conveyance or place, or any portion of any house, room, conveyance or place, which is used for purposes of sexual exploitation or abuse for the gain of another person or for the mutual gain of two or more prostitutes (*The Immoral Traffic (Prevention) Act* 1956, Section 2(a).
4. James Q Wilson (1989/2000), ibid.
5. Joly Miller and Dheenan Jaya Sundera, 'Prostitution, Sex Industry

and Sex Tourism' in *Current Perspectives on Sex Crimes,* (2002) (ed.) Ronald M. Holmes and Stephen T. Holmes, Sage Publications.
6. Daryl A. Hellman (1980), *The Economics of Crime,* St. Martin's Press, New York.
7. Rogers (1973), ibid.
8. Stephen D Levitt, et al (2009), ibid.
9. Stephen D Levitt, et al (2009), ibid.

Chapter 15: Beta Regulations: The Coaseian Alternative

1. Suresh Mishra, Sapna Chadah, Mamta Pathania (eds.) (2012), *Consumer Protection in India,* IIPA and Concept Publishing Company, New Delhi.
2. Mishra *et al,* ibid.
3. The Informal Sector Survey by the NSSO (1999-2000), www.mospi.nic.in, estimates the number at 45 million with a substantial %age (30%) not having a fixed location.
4. Dreze and Sen (2013), ibid.
5. Ronald Coase, 'The Problem of Social Cost', *Journal of Law and Economics,* 3:1-44 (October 1960).
6. Daniel S. Jones (2012), ibid, p. 467.
7. Lott Jr. (2007), ibid.

Chapter 16: Infrastructure and Public Health

1. Vi Ostrom and Elinor Ostrom (1999), *Public goods and Public Choices,* Polycentricity and Social Public Economies, *Readings from Workshop in Political Theory and Policy Analysis,* Indiana University (ed.) Michael D McGinnis, at scisoc.colorado.edu.
2. Landsburg (1993), ibid.
3. Thaler, et al (2008), ibid.
4. Thaler, et al (2008), ibid.
5. M. Gladwell (2000/2010), ibid.
6. Sheela Rani Chunkath (2008), 'Reducing Maternal Mortality and Female Infanticide, The Tamil Nadu Experience', in *Splendour in the Grass: Innovations in Administration,* Department of ARPG, GoI, Penguin Books India.

Chapter 17: School Education: 'Predation' of The Right to Educate

1. Banerjee and Duflo (2011), ibid.
2. Nandan Nilekani (2008), *Imagining India: Ideas for the New Century,* Penguin/Allen Lane.

3. R.N. Gupta, et al (2009), ibid.
4. McKinsey Report (2007), *How the world's best performing school systems come out on top* (www.mckinseysociety.com).
5. Banerjee and Duflo (2011), ibid.
6. Sendhil Mullainathan and Eldar Shafir (2013), *Scarcity: Why Having Too Little Means So Much*; Allen Lane/Penguin Books.
7. NSSO 61st Round; Report No. 517, *Status of Educational and Vocational Training in India.*
8. Sachidanand Sinha (2012), *Status of School Education in Punjab,* Institute for Development and Communication, Chandigarh.
9. Gupta et al (2009), ibid.
10. Abdul Latif Jameel Poverty Action Lab, www.povertyaction-lab.org.
11. *How the World's Most Improved School Systems Keep Getting Better* (www.mckinseysociety.com).
12. Jean Dreze and Amartya Sen (2013), ibid.
13. Arvind Panagariya, 'What Right To Education?' *The Times of India*, 6 April 2013.
14. Mancur Olson (2000), ibid.
15. 'Just as a man may be said to have a right to his property so he has a property in his rights' – James Madison (Olson, 2000 ibid, p. 42).

Chapter 18: Higher Education: More Regulation Equals Less Competition

1. Deepti Gupta and Navneet Gupta (2012), 'Higher Education in India: Structure, Statistics and Challenges', *Journal of Education and Practice*, ISSN 2222-1735 (Paper) ISSN 2222-288X (Online), Vol. 3, No. 2, (www.iiste.org).
2. Nilekani (2008), ibid.
3. www.chea.org.
4. Milton Friedman and Rose Friedman (1980/90), ibid.
5. Nilekani (2008), ibid.
6. V. Shantha Kumar (2011), ibid.
7. Milton Friedman and Rose Friedman, et al (1980/90), ibid.
8. Richard O. Zerbe Jr and Howard Mc Curdy (1999), 'The Future of Market Failure', *Journal of Policy Analysis and Management* 18(4): 558.

Chapter 19: Donation of Human Organs: Incentives for Altruism

1. Vangal R Murlidharan, Stephen Jan and S. Ram Prasad (2006),

'The Trade in Human Organs in Tamil Nadu: The Anatomy of Regulatory Failure', *Health Economics: Policy and Law* 1:41-57.

2. *The Report of Transplant of Human Organs Act Review Committee*, 25 May 2005.
3. Thaler, et al (2008), ibid.
4. Daniel M. Davis, 2013, *The Compatibility Gene*, Allen Lane/ Penguin Books.
5. Alvin E. Roth, Tayfun Sonmez, M. Utku Unver, 'Kidney Exchange', *The Quarterly Journal of Economics*, May 2004.

Chapter 20: Crime and Punishment: 'Nudges' for Police, Victims, and Criminals

1. Malcolm Gladwell (2000/2010), ibid.
2. Matt Ridley (2003), *Nature via Nurture*, Fourth Estate UK, p. 267.
3. Eugene Mc Laughlin and John Muncie (eds.) (1996/2001), *Controlling Crime (Introduction)*, Sage Publications in association with Open University.
4. Rogers (1973), ibid.
5. Gary S. Becker, 'Crime and Punishment: An Economic Approach', *Journal of Political Economy*, Vol. 76, No. 2 (March–April 1968, pp. 169–217).
6. David Friedman extends the approach of Gary Becker to Crime in this article (www.davidfriedman.com).
7. Stephen D. Levitt, et al (2005).
8. John R. Lotte Jr (2007), *Freedomnomics*, Regnery Publishing, Washington.
9. Lotte (2007), ibid.
10. James Q. Wilson and George L. Kelling (1982), 'Broken Windows: The Police and Neighborhood Safety', *The Atlantic Monthly* (March): 29–83.
11. Malcolm Gladwell (2013), *David and Goliath: Underdogs, Misfits and the Art of Battling Giants*, Allen Lane/Penguin Books.
12. Daniel Kahneman (2011), ibid.
13. *India Corruption Study* (2005), Centre for Media Studies and *TI India* (www.tiindia.in).
14. Lotte Jr (2007), ibid.
15. Lotte Jr (2007), ibid, p. 116.
16. J.K. Tripathy (2008), *Reaching Out to People, TRICHY Community Policing Experiment, Splendour in the Grass*, Department of Administrative Reforms and Public Grievances, Government of India, Penguin Books, India.
17. *India Corruption Study* (2005), ibid.

18. Shankkar Aiyyer (2012), ibid.
19. *National Crime in India* (2011), National Crime Records Bureau, ncrb.nic.in/PSI-2011.
20. ibid.
21. www.hrln.org/hrln/prisoners-rights.html.
22. blog.lbj.org/tag/undertrial.
23. Hanson and Bussiere (1998), 'Predicting Relapse: A Meta Analysis of Sexual Offender Recidivism Studies', *Journal of Consulting and Clinical Psychology*, 66, 348–62 (quoted in) 'Where Should We Intervene? Dynamic Predictors of Sexual Offenses Recidivism', R. Karl Hanson and Andrew J.R. Harris, *Current Perspectives on Sex Crimes* (2002), (ed.) Ronald M. Holmes and Stephen T. Holmes, Sage Publications.
24. 'Effective Recidivism Reduction and Risk Focused Prevention Programme', February 2008, RKC Group by Roger Przybylski (www.dcj.state.co.us/org/pdf/docs); Report for Colorado Division of Cr. Justice.
25. *National Crime in India* (2011), National Crime Records Bureau.
26. Ibid.
27. James Watson (2003/2004), *DNA, The Secret of Life*, Arrow Books, UK.
28. Thaler, et al (2008), ibid.
29. Ridley (2003), ibid.
30. James Watson (2003/2004), ibid.
31. United Nations (2006), UN office on Drugs and Crime, New York.
32. Ludwig Von Mises (1944/2002), ibid.

Chapter 21: Managing Environment: Information, The Key Incentive

1. Jared Diamond (2005), *Collapse: How Societies Choose to Fail or Survive*, Allen Lane/Penguin Books.
2. Yochai Benkler (2011), ibid.
3. Daniel Goleman (2009/10), *Ecological Intelligence: The Hidden Impact of What We Buy*, Broadway Books, New York.
4. Jared Diamond (2005), ibid.
5. Tim Harford (2011), ibid.
6. Tim Harford (2011), ibid, Chapter on 'Climate Change or Changing the Rules for Success'.

Chapter 22: Corruption: The 'Moral' of Incentives

1. P. Mauro (1995) 'Corruption and Growth', *Quarterly Journal of Economics*, Vol. 110, No. 3, pp. 681–712.

2. Schleifer Andrei and Robert W. Vishny (1993) 'Corruption', *Quarterly Journal of Economics*, August 1993 108 (3) pp. 599–617.
3. Alan Beattie (2009), *False Economy*, Viking, Penguin Books, p. 165.
4. 'International Cooperation against Corruption, Finance and Development', March 1998 www.imf.org/external/pubs/ft/fandd/03/pdf/klitgaar.pdf.
5. Vikram Karve@karvediat.blogspot/212/10.corruption-in-nutshell-part-formula.html.
6. *India Corruption Study* (2005), Centre for Media Studies/TI India, www.tiindia.in.
7. Debroy, et al (2012), quoting a newspaper *Prabhat Khabar* (15 November 2003) provide an estimate of bribery in different services.

Bribery per Application/Unit	
Birth Certificate	Rs. 300-500
Death Certificate	Rs. 150-200
Electricity Connection	Rs. 3000-10000
Water Connection	Rs. 2000-4000
Sewerage	Rs. 300-500
Vehicle RC	Rs. 300-500
Driving Licence	Rs. 1000-1500
Construction Plan approval	Rs. 500-1000 (Multi-storey Rs. 2000-5000 per flat)
Land Registration	Rs. 2000-5000 per deed (as under estimate in our opinion)

8. Lipsky (1980), ibid.
9. Ronald Coase (1937), 'The Nature of the Firm', ibid.
10. R.N. Gupta (2001), 'Indian Bureaucracy and Corruption: Hunting the Hounds', *Social Sciences Research Journal*, Punjab University, Vol. 9, No. 3.
11. James Q. Wilson (1989/2000), ibid, p. 343.
12. Tim Harford (2006), *The Undercover Economist*, Little Brown, UK.
13. Steven E. Landsburg (1995/2009), ibid.
14. Tim Harford (2011), ibid, differentiates among the three – unintended 'slip', deliberate 'violation' of the law/practice and 'mistake—a deliberate act' leading to unintended consequences.
15. Neil H. Jacoby, Peter Nehemkis, Richard Ells (1977), *Bribery and Extortion in World Business*, Macmillan Publishing, New York.
16. Mancur Olson (1965), The *Logic of Collective Action*, Harvard University Press, Cambridge, MA.
17. Johan Graf Lambsdorff, 'Good Governance and the Invisible Foot' in Kerstin Kotschau and Thilo Marauhn (eds.) (2008), *Good*

Governance and Developing Countries, Peter Lang Internationaler Verlog Development Wissenschaften Frankfurt.

18. Stiglitz (2006), ibid.
19. Banerjee and Duflo (2011), ibid.
20. Dan Ariely (2008), *Predictably Irrational*, Harper Collins, USA, p. 204.
21. Benjamin Olken, 'Monitoring Corruption: Evidence from a Field Experiment in Indonesia', April 2007 quoted in Banerjee and Duflo (2011), ibid.
22. Dan Ariely (2008), ibid.
23. Robert Wade (1985), 'The Market for public office', *World Development*, Vol. 13, No. 4.
24. Daniel Kahneman (2011), ibid.

Chapter 23: Poverty Alleviation: Harnessing 'Wisdom of The (Poor) Crowds'

1. N. Ferguson (2008/9), ibid, quoting *Illustrated London News* in 1867.
2. N. Ferguson (2008/9), ibid.
3. Milton Friedman and Rose Friedman (1980/90), ibid.
4. Milton Friedman and Rose Friedman, 1980/90, ibid.
5. Sabina Alkire and Emma Maria Santos, 'Acute Multidimensional Poverty: A New Index for Developing Countries, OPHI', Working Paper 38, July 2010.
6. *The Economist*, 31 July 2010.
7. *The Economist*, 31 July 2010.
8. admis.hp.nic.in/ehimapurti/schemes.htm.
9. downtoearth.org.in.
10. Lane Kenworthy (2011), *Progress for the Poor*, Oxford University Press, UK.
11. Lane Kenworthy (2011), ibid, p. 3.
12. Reetik Khera (2008), 'Access to the Targeted Public Distribution System: A case study in Rajasthan', *Economic and Political Weekly* 43(44): 51–6.
13. R.N. Gupta, et al (2009), ibid.
14. planningcommission.nic.in/reports.
15. Dreze and Sen (2013), ibid (Chapter on 'Poverty and Social Support').
16. www.oxbridgewriters.com/essays/economics/public-distribution-system.php.

17. Mancur Olson (1965), *The Logic of Collective Action*, Harvard University Press, Cambridge MA.
18. Malcolm Gladwell (2000/2001), *The Tipping Point*, Abacus/Little Brown, London, p. 175.
19. James Surowiecki (2004/2005), *The Wisdom of Crowds*, Abacus, Little Brown, UK.
20. James Surowiecki (2004/2005), ibid.
21. Muhammad Yunus, (1999/2007), *Banker to the Poor*, Penguin Books, New Delhi.
22. Atul Gawande (2010/2011), *The Checklist Manifesto*, Introduction, Penguin Books.
23. Daniel Kahneman (2011), ibid, pp. 226–7.
24. Surowiecky (2004/5), ibid.
25. Charles Mackay (1993, reprint of 1852 edition), *Extraordinary Popular Delusions and the Madness of the Crowds*, Barnes and Noble, New York.
26. Irving Janis (1983), *Group Think*, revised 2nd ed. Houghton Mifflin, Boston.
27. Banerjee and Duflo (2011), ibid, p. 24.
28. Banerjee and Duflo (2011), ibid, p. 39.
29. Mullainathan et al. (2013), ibid.
30. Dan Ariely (2008), ibid.

Chapter 24: Micro Rules and Institutions: Problems, Possibilities and Prospects

1. Tim Harford (2011), ibid.
2. www.indiakanoon.org.
3. Duflo and Banerjee (2011), ibid.
4. Dreze and Sen (2013), ibid.
5. Ariely (2008), ibid.
6. *Study on Drug Abuse in the Border Districts of Punjab* (2010), IDC, Chandigarh.
7. V.K. Arora and Rajnish Gupta, 'DOTS Strategy in India', *Current Medical Journal North Zone*, Vol. VIII, No. 4, July 2002 (lvsitbrd.nic).
8. Michael Lipsky (1980), ibid, p. 34, 2nd ed. Russell Sage Foundation, New York.
9. Taleb (2012), ibid.
10. *The Times of India*, 10 October 2013.
11. Tyler Cowen (2006); *Discover Your Inner Economist*, Dutton/Penguin Books.

25. Conclusion: Designing Institutional 'Nudges' for Public Services

1. Tyler Cowen (2006), ibid.
2. Alan Beattie (2009), *False Economy*, Viking/Penguin books, p. 165.
3. Michael Lipsky (1980/2010), ibid.
4. Lipsky (ibid).
5. Malcolm Gladwell (2008), *Outliers: The Story of Success*, Allen Lane/Penguin Books, p. 183.
6. Patricia W. Ingraham and Lawence E. Lynn (2004), *The Art of Governance: Analysing Management and Administration*, Georgetown University Press, Washington DC. The authors trace the change from 'hierarchies' and 'markets' to 'networks', and provide a 'reduced – form expression' consisting of O = *f* (E, C, T, S, M), where
   O = outputs/outcomes (individual or organizational);
   E = environmental factors (political, economic, and so on);
   C = client or consumer characteristics;
   T = treatments (primary work, core processes, or technology);
   S = structures (administrative or organizational); and
   M = managerial roles, strategies, or actions.
7. Benkler (2011), ibid.
8. Tim Harford (2006), *The Undercover Economist*, Little Brown, UK.
9. Cassidy (2009), ibid, p. 100.
10. Harford (2011), ibid.
11. www.archive.org/details/sims_evolved_virtual_creatures_1994.
12. Harford (2011), ibid.
13. Banerjee and Duflo (2011), ibid.

Name Index

Subject Index